Boycott Theory and the Struggle for Palestine

Off the Fence: Morality, Politics, and Society

The series is published in partnership with the Centre for Applied Philosophy, Politics & Ethics (CAPPE), University of Brighton.

Series Editors:

Bob Brecher, Professor of Moral Philosophy, University of Brighton
Robin Dunford, Senior Lecturer in Globalisation and War, University of Brighton
Michael Neu, Senior Lecturer in Philosophy, Politics and Ethics, University of Brighton

Off the Fence presents short, sharply argued texts in applied moral and political philosophy, with an interdisciplinary focus. The series constitutes a source of arguments on the substantive problems that applied philosophers are concerned with: contemporary real-world issues relating to violence, human nature, justice, equality and democracy, self and society. The series demonstrates applied philosophy to be at once rigorous, relevant, and accessible—philosophy-in-use.

The Right of Necessity: Moral Cosmopolitanism and Global Poverty, by Alejandra Mancilla

Complicity: Criticism between Collaboration and Commitment, by Thomas Docherty

The State and the Self: Identity and Identities, by Maren Behrensen

Just Liberal Violence: Sweatshops, Torture, War, by Michael Neu

The Troubles with Democracy, by Jeff Noonan

Against Borders: Why the World Needs Free Movement of People, by Alex Sager

Digital Working Lives: Worker Autonomy and the Gig Economy, by Time Christiaens

The Other Enlightenment: Race, Sexualist and Self-Estrangement, by Matthew Sharpe

Boycott Theory and the Struggle for Palestine: Universities, Intellectualism and Liberation, by Nick Riemer

Boycott Theory and the Struggle for Palestine

Universities, Intellectualism and Liberation

Nick Riemer

ROWMAN & LITTLEFIELD
Lanham • Boulder • New York • London

Published by Rowman & Littlefield
An imprint of The Rowman & Littlefield Publishing Group, Inc.
4501 Forbes Boulevard, Suite 200, Lanham, Maryland 20706
www.rowman.com

86–90 Paul Street, London EC2A 4NE

Copyright © 2023 by The Rowman & Littlefield Publishing Group, Inc.

All rights reserved. No part of this book may be reproduced in any form or by any electronic or mechanical means, including information storage and retrieval systems, without written permission from the publisher, except by a reviewer who may quote passages in a review.

British Library Cataloguing in Publication Information Available

Library of Congress Cataloging-in-Publication Data Available

ISBN 9781538175866 (cloth)
ISBN 9781538175873 (pbk.)
ISBN 9781538175880 (ebook)

Contents

Preface   vii

   Introduction   1

1   Institutions of Occupation and Resistance   13
   The Amputation of Higher Education in Palestine   14
   Universities as Tools of Occupation   21
   Individuals versus Institutions   28

2   The Academy and Its Freedoms   35
   Singling Out Israel   36
   Freedom to Boycott   41
   Boycott or Counter-Boycott?   49
   What Is a University For?   52
   Collaboration and Community   53

3   Little Israels   57
   Denying Politics   59
   Democracy and Campus Exclusion   63
   States of Enclosure   66
   Discretion and the Institution of Critique   69
   Zionist Universals   72

4   Disruption, Protest, Democracy   77
   Speech and Social Conflict   79
   What Is Speech?   84
   Speech, Communication, Emotion   86
   Speech as Interpellation   91

Redistributing Speech 98
　　　The Heckler's Veto and the Tactics of Disruption 100

　　　Appendix: Speech, Practices, Power   103

5　The Politics of Regressive Research   109
　　　Inherently Progressive? 111
　　　Boycotting the Non-Governmental Organizations 114
　　　Footnotes against Hate 118

6　The Opium of the Educated   129
　　　The Drag of Theory 131
　　　Thought and Inaction 135
　　　Stopping to Think 137
　　　Against Smartwashing 141
　　　In Praise of Groupthink 143
　　　The Anti-Intellectualism We Need 147

Notes   151
Index   205
About the Author   213

Preface

Universities are in many ways at the forefront of the Palestine solidarity movement in the west – a situation that shows in a nutshell just how far the movement still has to go before justice for Palestinians is likely to be achieved. This book's focus is on just one aspect of Palestine solidarity on campus: the institutional academic boycott of Israel, a branch of the Boycott, Divestment and Sanctions (BDS) campaign. If Israel's apartheid practices are to end, the intensity with which BDS is often debated in higher education will have to be matched outside it. One of the ways this can happen, perhaps, is by normalizing the boycott in academia, in order to establish universities as precedents for the kind of principled solidarity with Palestine that should be encouraged in other contexts. My hope is that this book can contribute to this goal.

More specifically, the chapters that follow have the ambition of advancing the academic boycott of Israel in three ways: by presenting a comprehensive justification for the boycott in itself, by analyzing the university contexts in which the call to boycott is made and by relating it to various questions within contemporary political and intellectual life, in recognition of the fact that, more than simply the main expression of support for Palestine in academia, the academic boycott is also one of the most divisive topics in the politics of knowledge today.

The book is intended for anyone who is at least open to the possibility that the academic boycott of Israel is politically and intellectually justifiable. Its starting point is the observation that BDS overall appears to be easily the most powerful tactic that the Palestine solidarity movement currently has. This is a premise of the argument that follows, so I will not be offering either any speculation on the boycott's utility in comparison to other tactics that Palestinians and their allies might adopt or any assessment of specific academic boycott achievements or failures. This should not be taken as any sign of overinvestment in the academic boycott or overestimation of its political possibilities. Justice for Palestinians will obviously not be achieved by any kind of activism among academics or students on their own – which is why people involved in BDS on campus are also typically active in other Palestine solidarity (and wider antiracist and decolonization) efforts. These wider efforts are not my concern here: while I often use the term "BDS" as shorthand to refer simply to the academic boycott, I have little to say about wider campaign activity beyond it, whether student activism, university divestment campaigns or other forms of Palestine solidarity on or off campus. This selectivity does not come from any lack of appreciation of these other activities' importance. Rather, by homing in on a small facet of the wider BDS campaign, I hope to suggest just how robust and intellectually rich the justification for Palestine solidarity more generally is: if, as I argue, it makes political sense to boycott Israeli universities, which pursue work that they regularly claim is indispensable to peace efforts in Palestine-Israel, then boycotting cultural and consumer activity, where the same claim is much less plausible, immediately becomes easier.

This book has been a long time in the making, and I have relied more than usual on friends and colleagues for help in writing it and advice on how to publish it. I'm extremely grateful to the numerous academics throughout the West Bank, most of whom need to remain unnamed, who have helped me to understand the experience of Palestinian universities under occupation in finer detail. Without their generosity, the analysis here would have been greatly impoverished. I'm also especially grateful to everyone who read the manuscript in its entirety or in part, supplied details or clarifications or helped in other ways with the development of aspects of the argument or with the book's journey into print: Abaher El-Sakka, Ahmed Beshtawi, Aurélien Mondon, Briony Neilson, Bruce Robbins, David Brophy, Eran Asoulin, Fahad Ali, Gavan Titley, Jacqueline Léon, James Godfrey, Jean-Michel Fortis, Jumana Bayeh, Lana Tatour, Marcelo Svirsky, Mark Johnston, Mazin Qumsiyeh, Nadine El-Enany, Nina Riemer, Osama Jarrar, Robert Boncardo, Sam Jones, Sarah Keenan, Saree Makdisi, Sebastian Budgen, Simon During, Sol Salbe, Stefan Mattesich, Steven Salaita and Tom Riemer. Their generosity has significantly improved the result. I'm grateful to Eran Asoulin and Benedetto Passaretti for their meticulous research-assisting and manuscript-preparation work and to Bob Brecher for his generous and astute advice on the manuscript and for going above and beyond in facilitating the book's publication. I'd also like to thank the two anonymous readers for Rowman and Littlefield for their valuable comments. It goes without saying that no one mentioned is responsible for any mistakes or misinterpretations and certainly shouldn't be assumed to share any of the ideas in the book.

I'm grateful to audiences at Maynooth University, Ireland; at the University of Sydney English department seminar; and at the 2017 BDS: Driving Global Justice for Palestine conference, also at the University of Sydney, for their reactions to oral presentations of some of these ideas, as well as to the students in various contexts with whom I've discussed questions relevant to the book. Some parts of the following chapters use material that has previously appeared in earlier versions, including in *Jacobin* (chapters one, two and three), *Australian Universities' Review* (chapter three) and *Overland* (chapter six).

In her essay "The Academic Boycott and Beyond: Towards an Epistemological Strategy of Liberation and Decolonization," Yara Harawi notes that "the voices of academic allies cannot and should not replace Palestinian voices." With Palestinians all too often excluded from debates on their own people's liberation, it is essential that they be front and center of discussion of the academic boycott. But they should not be left to struggle alone. To be real, solidarity with Palestinians must be active; the more the case for boycott is strengthened, the less will silencing and exclusion of Palestinians be possible. My intention in this book, as I hope will be clear, is to echo and reinforce, not to replace, the calls for boycott and other forms of solidarity and the analysis of its politics that Palestinians themselves have so powerfully and lucidly made – not just with their words but also with their bodies and, all too often, their lives. So the chapters that follow are dedicated to the proud Palestinian resistance, both in Palestine itself and outside it, and to the countless Palestinians, including students and academics, whose lives have been ruined or taken by Israeli colonial violence, with the support of its universities, in the years I have been writing.

Introduction

"We call upon academic institutions and academics worldwide," academics at Birzeit University in Palestine wrote in a 2018 official statement, "to boycott Israel and its complicit academic institutions, until it complies with its obligations under international law."[1] For decades now, Palestinians and their supporters have been making that same, simple request. During this time, the boycott movement has been growing. It will continue to do so. Nevertheless, only a small minority of academics have publicly undertaken to cut ties with Israel. Even after the brutal Zionist violence of May 2021 – attacks on worshipers in the Al-Aqsa mosque, accelerated ethnic cleansing in East Jerusalem, pogroms against Palestinians in Israel and a devastating air assault on Gaza which killed 256 Palestinians – fewer than half the solidarity statements issued by academics worldwide committed to Boycott, Divestment and Sanctions (BDS). And of that minority, some even stopped short of explicitly endorsing the academic boycott, even though this is the most relevant version of BDS in a university setting.[2] The reason is clear enough: almost everything in the politics and culture of higher education works against academics boycotting Israel. Quite aside from the fact that boycotting means forgoing professional opportunities and often involves a risk of reprisals, boycotts are a form of shunning, and so are the very opposite of the norms of professional "collegiality" and "civility" that academics frequently invoke, and sometimes even observe, in their working lives.

In the chapters that follow, we will explore these and other features of the academic boycott in its political, social and intellectual dimensions. The book's most important aim is to present the political and intellectual rationale for the boycott as thoroughly as possible, in the hope of winning new adherents to it. At the same time, we will analyze the university contexts in which the boycott intervenes, and the uptake and resistances it triggers. But, as we will see, it is impossible to do any of this properly without also addressing some of the questions that academic BDS raises, and that its best-known proponents frequently discuss, about the politics of intellectual life more broadly, both in universities and beyond them. In calling for the suspension of intellectual activity – in particular, conferences and academic exchanges – in certain carefully defined circumstances, BDS and academics' frequent reluctance to engage in it raise important questions about the connections between progressive thought and progressive action in the current moment. I hope that understanding these connections better will contribute to the Palestine solidarity movement by giving us a clearer picture of the social and political stakes of the call for BDS both in universities and beyond them.

In academic circles, boycotting scholarly activity, of all things, can seem particularly counterintuitive and unjustifiable. This impression is mistaken: as will become clear, the academic boycott follows from certain basic and readily justified intellectual and political considerations. By demonstrating this in the course of the book, I hope to strengthen the case not only for the academic boycott itself but also for the economic and cultural aspects of the wider BDS campaign. Critics of the consumer and cultural boycotts cannot reach for the same high-minded defenses as critics of the boycott's academic version, such as the necessity to maintain intellectual and scientific dialogue. But if these defenses fail and the academic boycott is in fact justifiable, as I will argue it is, then the justifiability of the other forms of boycott should be even more obvious.

Boycotts are, as Muhammad Ali Khalidi notes, "a ubiquitous political tactic and their moral credentials are rarely called into question when used in other contexts" than BDS.[3] Boycotting has been a recurrent component of Palestinians' resistance to Zionism for over a century; it was even central to the Zionist project in Palestine, as Abdel Razzaq Takriti has shown.[4] The most recent instantiation of the boycott tactic on a large scale dates to the call issued in 2005 by 173 Palestinian organizations – unions, professional associations, refugee and human rights organizations, charities and religious, cultural and community groups – for a campaign of BDS against Israel. Given Israel's insatiable, merciless and completely illegal persistence in the violent repression of Palestinians, and the unequivocal failure of "all forms of international intervention and peace-making," Palestinians called on international civil society, including people of conscience in Israel, "to impose broad boycotts and implement divestment initiatives against Israel similar to those applied to South Africa in the apartheid era," and to pressure governments "to impose embargoes and sanctions against Israel."[5] The call stipulates that

> these non-violent punitive measures should be maintained until Israel meets its obligation to recognize the Palestinian people's inalienable right to self-determination and fully complies with the precepts of international law by:

1. Ending its occupation and colonization of all Arab lands and dismantling the Wall
2. Recognizing the fundamental rights of the Arab-Palestinian citizens of Israel to full equality; and
3. Respecting, protecting and promoting the rights of Palestinian refugees to return to their homes and properties as stipulated in UN resolution 194.[6]

In a situation where official diplomatic and legal mechanisms have spectacularly failed to secure these goals, the BDS campaign proposed to change tack. Bypassing the sclerotic institutions of international law, it would return some leverage over global justice to ordinary people. It is hardly surprising, as a result, that no other campaign has ever received as comprehensive a mandate from Palestinians themselves. Those who reject BDS, then, are turning their backs on the overwhelming request of Palestinian civil society, among the most strangulated and oppressed on the planet.

Universities have been center stage throughout the history of BDS. Along with the cultural boycott, the academic arm of the campaign was the first to take shape. For many years, the Palestinian Council for Higher Education had banned cooperation with Israeli academia in protest at the denial of academic and other freedoms to Palestinians. In 2002, several hundred European academics and researchers called for a moratorium on European funding of Israeli cultural and research institutions; at the end of that year, the University of Paris 6 voted to call for the nonrenewal of the European Union's (EU) research funding agreement with Israel.[7] The following year, Palestinian academics and intellectuals issued their own boycott call. Then, in 2004, the newly constituted Palestinian Campaign for the Academic and Cultural Boycott of Israel (PACBI) asked international academics to "comprehensively and consistently boycott all Israeli academic and cultural institutions as a contribution to the struggle to end Israel's occupation, colonization and system of apartheid." As well as institution-level action against Israeli higher education, PACBI also called for direct support for Palestinian academic and cultural institutions, "without requiring them to partner with Israeli counterparts as an explicit or implicit condition for such support."[8] Since this call was issued, the academic boycott has slowly been gaining adherents. Notably, the University of Johannesburg cut its ties with Ben-Gurion University in 2011.[9] Academic associations including the US American Studies Association, the National Women's Studies Association, the African Literature Association, the British Society for Middle Eastern Studies, the Middle East Studies Association and the Latin American Council of Social Sciences, have voted to endorse BDS. Academics from Australia to Brazil have signed pledges to uphold the academic boycott, which is promoted in many countries, including the US, UK and France, by ongoing organizing collectives. Prominent but so far unsuccessful campaigns for an endorsement of the academic boycott have been run in the Modern Language Association. Scores of student unions and associations around the world have voted to support different aspects of the boycott campaign.[10]

Boycotts in universities do not, of course, lead directly to justice for Palestinians. Instead, boycott activism contributes to this end in two related ways: by placing pressure on Israel and by expressing concrete solidarity with Palestinians. On the question of pressure, it is commonly acknowledged that Israeli society will not abandon its anti-Palestinianism of its own accord but will need to be compelled by outside forces. In the absence of internal, self-seeded change, the pressure the academic boycott places on Israel takes two forms. First, in directly targeting universities, academic BDS targets institutions that play a central role in the maintenance, planning and justification of Israeli state anti-Palestinianism. As detailed in chapter one, universities are an integral component of Israel's permanent war effort: in trying to institutionally isolate them, the boycott aims to undermine the war effort itself. In this context, it is crucial to appreciate that the academic boycott is not a blanket boycott of any and all Israeli academics. Quite the contrary, as discussed in chapter one, the official guidelines to the academic boycott issued by PACBI make it clear that mere affiliation to an Israeli university does not qualify any academic for boycott. It is only official institutional leaders – university presidents and deans acting in their official capacity – and Israeli university-sponsored academic structures such as conferences and exchange programs that are boycottable. The boycott, therefore, targets *only* those individuals who have freely chosen to make themselves accountable, through their leadership positions or their use of official university-level structures, for their institutions' commitment to maintaining anti-Palestinian apartheid in Israel.

The second form of pressure academic BDS places on Israel is ideological. As we will explore in chapter four, Israel has set great stock in its membership of a notional liberal, democratic, western community of nations, of which it traditionally saw itself as an outpost, radically demarcated from the authoritarian regimes of much of the rest of the Middle East. Despite the dominance of the far right in Israel's current political culture, this liberal image is still central to Zionist ideology. In isolating Israeli universities' official activities, the academic boycott aspires to shatter the myth of Israeli democratic liberalism and highlight its flagrant violation of the most elementary considerations of justice. It sets out to do this within a community – university teachers and researchers – that is a powerful vector of Israel's international image. By isolating its complicit higher education institutions and challenging the soft global power that Israel exerts on the world scene through them, the academic boycott aims to foster a realization in Israeli civil society and among Zionists worldwide of the untenability of their present policies.

The other principal rationale of the academic boycott is its status as an expression of solidarity with Palestinians. Among close observers of Palestinian affairs, it is commonly believed that the popular, democratically led BDS campaign has done more than any other recent political initiative to advance Palestinian rights. Certainly, it has done far more than the decades of collaborationism shown by the official Palestinian leadership. When an oppressed political community asks for solidarity and says what it wants its supporters to do, there is every reason to do exactly as it asks, especially when, as in the case of BDS, there is no alternative strategy remotely as effective on the horizon. Just as implementing the boycott is meant to undermine Israelis' confidence in their own political choices, so too, by showing Palestinians the solidarity they have asked for, allies contribute to the momentum and vigor of Palestinians' liberation movement. To ignore Palestinians' request to boycott is to inflict a further humiliation on a subject population that has every right to expect the support of people of conscience.

This is all a long game, and no one should expect BDS tactics to bear fruit rapidly. It took decades for a boycott movement to help overturn apartheid in South Africa, a significantly less complex political challenge. Nor, as with any other political campaign, is there any absolute guarantee of the effectiveness of BDS. If politics were deterministic, it would not need to exist. Neither the course nor the details of any aspect of the Palestine solidarity campaign can be predicted in advance. But none of this is any reason not to embrace the political tactic that Palestinians themselves have so decisively chosen. In allowing the boycott to attain critical mass, full commitment to BDS by supporters of global justice would substantially accelerate the tempo of Palestinian struggle. It would make it possible to appreciate the longer-term virtues and weaknesses of BDS sooner so that tactical and strategic adjustments could be made – or, if necessary, boycotting abandoned in favor of something else. As we will see in the following chapters, there are at present *no* good arguments against any aspect of the academic boycott. But even if the picture were less clear-cut, misgivings about BDS's soundness as a tactic would not be good enough a reason to refrain from implementing it, since it is only by fully testing the strengths and limits of a current tactic that Palestinians can know whether their liberation struggle is on the right track. Those who withhold support from BDS because they are uncertain that it is the right thing to do are thus obstructing the collective process of tactical trial and error on which all political movements depend.

It is also important to note that the BDS campaign is silent on the concrete form that justice for Palestinians should take. Its three demands – the end to the occupation of the West Bank and the siege of Gaza, equal rights for Palestinian citizens of Israel and acceptance of Palestinian refugees' right to return – do not include any stipulations about the political arrangements that could make any of them a reality. As Israeli colonizing activity through settlements turns a two-state model into a grotesque anachronism, it is up to Palestinians themselves to decide the kind of political structures they demand. BDS gives Israel an incentive to take Palestinians' demands seriously but recognizes that, even if they have a crucial role in making genuine dialogue possible, Palestinian allies have no part to play in its outcome, which is a matter for Palestinians and Israelis alone.

Despite regular proclamations of its "failure," there is at least one reason to be confident in BDS as the current principal tactic of the Palestine solidarity movement: the overwhelming resources deployed by Israel to quash it.[11] On its own, the budget devoted to BDS countermeasures – $72m was committed in 2017[12] – gives a sense of how serious a threat the boycott movement constitutes in Israel's eyes. This money is spent on a variety of lobbying, "lawfare" and hasbara (propaganda) initiatives, which have played no small role in undermining democratic norms in the states in which they are applied. The anti-boycott legislation currently in place in over thirty US states, the witch-hunt against UK Labour leader Jeremy Corbyn and the widening adoption of the definition of anti-Semitism promoted by the International Holocaust Remembrance Alliance, which treats criticism of Israel as anti-Semitic, are three examples of the intensity of Israel's counterattack on the Palestine solidarity movement in general, and of its exemplary contribution to the rapidly escalating, and highly dangerous, illiberalism and authoritarianism of supposedly democratic western states. With Israel now a rallying point for far-right politics the world over, Palestine and BDS activists are taking a position on a flashpoint issue for the international right, pressing demands of justice and democracy whose relevance goes far beyond the geographical and ideological boundaries of the Mediterranean and the Jordan. The enthusiasm shown for Israel by the planet's Trumps, Modis, Bolsonaros and Orbáns – to say nothing of its Macrons, Johnsons and Trudeaus – makes opposing it a significant political priority and ties antifascist struggles in many countries to Palestinians' own resistance to Zionism.[13]

The stakes of the Palestine justice campaign, then, go well beyond the confines of the Middle East. In addition to its antifascist and anti-authoritarian dimensions, Palestinians' status as the Indigenous victims of Israeli settler-colonialism is another factor that confers wider political import on their struggle. It would be evasive and hypocritical, to say nothing of counterproductive, to support Palestinians but not other victims of settler-colonial violence; living as I do in Sydney, I am keenly aware of the affinities between Israel and Australia as settler-colonies, and of the intensity of the support that the mainstream political consensus in Canberra, as in so many other parts of the west, lavishes on Israel. The Palestine solidarity movement in Australia, like in other settler-colonies has, accordingly, put antiracism, decolonization and

Indigenous rights at the heart of its political self-definition. As Steven Salaita notes in relation to the academic boycott specifically, "BDS represents not the misguided inclinations of radical scholars but the will of the Palestinian people. We listen to the colonized. We hear the colonized. We heed the colonized. This is the first necessity of decolonization."[14]

Since Israeli settler-colonialism is at the origin of intense and murderous racism against Palestinians, anti-Zionism is intrinsically linked to wider antiracist struggles in other societies. It would be politically unprincipled to support Palestinians against the racist oppression to which they are subject but not support antiracist struggles in other contexts, such as the Black Lives Matter movement or the Indigenous justice movements in Australia, North America or New Zealand. In particular, the Palestine justice campaign has a special interest in Islamophobia. Not all Palestinians are Muslim, of course, but the lack of real support for the Palestinian cause in the west is reinforced by deeply entrenched anti-Muslim prejudice, a phenomenon that has only intensified since 2001, and which means that Palestinians have to battle the same fundamentally orientalist and colonialist premises that drive western governments' attitudes to other Middle Eastern people, including those living in the west. Asserting the necessity of freedom for Palestinians can serve, then, as a reminder of the fact that the universality of justice must not be suspended for Muslims, whether in Palestine or elsewhere.

Just as Islamophobia has been politically instrumentalized in the service of neocolonial control of Muslim populations, anti-Semitism currently provides the excuse for a heavy-handed and highly irrational assault on fundamental democratic liberties. This takes the form of the severe legal penalties increasingly leveled against expressions of Palestine solidarity on the grounds that they are instances of racism against Jews, or of witch-hunts against Palestine supporters on the grounds of their supposed anti-Semitism – the vendetta against Jeremy Corbyn in the UK Labour Party being the most flagrant example.[15] Facebook even considers the term "Zionist" as potentially anti-Semitic – particularly clear evidence of the rational and moral dead end into which Zionists' efforts to defend their ethno-state inevitably lead.[16] As we will explore in the last chapter of the book, overcomplication and excessive subtlety can easily sound the death knell of progressive politics. So it is important to assert the self-evidence and the *lack* of nuance with which two simple facts should be stated: *anti-Zionism is not the same as anti-Semitism*, and *objecting to Israel's anti-Palestinian policies, as many Jews do, is not anti-Semitic*. It is not anti-Catholic or anti-Latino to criticize the policies of Costa Rica, where Catholicism is a state religion, just as it is not Islamophobic or anti-Shia to criticize Iran or anti-Buddhist or anti-Asian to criticize Cambodia. In just the same way, objecting to Israel's anti-Palestinianism is not anti-Jewish racism. What *would* be anti-Semitic would be to oppose

Israeli policies and measures on principle, simply because they are decided on and enacted by Jews – the exact *opposite* of the stance adopted by BDS. Once the three demands of BDS are met – an end to the occupation and siege, equal rights for Palestinian citizens of Israel and recognition of refugees' right of return – there is no longer any need for a boycott campaign.

Zionists typically retort that the third BDS demand, the right of refugees to return to the homes from which they were – and continue to be – expelled, is, given the demographic realities in play, tantamount to a demand for the dissolution of Israel *as a Jewish state* and is therefore indeed anti-Semitic.[17] Once again, the rebuttal should be simple. BDS is an anti-Zionist movement, but it does not call for the "destruction" of Israel, as is so often claimed; as a democratic and antiracist campaign, it does not raise a single obstacle to any Jewish person who wishes to practice their religion in Israel, Palestine or, indeed, anywhere else in the world. Instead, it is working toward a situation in which everyone who lives between the Jordan and the Mediterranean enjoys full civil liberties and democratic prerogatives, including freedom of religion. What BDS does deny, on exactly the same democratic grounds, is that Jewish people have, under the guise of a claim to "self-determination," a right to an exclusivist ethno-state that not only denies its Palestinian victims the most basic rights but also systematically represses, dispossesses, tortures, imprisons and kills them. If anti-Zionism is anti-Semitic, then many anti-Zionist Jews in Israel and around the world are anti-Semitic, including many of the original Jewish inhabitants of Palestine, who frequently opposed Zionism on religious grounds.[18]

In addition to its antifascist, antiracist and anticolonialist dimensions, a further universalistic dimension of the Palestine solidarity campaign is its demand for refugee rights. Whatever the details of how the right of return is implemented, acknowledging it would be a powerful victory not just for Palestinians but also for refugees and refugee rights movements around the world. With increasing numbers of people being forced from their homes by war and global heating, the resolution, in the refugees' favor, of the decades-long refugee crisis in Palestine would represent a major victory for intergenerational refugee rights and establish a precedent that could be invoked in many other situations. In this as in so many other ways, the achievement of justice for Palestinians would have an agenda-setting impact on the struggles of oppressed people around the world.

The six chapters that follow take us from the most particular to the most general aspects of the politics of the boycott in universities. In chapter one, we start with a detailed description of the daily reality of university life in occupied Palestine, documenting the effects of the Israeli occupation on academics and students. The chapter then goes on to detail Israeli universities' role as tools of occupation and apartheid and the ways in which they support

Israeli anti-Palestinianism. In the chapter's final section, I tie these strands together by addressing a key – and often misunderstood – strategic feature of the academic boycott campaign, the institutional character of boycott targets. Overall, the chapter aims to provide as full a survey as possible of the Israeli universities that the academic boycott aspires to affect and the Palestinian ones it aims to benefit.

If Palestinians' appeal to boycott Israeli universities is to have any chance of being widely adopted, BDS supporters will have to defeat the argument that the Israel boycott is an unacceptably selective violation of some academics' "academic freedom" and break the myth of the exceptionality of boycott as a practice in academia. These are the aims of chapter two. I begin by making a thorough case for the legitimacy of a selective boycott of Israel, showing why it is perfectly valid to call for a boycott of it without necessarily also calling for a boycott of any other states. The chapter then discusses the central question of academic freedom, highlighting the ways in which academia is inherently not a sphere of "freedom" but operates instead through multiple systems of exclusion. Furthermore, in contrast to the standard ideology of the "academic community" – a homogeneous, fundamentally consensual body pursuing knowledge in politically neutral ways – actual university life is riven with competing interests and constituted in its essence by the struggle of various "counter-communities." In this situation, political boycotts are an entirely predictable – and unobjectionable – feature of academic life – a conclusion that is confirmed by the existence of the numerous political boycotts other than BDS that are currently taking place in universities. Far from a violation of the ordinary norms of the academy, boycotting is in fact a constitutive and deeply embedded, though strongly disavowed, feature of academic professionalism. In the final sections of the chapter, I argue that boycotting is far from inappropriate as a mode of academic behavior, since regulation through exclusion is an intrinsic aspect of academic self-governance. If the ideas I defend in this chapter are correct, two of the most powerful arguments against the academic boycott – the claims that it is a scandalous exception to the norms of academic conduct and that it constitutes an illegitimately selective attack on Israel and its supporters' academic freedom – simply disappear.

Steven Salaita argues that "one cannot endorse academic boycott without also implicitly staking a position on questions of faculty engagement. For this reason, it is important to couch boycott in an analysis of various unjust campus practices, from exploited labor to militarism to inadequate protection against sexual assault and racism."[19] Exactly this is the aim of chapter three, which examines the manifold authoritarian tendencies of contemporary higher education and the dispositions of compliance and exclusion latent in the way it operates, documented with examples and case studies from the UK, Europe, Australia and North America. This will give us a better fix on the resistance to Palestine justice campaigns, especially BDS, that is encountered in the academic arena. The chapter particularly considers the humanities and social sciences, the areas in which BDS activities are most vigorous. The aim is to understand two of their contradictory effects: on the one hand, the fact that they foster counter-hegemonic, emancipatory initiatives like the boycott itself; on the other, their role in simultaneously reconciling students to the world and its existing imbalances of power, thereby contributing to the social relations that support domination, including over Palestine.

Chapter four turns to one of the best-known hallmarks of BDS activism internationally, the active disruption of Zionists invited to speak at universities. Palestine solidarity activists engaging in this tactic regularly attract criticism for their supposed hostility to the "free" exchange of ideas. Disruption raises questions that are crucial for grassroots politics beyond BDS, and it is important that activists' approach to it should be grounded in a realistic and objective understanding of the nature of public speech events, not in an idealist fantasy of them. Far from the abstractions on which liberal freedom of expression arguments rest, chapter four therefore offers an account of speech, disruption and silencing anchored in a materialist conception of speech. The chapter is predicated on the fact that disruptive protest has regularly been an instrument of social progress. In exploring the contradiction of BDS critics' refusal to tolerate episodic obstruction of Zionists' speech while tolerating the structural obstruction of Palestinians', it references a number of case studies of campus disruptions by BDS and antifascist protesters in Europe, the US and elsewhere. In doing so, it tries to counter perhaps the most serious ideological impediment to assertive progressive politics, whether over Palestine or other issues.

Palestinian intellectuals have frequently stressed the need for Palestine activism in universities to break out of a narrowly intellectualist, idealist mode and to engage with the material forces at work in the academic sphere. Inspired by those reflections, chapters five and six take up more general questions that the academic boycott raises about the politics of intellectual activity in universities and outside them. Academics promoting the boycott are regularly confronted with questions about the nature of academic and political activity, their points of crossover, their antagonisms and the contributions they can make, separately and jointly, to progressive change. Boycott opponents insist that intellectual work in universities is essential to social progress and must be allowed to continue. But asserting their right to pursue academic exchange by attending Israeli conferences and participating in Israeli exchange schemes *no matter what* only reinforces academics' already considerable social privilege: even when Palestinians are being brutally dispossessed, imprisoned and murdered, the need not to sacrifice the slightest prerogative of intellectuals' academic employment, for Zionists and their allies, trumps all other political considerations. Stated like that, the widespread academic resistance to BDS sounds absurd and draws attention to the regressive political potential of academic research. As the boycott campaign in academia suggests, the unimpeded pursuit of intellectual activity – whether through the official circuits of scholarly exchange or otherwise – is often not the most urgent task facing progressives, even progressive intellectuals. This important point is illustrated in chapter five by an examination of recent debates about the political stakes of intellectual analysis in two contexts without direct relation to BDS. Case studies of the publication of a much-reported scholarly edition of Hitler's *Mein Kampf* and of institutional collaboration between researchers and security forces responsible for torture raise parallel questions of the political effects of academic research to those raised by the academic boycott and allow us to see more clearly what is at stake in the boycott's refusal of intellectual engagement. As these case studies demonstrate, even ostensibly progressive intellectual work does not necessarily benefit society by contributing to increased public enlightenment, as BDS opponents would like us to believe. As a result, the boycott cannot be opposed on the grounds that intellectual work in universities is *always* socially beneficial and therefore *never* to be obstructed.

Having examined two instances of regressive research in chapter five, the book's final chapter considers the ways in which intellectual work can, *in itself*, exert a conservatizing and anesthetizing impact, regardless of whatever progressive effects it is meant to have. The chapter starts by discussing intellectualism's disconnection from the social mechanisms of political power and academics' status as political commentators or spectators rather than players. Challenging the wishful thinking that sees intellectual analysis as *in itself* a political act, or at least as having significant political functions, we will see that intellectuals' non-engaged status is often central to the very conception of intellectual activity: political disengagement, I argue, is deeply embedded in the culture of theoretical reflection and needs to be confronted if we are to successfully "dislodge academics from the fantasies of disinterested observation" on which they are so fixated.[20] In the latter parts of the chapter, I draw a contrast between the disengagement of academic intellectual activity and the kinds of collective thinking – "groupthink," in a novel, positive sense of that expression – required in political organizing and campaigning, including for BDS. Political campaigning of the kind involved in BDS possesses, I will argue, a significant, and systematically underestimated, intellectual content. There is nothing unique to boycott politics in this. Disdained by liberal intellectuals though it often is, "concrete" political organizing of any kind illustrates a type of collective, distributed intellectualism – one that displays the very properties often considered typical of radical theorizing, and suggests a different politics of intellectual work. There is, in short, nothing "anti-intellectual" in preferring boycotts to the normal course of intellectual, academic or cultural exchange. Rejecting BDS on the grounds that keeping talking and thinking are, under all circumstances, necessary for progress, is unfounded.

Chapter 1

Institutions of Occupation and Resistance

An existence liberated from siege, military occupation and colonization; an end to a "program of racial hate elevated to the level of state policy," "animated by doctrines of racial self-segregation, racial exclusiveness, and racial supremacy";[1] the right to live in the home to which you are legally entitled: these are modest demands, less than the bare minimum for the kinds of lives that many westerners would consider normal. The goals of the broader Boycott, Divestment and Sanctions (BDS) campaign, of which the academic boycott is just a part, are no more than these. On the simple grounds of respect for justice, all university workers should support BDS, just as they should support other initiatives for global justice. But there is an extra reason for academics, in particular, to show solidarity with Palestinians through the academic boycott of Israel: the devastating effects of Israeli practices on school and higher education in Palestine. For years now, Israel's abuses of Palestinians have consistently been judged as meeting the legal definition of apartheid.[2] Israeli apartheid, which experts today judge as "far more sophisticated than that experienced by South Africans," constitutes an attack on the very *possibility* of school and university study for Palestinians.[3] For anyone committed to the universal importance of education, this scholasticide should be intolerable.

Palestinians have been informing the world for decades about the repression they face, including in universities. But the actual conditions of higher education in Palestine, along with Israeli universities' shared responsibility for them, are still not well known in the west, and Palestinian academics' call to join the academic boycott can often appear dauntingly remote from any situation with which western scholars are familiar. This is a significant obstacle in the way of international academic solidarity with Palestine. So we will begin our discussion of academic BDS with a description of the current impossible conditions of higher education in Gaza and the occupied West Bank, which we will follow with an account of Israeli universities' distinctive responsibility for the colonialist system that places the very existence of Palestinian higher education under threat. Acknowledging the agony of Palestinian universities, and Israeli universities' essential role in perpetuating it, should be a powerful incentive to join the academic boycott, described to me recently by one academic in Palestine as among the most positive steps forward for their people's rights *ever*.

THE AMPUTATION OF HIGHER EDUCATION IN PALESTINE

Palestine has a rich and ancient history of education and scholarship, but in the modern period, universities were initially not part of it: before 1967, Palestinian university students usually studied in Jordan, Lebanon, Egypt or Europe; in Palestine itself, at most only two years of tertiary education could be undertaken, the Zionist authorities believing that educated Palestinians constituted a "problem" for Israel.[4] After the Six-Day War and the occupation of the West Bank and Gaza Strip, Israel started obstructing Palestinian students' travel and often detained Palestinians returning from abroad. This interference with Palestinians' freedom of movement made domestic universities in the occupied territories increasingly necessary. Without universities in Palestine, the Israeli occupation would have made it impossible to realize a basic precondition of students' academic freedom: the possibility of tertiary study itself. In establishing Palestinian universities, the ambition was not just to provide higher education within the existing terms of the occupation but also, in the words of the cofounder of Birzeit University, Gabi Baramki, to build "a road to freedom." "Having a university was crucial if we were to resist the occupation," Baramki wrote. "We would produce well-educated, confident graduates, proud of their Palestinian national identity and eager to contribute to the development of their homeland. Moreover, university life would create a haven for the practice of democracy in a situation of political oppression."[5]

The very project of founding Palestinian universities, then, has to be understood as an expression of resistance to oppression at the hands of Israel: the president of An-Najah University in Nablus described his institution in 1985 "as a symbol of the Palestinian people's determination to strengthen its hold over its homeland."[6] University creation in the West Bank and Gaza was not helped by the fact that between 1967 and 1990, the Israelis systematically expelled around two thousand members of Palestine's cultural, intellectual and professional elite, including academics and students, whom it saw as sources of resistance to their control.⁷ Birzeit University's inaugural president, Hanna Nasir, was among them. Israel's decision to permit any universities at all in the Palestinian territory it occupied, especially at a time when it opposed the creation of other national institutions,⁸ is sometimes suggested to have been motivated by the desire to create a brain drain of Palestinian graduates from historic Palestine to the Gulf oil boom, thereby supporting the wider project of Zionist ethnic cleansing.⁹ On the Palestinian side, by contrast, the opening of higher education institutions was often seen as a way of *stemming* the forced exodus of graduates abroad, since higher educational levels in the West Bank and Gaza, as well as in the surrounding countries, were taken to be a prerequisite for national liberation.[10]

The nation-building ambitions of Palestinian higher education have remained a constant of its modern history. In the face of the attempted Zionist erasure of Palestine, "the transmission and preservation of Palestinian history, heritage and culture" in the service of national liberation was a fundamental aim of the Palestine Liberation Organization, which funded universities, and of the universities themselves.[11] Palestinian universities were, in other words, founded "with the goal of producing anticolonial knowledge."[12] Conviction about an "indissoluble link" between education and emancipation drove university founders;[13] the first director of the Council for Higher Education in the West Bank and Gaza spoke of universities' mission as guiding Palestinian society's "metamorphosis from a colonial to an independent community with as little disorder and dislocation as possible."[14] "Patriotic" considerations fall among Birzeit University's responsibilities, a recent annual report states.[15] Indeed, *failure* to foster students' political development would be a serious dereliction of universities' duty: "What kind of people will the Palestinian graduates be," asked the *Al Fajr* newspaper in 1987, "if they are not allowed to think and express their own and their people's political aspirations?"[16]

"In reality," Abaher El Sakka comments in relation to Palestinian universities, "the academic field is an extension of the political field."[17] Different political groups play a central role in Palestinian higher education: Al-Azhar University in Gaza was established by Fatah and the Islamic University by Hamas. Both are heavily involved in university life.[18] In the absence of a Palestinian state, universities also assumed embryonic state functions for the population of the occupied territories, taking responsibility in such domains as literacy development, pharmaceutical certification and primary health care; the majority of the Palestinian negotiating team at the 1991 Madrid conference were Birzeit University staff. Universities also function as theaters of competition for Palestinian political groups, with student elections consciously modeling the democratic protocols of a future free Palestine. Universities have been central hubs and incubators of politics from the moment of their foundation – An-Najah's graduation ceremonies, for a recent observer, "looked less like graduation ceremonies and more like Fatah rallies."[19] As a result, student leaders are continually targeted by Israel: between 2012 and 2018, for instance, over twenty members of the Birzeit student council were arrested, including four of its heads.[20] The Israel Defense Forces (IDF) and other security forces regularly make armed incursions onto campuses, which they treat as their hunting grounds; live ammunition is regularly fired.

The West Bank occupation and blockade of Gaza constitute massive obstacles to Palestinians' access to school and university. Walls, buffer zones, ubiquitous checkpoints and, in Gaza, recurrent power shortages severely disrupt the day-to-day life of students, staff and institutions. Students' education is, of course, undermined long before university. Palestinian school students in East Jerusalem suffer from an acute shortage of classrooms.[21] Gazan school students, in the words of Saree Makdisi, are academically stunted because they "cannot concentrate – or, even if they can, because they are trying to study and learn in circumstances that no child should have to endure."[22] In the West Bank, checkpoints turn the journey to and from university into a punishing, humiliating ordeal and significantly reduce the proportion of the day in which classes can be held: what should be a twenty-five-minute car trip can involve crossing no less than four checkpoints and become a three- to four-hour nightmare.[23] Many Birzeit students have to cross the Qalandia checkpoint, the biggest on the West Bank, to get to and from the university. This process can take many hours – a massive theft of time and dignity that could be invested in study, leisure or work. The bus from Bethlehem to Jerusalem passes through a checkpoint at which students are sometimes stopped for four to five hours – a situation that can lead parents to think that their daughters and sons shouldn't be at university at all. Harassment at checkpoints (sometimes, women in headscarves are told they cannot cross without uncovering themselves),[24] the sheer time taken to travel from one city to another in a country strangulated by an occupying army, the need to help defend the family home from Israeli settlers – all these mean that it is never clear how many students will be able to attend class from one day to the next, a serious disruption to the continuity that effective teaching and learning require. One of the checkpoints regularly set up by the IDF outside university gates across Palestine, especially at exam times, is at Abu Dis, an East Jerusalem suburb where Al-Quds University has a campus; exams or not, the campus is continually monitored by Israeli surveillance cameras.[25] Given that a majority of Palestinian students are women, this harassment is sexist as well as racist.[26] The difficulties of travel mean that universities increasingly draw their students, and to a certain extent their staff, just from their local regions.[27] Seventy per cent of Birzeit students come from the Ramallah and Jerusalem areas and, according to one academic, speak of Hebron, a mere 50 kilometers away, as though it's the

US. In a country trying to cultivate a national culture and to open its students to the world, this is a serious problem.

The occupation also severely complicates the international exchange and recruitment that are essential to academic life. Even though Tel Aviv airport is not far away, West Bank academics who want to travel overseas have to fly out from Amman in Jordan. Leaving the West Bank itself necessitates crossing the King Hussein (Allenby) Crossing, an often fraught and uncertain process that increases the time and the cost of each trip abroad. Travel restrictions also affect staff without West Bank residency permits – foreigners and even some Palestinians themselves. Given that PhD programs are currently offered in only a tiny number of Palestinian institutions, recruitment of foreign-trained staff is a necessity, but it too is severely disrupted by the arbitrary conditions on movement imposed by Israel.[28] Restrictions on travel into and out of Palestine preclude any certainty about whether staff and students without Palestinian residency permits will be allowed in, thereby straightjacketing institutions into local enclaves: in the 2017–2018 academic year, for instance, denial or delay of work visas for foreign staff affected scores of lecturers; as many as half of the sixty-four foreign academic and other staff members employed by nine Palestinian universities were reported to have been subjected to visa denial or restriction in the two years to 2018.[29] At Birzeit University alone, fifteen academic staff members had their visa requests refused or significantly delayed. One English literature academic was forced to leave the country outright, as was a history academic who had worked at the university for the past four decades.[30] According to Academia for Equality, twelve departments at Birzeit University or affiliated institutions faced losing faculty members at the start of the 2019–2020 academic year; as of September 2020, five international faculty members had to end their contracts with Birzeit because Israel refused to admit them back into the West Bank.[31] The screw tightened even further in 2022, with Israel announcing that the military administration of the occupied territories would now vet all applications from foreign academics to teach at West Bank universities, with no more than one hundred visas to be issued, all under highly restrictive conditions concerning both eligibility and duration of stay. Visas for international students would also be reduced to a minuscule quota.[32] Under these conditions, without even the most basic staffing continuity, university planning is continually in damage-control mode. Trying to circumvent or adapt to the expulsion of foreign staff is a permanent drain on university resources and has had major detrimental effects: to give a single example, in the 1980s, foreign staff made up over a third of Birzeit's Cultural Studies department, but the continual denial of entry permits almost forced the department's closure and necessitated significant restructuring.[33]

Given the extreme youth of Palestine's population – forty-six per cent of the West Bank, and sixty-one per cent of Gaza are under eighteen – Israel's entire post-1967 regime can in itself be considered as an attack on education.[34] Unlike the other targets of Israeli oppression, education is intangible and cannot be stolen or demolished. This means it is avidly sought after by Palestinians: Palestinian prisoners in Israeli jails even went on hunger strike in 1992 in order to win the right to university study.[35] (Today, Israel has completely banned higher education for Palestinian prisoners through the Open University of Israel, the only option available to them, and regularly obstructs the instruction offered by prisoners themselves in partnership with Palestinian institutions.[36]) In a society engulfed by a hostile military power, education is sometimes seen as all that is left.[37] But if higher education throws a lifeline to the occupied and besieged Palestinian population, Israel still finds many ways to sever it. Derar Elyan, vice president of the Palestine Technical University, described the situation at the institution's Tulkarm campus in the following terms in a 2016 appeal:

> Since 2002, the army has used a shooting range built on confiscated university land, with firing oriented in the direction of the university buildings. Moreover, since October 2015, the army has responded aggressively and disproportionately to demonstrations against the occupation, storming the university's campus 130 times over 85 days, injuring 138 students and staff members with live bullets. In addition, the army fired tear gas grenades causing 850 cases of suffocation and destroyed greenhouses used by the students. These incursions into [the] campus also included shooting at walls, windows, and lamps; using so-called "skunk water;" and preventing the use of the library for weeks. To date, 12.5% of the total study days have been disrupted this year, as the university was forced to suspend study 12 times and to close its doors for two days to maintain its students' lives and safety.[38]

The closure of campuses has been a frequent measure, sometimes for years on end – Birzeit was closed for four years from 1988.[39] Closures do not just prevent classes being held but lead to the destruction of laboratory samples that need constant attention. Staff and students are regularly arrested and detained: in November 2019, eighty students from Birzeit were in Israeli jails.[40] In 2019, Birzeit and the Addameer Prisoner Support and Human Rights Association reported a "growing number of cases of severe physical torture during the interrogation of students" by Israel.[41] At Bethlehem University, as on other Palestinian campuses, many students are politically active: during exam periods they don't return home but go into hiding in Bethlehem instead in order to avoid being arrested and prevented from finishing their year. These conditions stifle student life on campus: in non-exam periods, everyone goes home to their village after class. There is no student housing or shared houses: students live with their parents, who sometimes pick their children up from the checkpoints – a practice which some lecturers find infantilizing. According to Baramki, almost *every* Birzeit lecturer in 2010 had been "held by the military for some length of time";[42] between 2002 and 2010, 436 Birzeit employees and students were imprisoned.[43] Al-Quds University astrophysicist Imad Barghouthi has been detained on multiple occasions; he served over six months' administrative detention, without charge or trial, in 2016, and was arrested again and detained indefinitely in 2020, periods during which his teaching had to be postponed;[44] An-Najah physics professor Essam al-Ashqar was detained for almost a year in 2016–2017; in September 2019, media studies professor Widad Barghouti was detained and later released on house arrest.[45]

Israeli taxation and the withholding of building permits place onerous restrictions on universities' ability to function, let alone expand. Censorship and delays in supply of books, journals and equipment are common: since the uncensored Arabic books available in Lebanon cannot be imported, Palestinian universities have to use the doctored versions of texts available in Jordan, Egypt or elsewhere.[46] Because of postal restrictions, Palestinian universities can typically receive books and other parcels only at addresses in Jerusalem, greatly complicating the process of communication with the outside world. Funding is a constant problem: the throttled Palestinian economy cannot reliably generate the tuition fees, which constitute between sixty and eighty per cent of chronically underfunded universities' budgets.[47]

A selection of incidents in a recent single period – December 2017 to December 2018 – exemplifies the full extent of Israel's day-to-day assault on education in Palestine.[48] On December 12 and again on December 17, 2017, students protesting at the Tulkarm campus of the Palestine Technical University against the US decision to move its embassy to Jerusalem were attacked by Israeli soldiers, who fired tear gas and rubber-coated steel rounds at them. On December 14, the IDF raided the Abu Dis campus of Al-Quds University, prompting clashes with local residents. The IDF destroyed, removed or damaged three hundred exhibits being prepared for an exhibition at a campus museum presenting the experiences of Palestinian prisoners and damaged hundreds of books.[49] The same day, the Birzeit campus north of Ramallah was also raided, with banners and other student material seized. On the 17th, in addition to the second Tulkarm attack, Israeli forces fired tear gas into the Palestine Technical University campus in Al-Arroub, north of Hebron, causing multiple cases of suffocation. On January 15, 2018, the Al-Quds Open University student Ahmad Abd al-Jaber Muhammad Salim, secretary of the Democratic Front for the Liberation of Palestine (DFLP) student bloc, was killed by the IDF in Jayyous.[50] On March 4, rubber-coated steel bullets and tear gas canisters were used by the IDF on students on the same campus. The university's director was reported by the WAFA news agency as saying that Israeli forces deliberately provoke students "through their almost daily presence at the university's entrance; and the searching and interrogating of students, which provokes clashes."[51] On March 6, a twenty-year-old Jenin university student was abducted by the IDF.[52] On March 8, armed Israeli soldiers disguised as students made a violent intrusion onto the Birzeit University campus and abducted the head of the Student Council, Omar al-Kiswani, who was pinned to the ground outside the Student Council building; live rounds were fired. In the first month of Kiswani's detention at the Al-Maskobiyya interrogation center in occupied Jerusalem, he endured interrogations that lasted for eighteen to twenty hours a day, was prevented from sleeping and was banned from seeing his lawyer for twenty-five days.[53] A student march protesting against the kidnapping was attacked with live ammunition several days later; at least eight students were injured, one of them seriously. On April 23, the IDF shut down two schools, a vocational college and an area around the Abu Dis campus of Al-Quds in order to seal holes that had been drilled in the separation wall.

The following day, the dean of students at Bethlehem University, Mahmoud Hammad, was arrested. On April 25, Ibtihal Khader Ibreiwish, a twenty-year-old student at the Al-Arroub branch of the Palestine Technical University, was abducted by the IDF as she left the campus.[54] The next day, Israeli soldiers sealed the campus entrances, preventing staff and students from entering it, and wounded four of them.[55] Another arrest of an academic, Ghassan Thouqan, a lecturer at An-Najah National University in Nablus, followed on July 11. On September 5, Israeli forces sealed off the Abu Dis campus of Al-Quds University. Dozens of students suffered from tear gas inhalation.[56] On September 20, a Palestinian student, Ola Marshoud, was finally released after seven months' detention.[57] On October 2, two university students were shot and injured with rubber-coated steel bullets, and many others suffered from tear gas inhalation in an attack by the IDF on students demonstrating the nation-state law and the planned demolition of the Khan al-Ahmar Bedouin community. On November 19, the new head of the Birzeit Student Council, Yehya Rabie', was taken into custody, joining sixty other Birzeit students in Israeli prisons, often without charge.[58] On December 5, Israel announced that it would no longer recognize social work degrees from Al-Quds University, effectively voiding that degree of its professional utility.[59] On December 12, the IDF ransacked a number of faculties and offices at the Al-Quds Abu Dis campus.[60] On December 23, Israeli soldiers again sealed the gates of the Al-Arroub campus of Palestine Technical University and prevented the students from entering or leaving it.[61]

This litany of attacks comes in addition to the daily obstructions with which staff and students must contend simply in virtue of living in the occupied territories. Already in 2010, according to Saree Makdisi, "three Gazans in four are unable to pursue a university education because there is no room for them in the system – and because they can't get out of Gaza."[62] Israel's periodic attacks on Gaza increase the hardship of students and university staff even further. Students accounted for more than a quarter of civilian deaths during Israel's war on Gaza in the summer of 2014. Sixty-six per cent of students at Al-Azhar University – almost four thousand people – lost their homes in the war. Many of the university's buildings, including its entire agricultural college, were destroyed by armored bulldozers and airstrikes. Israeli tanks shelled the Arab College of Applied Sciences, the University of Palestine, the University College of Applied Science, Al-Quds Open University and Al-Azhar New Campus. The Palestine Technical College underwent direct impact from a drone. The Islamic University suffered major structural damage when targeted by an Israeli airstrike.[63] Israeli bombardment caused yet more damage and closures to universities, schools and cultural institutions during the assault on Gaza in 2021.[64] Gaza exemplifies in graphic form the deeper reality: "scholasticide" – the violent suppression of education – is a key strategic objective of Israeli policy toward Palestinians.[65]

UNIVERSITIES AS TOOLS OF OCCUPATION

Judith Butler argues that academic freedom is a "conditioned freedom," in that it can exist only under the conditions of "institutional structures that make [it] possible and protect its ongoing exercise." What Butler has in mind are simply the kinds of stable academic organizations and the social arrangements that support them which people in the west expect.[66] In systematically undermining, attacking and destroying the structures that enable Palestinian universities to function, Israel imposes a militarized blockade of Palestinian academic freedom and the very possibility of higher education in Palestine.

Opponents of BDS frequently claim that in targeting Israeli universities, the boycott "silences" "one of the major sources of antigovernment critique" in that country.[67] In fact, the opposite is true: far from being a haven of critique, dissent or antiracism, Israeli higher education has anti-Palestinianism as a central plank, notwithstanding the views of individual Israeli academics. Israeli universities are often described as "complicit" with the large-scale violation of Palestinians' rights, in the minimal sense that they do not officially protest against those violations.[68] But this is not nearly strong enough: in their institutional support for the Zionist project, more than simply being complicit with anti-Palestinianism, Israeli higher education is a central *instrument* of it.[69]

This is a role Israeli universities have played from the outset. Like Palestinian ones, Jewish universities in Palestine were also created in an explicit state-building perspective. The earliest Jewish institution in the region, Haifa's German-sponsored Technion, was envisaged as a university that would "precede, create, shape, and protect a modern state."[70] Although the original impetus behind the Technion was not itself Zionist, the institution soon established itself as central to Zionist ambitions and was described by Ben-Gurion as "the cornerstone of the State of Israel."[71] The opening of the Hebrew University of Jerusalem (HUJ) in 1925, over two decades before the 1948 Nakba created a Jewish state, represented the accomplishment of one of the Zionist movement's most important aspirations. "In the university," the then president of the World Zionist movement, Chaim Weizmann, declared, "the wandering soul of Israel will reach its haven."[72] The "load of religious and messianic expectations with which the cultural and secular project of university founding was freighted was massive," according to one commentator.[73] The 1948 Zionist takeover of historic Palestine means that university education in Israel takes place in areas from which Palestinians have been expelled, or where they are second-class citizens: Ben-Gurion University is located in Beersheba, occupied by Israel on October 21, 1948, with the population of five thousand being driven out at gunpoint to Hebron and many of them shot; the University of Tel Aviv lies on the ground of the destroyed Palestinian village of Al-Shaykh Muwannis, one of whose last remaining houses is now the faculty club; most famously, the Mount Scopus campus of HUJ is on expropriated Palestinian land just beyond the Green Line.[74]

A common narrative today stresses HUJ's status as "a pioneer in establishing contacts with Palestinian scholars" and a contributor to "the political movement towards peace."[75] The university was, indeed, the first to recognize the Palestinian matriculation examination and offers preparatory courses for Palestinian students. Because of movement restrictions in the West Bank, Palestinians from East Jerusalem are being increasingly driven out of Palestinian universities and into HUJ – where, as we will see, they are second-class citizens – exacerbating the balkanization of Palestine.[76] But the very *existence* of HUJ in Jerusalem, whether beyond or within the Green Line, derives from a project of Palestinian educational dispossession: in 1922, a proposal by the British governor of Jerusalem for an English university intended for a mixed student body of Arabs and Jews alike fell afoul of the Zionist movement, which refused to participate on the grounds that it "constituted a threat to Hebrew culture in Palestine" and to the future Hebrew University in particular.[77] Nothing came of the British proposal, nor of a subsequent one for an institution embodying the ideal of "Palestinism."[78] Zionists' preference for exclusivity in education regularly obstructed the creation of mixed Jewish Arab institutions, creating an obstacle to educational opportunity for

Palestinian students by requiring them to go abroad if they wanted to pursue university study.[79] Even today, most Israeli universities lack Arabic signage, and Arabic is largely missing from university websites.[80] Use of Arabic has sometimes even been forbidden on campus, as have displays of the Palestinian flag.[81] The first Arabic-language conference in the ninety-year history of HUJ was held only recently. Historically, HUJ enacted Palestinian dispossession in other ways, too: after 1948, books plundered from Palestinian households became the core of the Hebrew University's collection.[82]

Institutional Zionism is matched by intellectual. Academic work everywhere is often closely tied to the national priorities of the states in which it is conducted and funded; Israel is no exception. The scientific and ideological service to the Zionist project provided by disciplines like history, archaeology, sociology and Middle Eastern studies has been documented in detail by many researchers.[83] Even an apparently purely "academic" discipline like philology played an ideological role in orientalizing the Arabic world in the eyes of western Europeans. German-trained philologists at the early HUJ participated in the systematic portrayal of Palestinians as backward and degenerate by discrediting the Arabic spoken by their students as non-classical – an early instance of what has been described as "the securitization of Arabic studies among the Jewish people," with Arabic emerging "as a language that is *spoken* by Arab people but is *controlled* by Jewish-Israeli experts."[84] One of the HUJ orientalists, the German Jewish scholar Martin Plessner, later complained that native Arabic-speaking students didn't have a good-enough accent; he taught Arab students reluctantly, in the belief, in Amit Levy's words, that "they had no knowledge of their own language, and that they wanted to get good grades without making an effort."[85] Archaeology, in particular, has been identified as central to the ongoing construction of Israel's origin myth, with pro-settlement organizations regularly funding digs, including in the West Bank, in contravention of international law:[86] as Nadia Abu El-Haj documents, archaeology "substantiated the nation in history and produced Eretz Yisrael as the national home."[87] The Israeli non-governmental organization Emek Shaveh opposes the politicization of Israeli archaeology, with the aim of challenging "those who use archaeological sites to dispossess disenfranchised communities," and campaigning against the use of "the ruins of the past . . . [as] . . . a political tool in the Israeli-Palestinian conflict" and the fact that, despite the frequent involvement of Israeli universities, "archeology in the West Bank is treated as a military activity and not as academic research."[88]

Ilan Pappé has described the successful opposition in Israeli universities to the "post-Zionist" scholars determined to bring critical perspectives to bear on Israeli history and society. He relates how previously critical "Israeli 'new historians' such as Benny Morris and post-Zionist philosophers such as Ilan

Gur-Ze'ev and others appeared with mea culpa statements, reasserting their allegiance to Zionism, declaring their distrust of the Palestinians and their animosity towards the Palestinian minority in Israel."[89] Pappé himself, who made no such declaration, was forced out of Israel entirely.[90] Opposition to the perceived excessive leftism of the Politics and Government department of Ben-Gurion University threatened it with closure in 2011.[91] Criticism of the Israeli academy's silence in the face of attacks on Palestinians are frequent: the Israeli academic Chen Misgav reports that "it seems oppression and the egregious violation of the freedom of Palestinian academics produce mainly yawns" from his colleagues.[92] According to Gabi Baramki, Israeli academics took three decades to protest collectively against restrictions to Palestinian academic freedom – and when the first protest was made, it was not signed by any university rector.[93] "Faculty members," a *Haaretz* journalist commented in 2017, "rarely involve themselves in issues not directly related to their employment conditions and responsibilities."[94] When the Committee of University Heads in Israel was asked in 2019 by thirty-three academics at the University of Haifa to protest against Israel's denial of visas to lecturers wanting to visit West Bank universities, it refused.[95]

Israeli universities play a vital role in the development of the material and intellectual supports of Palestinian oppression. In 1963, the occupation of the West Bank was planned at the Hebrew University's Givat Ram campus.[96] Following the 1967 invasion of the West Bank, eminent Israeli political scientists, sociologists and anthropologists contributed to a large-scale study of the newly occupied territories, designed to provide accurate information on the characteristics of their population with objectives that were "not academic but rather aimed to serve state interests," such as suppression of resistance and the departure of Palestinians to neighboring Arab countries.[97] Today, research cooperation between universities and weapons manufacturers binds Israeli higher education tightly into the state's military-industrial complex: Israeli universities are reliant for much of their income on IDF training and research funding.[98] The Technion, for instance, has close institutional links with Elbit Systems and Rafael Advanced Defense Systems, Israel's biggest arms manufacturers, and developed the remote-controlled bulldozer used to destroy Palestinians' houses.[99] The university's aerospace faculty maintains "exceptionally close ties" with these firms, as well as with Ministry of Defense research agencies and army and air force units.[100] During Operation Protective Edge in 2014, the Technion raised half a million dollars for those of its students involved in combat.[101] Ben-Gurion University cooperates closely with IDF logistics, cyber-defense, air force technology and computing units and trains IDF soldiers in engineering and exact sciences.[102] Its robotics lab has the IDF as an important "client and stimulus to research."[103] The Hebrew University's technology transfer company, Yissum, takes part in a long-term collaboration with Lockheed Martin, which supplies a very wide range of material, including fighter jets and artillery support, to the IDF.[104] Tel Aviv University facilitates the recruitment of its students by weapons companies, cooperates closely with Elbit Systems and, in 2022, established the Elrom Center, a joint venture with the Israeli Air Force to advance air and space power in Israel.[105] Given that Palestinians are privileged targets of IDF operations – Israel launched full-scale wars against Gaza in 2008, 2012, 2014 and 2021 – Israeli universities' ties with the military translate directly into attacks on Palestinians.

Universities also train students in the rehabilitation of Israel's tarnished reputation: the University of Haifa's "Ambassadors Online" course is aimed at the promotion of Israel's online international image. The program provides students with training in combatting "delegitimization" efforts online, in collaboration with the Israeli Ministry of Foreign Affairs.[106] At the private Reichmann University – formerly the Interdisciplinary Center (IDC) Herzliya – students can study for credit in the "Public Diplomacy" program, which provides training in online activism in favor of Israel and against BDS, in collaboration with Act.IL, an aggressive online hasbara organization which the university started.[107] The Technion's "Defense Strategy for International Markets" course prepares students to sell the weapons systems tested on Palestinians to global buyers. Students at HUJ can get credit for volunteering with the Zionist organization Im Tirzu, which intimidates and discredits pro-Palestinian academics.[108]

The University of Haifa educates "senior officials and high ranking officers" through the National Security Studies Program and the National Security Studies Center.[109] Tel Aviv University established and hosts the Institute for National Security Studies (INSS), which aims to shape Israeli national security policy. As at all such institutes in Israel, INSS staff are principally former senior IDF and other state security officers.[110] The INSS's 2018 "Plan" sketches a proposal for dealing with the "Palestinian threat," predicated on a unilateral move to "serve Israeli interests." It recommends completion of the separation wall, "ongoing construction in settlement blocs and their definition as essential to Israel in any future situation,"[111] refusal of Palestinian refugees' internationally established right of return and retention of IDF freedom of action throughout the West Bank – all presented as compatible with the aim of a "just" Israeli state.[112] Near the end of Operation Guardian of the Walls, Israel's attack on Gaza in 2021, a paper by the INSS's managing director recommended that "the entry of aid into the Gaza Strip should be made contingent on the existence of an effective mechanism for preventing a military buildup by Hamas and Islamic Jihad." Humanitarian relief, in other words, was to be used for military advantage.[113] Slightly earlier in the campaign, the same author – also an experienced IDF officer – had published an analysis recommending intensifying Israeli video propaganda to counter negative publicity over Gaza.[114] Another senior INSS figure, Gabi Siboni, a former IDF colonel and a senior research fellow at the institute, is a proponent of the "Dahiya doctrine" used to devastating effect in Lebanon and Gaza: the doctrine specifies that "with an outbreak of hostilities, the IDF will need to act immediately, decisively, and with force that is disproportionate to the enemy's actions and the threat it poses." "Such a response," it continues, "aims at inflicting damage and meting out punishment to an extent that will demand long and expensive reconstruction processes."[115]

The Moshe Dayan Center (MDC) at Tel Aviv University describes itself as "founded, in part, to bridge the gap between the Israeli intelligence apparatus and academia, and to provide research solutions to contemporary issues that the intelligence services did not have the time or capability to pursue." According to its website, it continues to "play a crucial role in safeguarding Israel's future," undertaking activities that "are not merely academic in nature. Instead, the MDC attacks real-world problems and helps to achieve real-world solutions."[116] Similarly, the BESA Center – the Begin-Sadat Center for Strategic Studies at Bar-Ilan University – produces policy recommendations for the Israeli political, military and foreign affairs communities and "conducts specialized research on contract to the Israeli foreign affairs and defense establishment."[117] Efraim Inbar, the center's former long-term director, has acknowledged that "political neutrality" is not an option for the center, which is Zionist in orientation.[118] A paper released by the center in 2018 argued that only "a fourth massive round of fighting against Hamas" would make Hamas realize that "that the pain to be suffered is so great, and the chance of eliminating the Jewish state so slim, as to render further violence pointless." "Now, alas," the paper concluded, "is the time for war."[119] After operation Guardian of the Walls in 2021, one BESA Center paper advocated boycotting Palestinians; another warned against any Israeli withdrawal from the West Bank.[120]

As declarations like these suggest, Israeli higher education takes place in a close structural symbiosis with the Israeli army and security apparatus, which supplies a significant proportion of universities' senior academic leaders and administrators.[121] Until 2018, Ariel University in the West Bank, disowned by much of Israeli academia, was effectively under the supervision of the IDF.[122] IDF soldiers have privileged access to higher education throughout Israel, thanks to the "Uniform to Studies" scheme, which provides generous scholarships for discharged combat soldiers, with plans to extend the scheme to anyone who has served in any capacity.[123] Since Palestinian Israelis do not serve in the IDF, they are ineligible for this significant reduction in the cost of university education. Bar-Ilan University tops up the "Uniform to Studies" scholarship so that IDF veterans can study fee-free.[124] Reservists, too, gain automatic academic credit with every eighteen days of annual service.[125] Tel Aviv University offered a year's free tuition to students who participated in the 2014 Gaza War.[126]

The formal instruction required for positions of responsibility in the IDF is dispensed through the university system, with the University of Haifa responsible for IDF officer training since 2018. In announcing this collaboration, the president of the university expressed his pleasure that the "University of Haifa [would be] responsible for the academic education of the Israel Defense Forces' core of command for the coming years."[127] Even before this arrangement, Haifa offered the previously mentioned Master's program in national security for members of the IDF, the police, Mossad, Shin Bet and other security and intelligence services. Bar-Ilan University offers a bachelor's degree for IDF and Shin Bet officers.[128] The Hebrew University of Jerusalem hosts the Talpiot program, which supplies the IDF with elite expertise in technology, as well the Military Medicine Program, applications for which are assessed by the army, with successful applicants' tuition fees being waived.[129] During the 2014 war on Gaza, HUJ declared that "the university is joining the war effort to support its warrior students, in order to minimize the financial burden" on them.[130] In 2019, the university took out a full-page newspaper advertisement to stress its commitment to its soldier students, stating that "we proudly support our faculty and staff that serve in the military reserves, who are parents of soldiers, or whose partners serve in the IDF, during peace time or under emergency. The university and the student union provide many special support programs for soldiers in both regular and reserve military service."[131] Details of Israeli university graduates have been forwarded by universities to the Shin Bet, allegedly for recruitment purposes.[132] In 2018, HUJ prompted further calls for boycott by hosting a day-long Shin Bet recruitment event for its students.[133] Israeli moral philosophers, James Eastwood shows, regularly "now supplement their academic work with teaching at military colleges, defense ministries, and officer schools."[134]

Israeli universities do not just supply the technical expertise on which the oppression of Palestinians depends, the training for the army that implements it and the ideological firepower needed to justify it in the battle of world opinion: their own campuses are sites on which Palestinian oppression is enacted. The Hebrew University, for instance, lets its rooftops be used for police surveillance of Palestinians in the adjoining East Jerusalem suburb of Issawiya.[135] Most significantly, this oppression is structural: Palestinian students, already subjected to significant discrimination in their schooling,[136] are significantly under-represented in Israeli higher education and are marginalized in many ways, including linguistically and in access to dormitories.[137] Israeli Palestinian staff, too, are in a tiny minority: a 2018 appointment of an Arab Christian is thought to be the first Arab Deanship in Israel ever.[138] Political activity by Arab students on Israeli campuses has often been banned or obstructed, including by Zionist students, as have conferences on topics deemed excessively pro-Palestinian.[139] In 2018, several Israeli universities voluntarily disrupted classes or otherwise supported protests against domestic violence, but nothing anywhere near such levels of institutional support for the Palestinian cause has ever been shown:[140] on the contrary, Israeli universities have blocked prizes being awarded to pro-Palestinian organizations and regularly suppress pro-Palestine and peace activism.[141] Their heads and other senior officials defend Israeli society against charges of apartheid, discipline or fail to defend pro-Palestinian faculty members and refuse to protest against violations of Palestinian academic freedom – instead denouncing BDS initiatives and initiating programs to counteract them.[142] Israeli university authorities often criticize and resist government policy on other matters, such as the requirement for gender-segregated programs for ultra-Orthodox students.[143] They have also sometimes asserted the independence of the Israeli faculty, including boycott supporters, against efforts by the state to interfere politically in university business through ethics codes or vetoes on appointments.[144] But they have never officially objected to the overall militarization of Israeli higher education or asserted the educational rights or academic freedom of Israel's subject Palestinian population. In 2019, Tel Aviv University shut down its Center for Peace Research, known for its cooperation with Palestinian organizations.[145] In 2022, Israel's university presidents accepted Ariel University into the Committee of University Heads, thereby reversing the decade-long boycott of the institution on the grounds of its location in an illegal West Bank settlement.[146]

INDIVIDUALS VERSUS INSTITUTIONS

Insofar as Israeli higher education is an instrument of anti-Palestinianism, it should be opposed, along with all other such instruments. But what does that mean in practice? Obviously, opposing Israeli universities as instruments of anti-Palestinianism doesn't mean that there shouldn't be universities in Israel at all. Instead, it throws into focus the question of the *ways* in which Israeli higher education contributes to Palestinian oppression and provides an immediate reason to oppose them with respect to those ways.

Israeli universities contribute to Palestinian oppression *as institutions* and it is as institutions that they should be boycotted. Universities are more than just the aggregates of their staff and students: they are institutional structures, defined internally by the hierarchical roles assigned to the individuals in them (president, dean, head of department, professor) and externally by their relations with the community, government, business and other institutions, particularly schools and other universities. There is a straightforward distinction between a university's institutional actions and the individual actions of its staff or students. When scientists in a university laboratory make a breakthrough, we usually do not say that the "university" has done so: we attribute it to the scientists who work there. The same applies, or should apply, when an academic writes a book or expresses a political opinion, or when students stage a demonstration or sit an exam: none of these cases counts as the *university* doing anything. On the other hand, there are many activities which can be attributed *only* to the university as an institution, or to one of its constituent structural components (departments, schools, etc.): admitting or graduating students, hosting conferences, signing contracts with industry or the state, putting on particular courses, publishing books or journals. All of these activities are ones, of course, in which individual academics play a role, but these are roles which they can discharge only in virtue of the position which they occupy in the institution's structure. As a mere academic, I cannot confer a degree, speak in the name of the university or enter into an exchange agreement with another institution: appoint me president or vice-chancellor, and suddenly this is exactly the kind of thing I can do. When officials at the University of Haifa moved in 2001 to strip a graduate of a Master's degree for his documentation of a 1948 massacre of Palestinians in Tantura, they did so in the name, and with the authority, of the institution, not as individuals.[147]

These may all seem to be obvious points, but the institutional character of university work is the crux of one of the most innovative and interesting aspects of the academic boycott campaign. While many of the individual academics involved in the activities described in the last section eminently qualify for a personal boycott outside the scope of BDS, their activities certainly don't justify a blanket boycott of *all* Israeli universities or academics. Weapons researchers, racists and warmongers can, unfortunately, be found on campuses around the world: if their activities were grounds for an all-out boycott of the universities at which they work, precious few institutions would be immune. As noted in the introduction, a key feature of the academic boycott strategy is that an academic does not qualify for boycott on an *individual* basis, solely because of their affiliation to a Israeli university: the boycott targets institutions, not individuals – complicity, not identity. Regardless of the anti- (or, for that matter, pro-) Palestinian activities of their individual staff members, the blanket institutional boycott of Israeli universities is justified because they are all *institutional* instruments of anti-Palestinianism. As institutions, Israeli universities all support the oppression of Palestinians through the facts described in the last section: the structural privileging of student soldiers; official, university-level links with the arms companies and military units directly responsible for attacks on Palestinians; the running of accredited university courses in hasbara; institutionally embedded ideological collaboration with government; policy-driven racism and political discrimination against Palestinian students; and the harnessing of universities' institutional social weight to defend Zionism and bestow an academic imprimatur on anti-Palestinian policy proposals.

The institutional nature of the academic boycott of Israel contrasts with the academic boycott of South Africa, which applied indiscriminately to all South African academics. It does not mean, however, that individual academics are never affected by boycott tactics. Universities are human institutions, and any boycott must necessarily affect people. The critical question is *which* people the boycott affects, and why. As an institutional boycott, BDS applies to the activities of two categories of people only: academics who have chosen to take on positions of institutional authority and in doing so have made themselves accountable for their universities' policies; and academics and students who draw on institution-level arrangements like exchange schemes, thereby harnessing the university's institutional identity. The philosophers David Rodin and Michael Yudkin correctly note that "academics, like other people, have the right not to be subject to morally inappropriate forms of discrimination in their professional activities."[148] As people who have thrust themselves into positions of political responsibility for their institutions and who therefore incur a moral accountability for universities' anti-Palestinianism, the discrimination which the academic boycott enacts against Israeli university leaders and other academics for freely associating themselves with universities' institutional identity is anything but morally inappropriate. Unlike the academic boycott of South Africa, which targeted individual South African academics, the principles of the academic boycott of Israel target complicity, not identity, and so exclude anyone being boycotted merely for being affiliated with an Israeli institution.[149] Unlike Palestinian academics, Israeli academics are not barred from attending overseas conferences, or from using funding from their institutions to do so.[150] This policy is often ignored by BDS critics.[151] By ensuring that individual academics are not targeted, not only are the principles of freedom of expression and academic freedom upheld, but the Israel boycott campaign also removes an important objection to academic boycotts in general: the concern that they may inadvertently target or alienate their own allies.[152]

Rather than individuals, then, the boycott targets the *official activities* of Israeli *universities*: the holding of conferences or collaboration with journals sponsored by Israeli institutions, student or staff exchange agreements to which Israeli universities are party, the hosting of addresses and talks by Israeli academic officials, inclusion of Israeli universities in world academic bodies and participation in review and refereeing for Israeli grants, hiring, promotion or tenure processes. All of these activities require individuals to partner with or support Israeli universities as *institutions*.

Even some BDS sympathizers, however, may hesitate over the call to boycott student exchange schemes: does it really contribute to justice in the Middle East, they may ask, to block the interchange of students between Israel and the rest of the world? Wouldn't doing so actually harm the opportunities for exposure to the world that might contribute to a shift in Israeli society's support for anti-Palestinianism? The idea that a boycott of Israeli universities could somehow proceed with *no* effect on their students is, on the face of it, absurd – what are universities, if not institutions, centrally concerned with teaching students? But it is important to recognize that, like the other activities targeted under the institutional boycott, blocking student exchange schemes with Israeli universities only harms Israeli students insofar as it withdraws a privilege they had previously enjoyed. This privilege is available to only a tiny fraction of the world's 207 million university students:[153] suspending it for students of Israeli institutions does no more than bring these students into line with the overwhelming international norm. Students are not immune from politics – indeed, many universities, as we have seen, actively implicate students in anti-Palestinianism. As an important source for the next generation of Israeli leaders, university students must not be exempted from Palestine justice efforts.

But what about the idea that boycotting international exchanges starves students of the exposure to diverse international viewpoints that could favor the development of pro-Palestinian sympathies among them? This argument is parallel to the one often raised against the cultural boycott, which objects that artists who refuse to perform or exhibit in Israel are isolating Israeli society from the international contacts it needs to be shaken out of its anti-Palestinianism. But the objection fails. In the first instance, student exchange schemes participate in the normalization of Israel – the reinforcement of the perception that Israel is not an apartheid state – that BDS aims to combat. Second, rather than placing any hopes in the vague possibility that exchanges will influence Israeli students' views on Palestinians, the far stronger and therefore more effective gesture in favor of Palestinian equality in Israel is for partner universities to show, by boycotting Israeli exchange schemes, that they are serious about bringing an end to Palestinian oppression. The much-remarked failure of political dialogue to bring a just peace to the region justifies considerable skepticism about the peace-making potential of conversations in students' classes, dormitories and bars, or that of concerts in Tel Aviv. As PACBI puts it:

> For those who say we need more dialogue and exchange of ideas, not less, we say that the boycott is a form of speech, a dialogic act that encourages

conversation, connections, dialogue, and exchange based on a set of shared principles of justice, based on an acknowledgement and recognition of the rights and the agency of the oppressed in any such conversation, and anchored in a principle of decolonizing the mind of the oppressor.[154]

Similarly, Rifat Odeh Kassis writes that "it is absurd and offensive to advocate for 'positive engagement' with an apartheid state, to 'convince' it to be more empathic with the people it subjugates, to construe the ultimate goal as 'mutual understanding' rather than an end to oppression itself."[155] We will explore this idea in later chapters.

Since the fundamental rationale for boycotting Israeli universities is countering the normalization of Israel, the boycott also applies to "any activity that creates the impression that Israel is a state like any other and that Palestinians, the oppressed, and Israel, the oppressor, are both equally responsible for 'the conflict.'"[156] This extends the boycott beyond Israeli academic officials to any academic initiative, Israeli or not, that obfuscates the political situation in Palestine by being premised on the idea that Palestinians are not an oppressed, subject population, but an equal "partner," just as responsible as Israelis for bringing peace. This presentation, which ignores Israeli responsibility for the annexation of the West Bank and the siege of Gaza, and encourages both parties to "meet each other half way," fails to represent the real structural dynamics of Israeli oppression, and therefore cannot contribute to ending it.

The consequences for Palestinian academics of "equal partner"-style collaboration with Israeli colleagues have been powerfully described by Gabi Baramki, commenting on European and US grants schemes which require joint Israeli participation as a condition of funding for Palestinian universities. "This is seen as promoting peace and understanding by the donors, but actually humiliates the potential Palestinian recipients without any real advancement towards peace," Baramki says.

> What donors fail to understand is that we will only cooperate on a basis of equality. Why should we want to sit alongside Israeli academics while we are hampered by Israel in our academic work and cannot even travel freely for academic purposes? Why should we pretend that doing academic work together in the current situation represents some sort of normality? All that this kind of cooperation does is make Israelis feel good.[157]

Opponents denounce BDS as a violation of the universality of intellectual exchange – the borderlessness of the understanding. The hypocrisy of this conception in a world of checkpoints, siege and apartheid has often been pointed out. But fully appreciating the political meaning of intellectual collaboration allows us to see how the situation described by

Baramki generalizes to anyone who participates in normalization projects. In rejecting normalization projects, and refusing admission to the intellectual community of the institutional actors complicit with apartheid, while maintaining access for individuals, BDS-supporting academics refuse the humiliation of Palestinians, both physical and symbolic, that normalization constitutes.[158]

Chapter 2

The Academy and Its Freedoms

Along with the charge of anti-Semitism, academic freedom holds pride of place among the themes deployed by Boycott, Divestment and Sanctions (BDS) opponents to counter the academic boycott. For BDS critics, the boycott of Israeli institutions is an unacceptable violation of academic freedom, a concept they typically understand as entailing the "free flow of ideas within the international scholarly community."[1] The fact that, as we saw in the last chapter, the "free flow" of academic ideas in Palestine is brutally obstructed by the occupation is a situation which BDS opponents typically show little interest in changing. Nevertheless, the accusation that BDS compromises academic freedom has been remarkably successful. Thanks to it, many liberals have held back from showing Palestinians the same solidarity that was historically shown to black South Africans and other victims of oppression.

The force of the academic freedom objection to BDS comes from the assumption that boycotts and other similar restrictions to the "free flow of ideas" are exceptional in academia. In an intellectual climate where the results of research in the sciences and elsewhere are regularly enclosed behind publishers' paywalls and often kept secret for commercial reasons, this is an implausible proposition.[2] Still, it might be thought that boycotts' exceptionality is exactly the source of their effectiveness: "justified boycotts must be exceptional," David Rodin and Michael Yudkin say, since "conceptually, the practice of a boycott can only have meaning against a background of substantially uninterrupted interaction and collaboration."[3] All this raises the question of exactly how the concept of academic freedom, with which boycotts are always contrasted, is to be understood and what, in real life, the norms governing academic exchange actually are. Are Rodin and Yudkin right about boycotts' necessary exceptionality in university life? What, empirically speaking, are the real norms, not just the imagined ones, that determine the flow of ideas in typical academic settings? If the appeal to boycott Israeli universities is to be widely adopted, it will help if BDS supporters can break the myth of the normality of academic freedom in universities and the exceptionality of boycotts as a practice. These are my aims in this chapter. Whereas boycotts are usually thought to be departures from the ordinary conduct of the academy, they are in fact *constitutive of*, and deeply embedded in, academic professionalism: in Steven Salaita's words, "boycotts in themselves are not especially controversial among academic communities . . . Criticism of Israel is controversial."[4] Once this is accepted, much of the case against the boycott of Israel simply disappears: if boycotts to achieve particular aims are expected in academic life, then the institutional academic boycott of Israel cannot be rejected as exceptional.

SINGLING OUT ISRAEL

Boycotts necessarily pit one sector of the university "community" against another. Talk of "communities," whether academic, scholarly or student, is common in universities. This talk usually relies on a conception of the communities in question as homogeneous, fundamentally consensual bodies pursuing knowledge in politically neutral ways. But in order to think accurately about academic BDS, it is vital to realize that this is a fantasy: actual university life is riven with competing interests and constituted in its essence by the competition of various "counter-communities" engaged in "a struggle to determine the conditions and criteria of legitimate membership."[5] These counter-communities are not just the well-known ones identified as the "conflict of faculties" (Kant) or the "two cultures" of humanities and sciences (C. P. Snow). Over and above these familiar divisions, universities embody a wide range of antagonistic interests: academics and students; management and employees; teachers and researchers; permanent and precarious employees; senior and junior, influential and marginalized ones; union members and union opponents; supporters of the status quo and dissidents; disciplinarily orthodox and heterodox academics. This variety is, indeed, exactly why a pro-boycott bloc can emerge in the first place, in opposition to dominant norms of university life.

As the debate over academic BDS shows, different counter-communities have different conceptions of how universities should be – including, often, different conceptions of "academic freedom" itself.[6] But if dissent and conflict over this and other questions are, as a matter of fact, thoroughly entrenched in academic life, they are also, as we will explore more fully in chapter three, often strongly disavowed. One of the ways in which this disavowal manifests itself most clearly is in the idea that, in universities, academics should behave apolitically and that the very act of taking sides over a political question is inappropriate. Given that, as Rima Najjar Kapitan points out, "one of the primary justifications for the . . . protection of academic freedom is the preparation of students for participation in the political realm," apoliticality is surely an unexpected requirement.[7] Nevertheless, an aspiration for apoliticality lies behind one of BDS opponents' most frequent complaints about the boycott: the charge that boycotting Israel is selective and therefore an affront to academic neutrality. Why, BDS critics ask, should Israel be "singled out" for special attention? Why not boycott institutions in other states responsible for human rights violations – China for its persecution of Tibetans and Uyghurs, Saudi Arabia or Iran for the situation of women and LGBTQ people, Myanmar for its persecution of the Rohingya, Turkey for its occupation of northern Cyprus, Australia for its crimes against refugees and Aboriginal people, Syria for its regime's devastation of entire cities? The list of potentially boycottable states is endless. Isn't it simply disproportionate, and therefore discriminatory – indeed, anti-Semitic – to target Israel? On the basis that the most severe crimes should be boycotted first,[8] surely, BDS critics ask, a number of these states outrank Israel as boycott targets? As a number of commentators have pointed out, the selectivity criticism is not leveled in order to suggest that all these other boycottable states should be boycotted too. Instead, BDS opponents' point is clearly to suggest that Israel is the *last* state to which boycott tactics should apply – sometimes with the implication that boycotting *anyone* is incompatible with a commitment to "academic freedom." The academic boycott is not the only target of this argument, which is regularly raised against all BDS activities in general.

What should we make of this? The first thing to note when a BDS opponent asks why boycotters are focused exclusively on Israel is that, as a matter of fact, they're not. BDS proponents typically participate, in differing degrees, in multiple campaigns, some of which also involve boycotts. Solidarity with Indigenous peoples subjected to settler-colonialism in places like the US or Australia is a central dimension of Palestine justice, and BDS, activism: one of the leading intellectuals and advocates of BDS, Steven Salaita, has devoted an entire book, *Inter/Nationalism: Decolonizing Native America and Palestine*, to exploring the connections between Palestine and Indigenous American solidarity. BDS supporters have often stated that they would support academic boycotts of other settler-colonial countries, were Indigenous people to call for them.[9] BDS-supporting colleagues at my own institution (the University of Sydney) are involved in campaigns for First Nations and refugee rights in Australia, the global solidarity movement for democracy in Syria, defense of the Uyghur minority in Xinjiang and Tamils in Sri Lanka as well as a range of other causes. This is entirely typical of BDS advocates. Still, a BDS opponent might reply, you're not actually calling for a *boycott* of anyone else, are you? Once again, this is, simply, factually untrue. Many older BDS activists are veterans of the boycott campaign against apartheid in South Africa. BDS supporters were among those who called for a boycott of international conferences in the US following Donald Trump's election and "Muslim ban" and even for a boycott of UAE universities following the 2018 arrest of a British research student.[10] Institutional boycotts of academic bodies complicit in Russia's 2022 invasion of Ukraine were widely welcomed by BDS supporters.[11] But even if no BDS activist had ever boycotted any other country than Israel, the charge of selectivity would still not be reasonable. Boycotting is a tactic, not a principle – a course adopted when there are grounds to believe that it will be effective, not an obligatory component of every global justice campaign. Because boycott is simply one tactic among many, there is no expectation that it should be universally applied, and no inconsistency involved if only a single campaign happens to involve it: there might be any number of reasons for which boycotts are presently the right approach for the campaign for Palestinian rights but not for others. The question is, precisely, tactical. In any case, if Israel is being "singled out," it is to advance the *universal* cause of justice: the academic boycott, like the rest of the BDS campaign, opposes Israeli anti-Palestinianism precisely *as* a flagrant instance of oppression and injustice, in order to contribute to the broader struggle for a more just world. As a landmark international justice campaign, the achievement of the goals of BDS – or even significant progress toward them – would have a precedent-setting value that could reset the bar for activism globally.

Charges of inconsistency, furthermore, cut both ways. When Zionist academics complain that the academic boycott violates Israeli academic freedom, they lay themselves open to exactly the same charge of selectivity they level, unjustly, against boycott supporters: why, we should ask them, do they insist so much more on Israelis' academic freedom – their right *not* to be boycotted – than on the academic freedom of others? Why are they not simultaneously arguing for the achievement of real academic freedom for *all* groups, including Palestinians, whose academic freedom is severely obstructed? In opposing the academic boycott, BDS critics are often, it is true, defending their own ability to participate freely in academic exchange. But all this shows is that they are committed to their personal self-interest, not to the universal right to academic freedom they claim to be upholding. Of course, faced with this accusation, Zionist opponents of BDS can protest that they do, in fact, support universal academic freedom. That claim should be tested: we should insist that Zionists provide evidence of the concrete, political measures they are taking to promote the academic freedom of groups to which academic freedom is currently denied. In many cases with which I am familiar, they will come up empty-handed: boycott opponents' principal activity with respect to academic freedom is, often, simply fighting the boycott. This selective defense of academic freedom for Israelis undermines Zionists' ability to criticize boycotters: if selectivity is a problem, then it is so at least as much for boycott opponents as for boycott advocates.

Many arguments have been made to justify singling Israel out for special attention in the way that BDS does: that "as human rights defenders and activists, we have limited resources and we have to use them strategically to achieve maximum impact to achieve our basic rights" (Omar Barghouti);[12] that international law highlights Israel's "state of exception – that [Israel] is already quite different and benefitting from that difference and transgressions" so that exceptional action in response is justified (Noura Erakat);[13] that Israel's violations "are so flagrant and the cause of so much suffering that . . . the proper criticism is the failure of the world to do more to stop them, not the sin of excessive attention" (Richard Falk);[14] that Israel *asks* to be judged by the standards of liberal democracies, and therefore should be (Eyal Sivan and Armelle Laborie);[15] that academics in western countries like the US or Australia, characterized by extreme levels of support for anti-Palestinianism, have a special obligation to develop civil-society responses against their own governments' extremism. In other areas of activism, the claim that a campaign with a particular objective – here, justice for Palestinians – is invalid because it does not simultaneously try to achieve other similar objectives – justice for other oppressed people – is patently ridiculous: in all political activism, campaign focuses are chosen as a function of particular circumstances, with a view to what can actually be achieved in any given context. Environmental campaigns against coal mining, for example, do not also target other environmentally damaging energy sources but cannot be reasonably criticized for not doing so. As a rule, it is no argument against a campaign position that it does not adopt the most general demands possible: if it were, there would be only a single, utterly ineffective campaign for global peace and justice. It is striking that a similar selectivity charge appears not to have been made against proponents of the academic boycott of South Africa. Nor are Tibetan solidarity activists accused of "singling out" China, as Ben White points out. "Only the Palestinians, it seems, are required to justify their right to existence and solidarity," White observes.[16] The argument that BDS is selective and therefore illegitimate is itself entirely selective and inconsistent, being applied to discredit Palestine solidarity only.

Cary Nelson has recently made a new argument for the unjustifiability of singling out Israeli universities for boycott, claiming that "most of the trouble in Palestinian universities has little to do with Israel," since "the most serious threats to academic freedom in Gaza and the West Bank come from Palestinian society itself."[17] The academic boycott is thus doubly mistaken in selectively focusing on Israeli universities, since the group that it seeks to benefit – Palestinians – is in fact the most responsible for its own troubles. This is because, for Nelson, Palestinian universities are characterized by "a culture of campus and campus-related violence that has been sustained for forty years and [that] will be very resistant to change."[18] For Nelson, Israel's military occupation and siege come a distant second to entrenched Palestinian "cultural values" that hamper university development.[19] "Palestinian universities," he says, "unfortunately never have been and still are not simply sites of intellectual exchange," since "a continuing reign of intermittent political terror by Palestinians themselves shapes the psychological environment and eliminates anything like academic freedom for political expression."[20] Palestinian universities function, Nelson says, as centers for the radicalization and recruitment of student terrorists, and so are "fundamentally different kinds of institutions" from western ones.[21] Given Israeli universities' embeddedness in Israel's military architecture, discussed in the previous chapter, the absurdity, and indeed the racism, of this argument need little commentary. It is, however, important to note that BDS does not require any idealization or endorsement of the current state of higher education in Palestine: it is simply predicated on the undeniable fact that Israel places intolerable constraints on Palestinian universities and that the removal of these constraints must be the priority for anyone who wants to see Palestinians' right to education upheld. This does not mean that there are no other constraints on universities in Palestine: leading BDS supporters are frequently, in fact, unequivocal critics of the Palestinian Authority and Hamas, both of which are responsible for serious repression against students and academics.[22] "The single most disturbing fact about Palestinian higher education," Nelson writes, "is that many Palestinian universities have substantial histories of student involvement in terrorism," a fact he describes as "definitional" of Palestinian higher education.[23] In claiming that *students'* involvement in *resistance* to Israel fundamentally compromises Palestinian universities, Nelson completely ignores the far greater, structural involvement of Israeli higher education *institutions* in war crimes, extrajudicial killings and state-terrorism against Palestinians, circumstances which should qualify Israeli universities for far harsher criticism.

For the academic boycott, the single-most persuasive ground for rejecting the selectivity objection lies in the fact that Palestinian academics continually ask their international colleagues to boycott Israel and that the academic boycott now has significant momentum. In that light, the criticism that BDS "unfairly" singles out Israel betrays a singularly perverse and intellectualized conception of politics. The only way the criticism makes sense is if political action is seen as an abstract space from which the individual is basically disengaged and which they therefore have the duty to survey dispassionately in order to decide, as if from scratch, what campaigns should and shouldn't exist. The BDS opponent who objects to boycotters' selectivity is asking us to adopt an essentially abstract attitude, as though surveying the scenery of global oppression and its resistance from on high. From that elevated and uninvolved vantage point, the fact that Israel is a boycott target and other countries are not appears problematic. What this misses is that Palestinians themselves are directly asking the world for solidarity and that an energetic and growing campaign has emerged in response, with the original BDS call frequently renewed and endorsed by numerous civil society organizations in Palestine.[24] Once that is accepted, the question for academics becomes not whether it's reasonable that Israel alone is currently being boycotted, but whether or not we are going to be part of an *actually existing campaign* to reverse one of the world's many historic injustices. The charge that Israel should not be boycotted because doing so is selective springs from a bizarre denial of what we can refer to as the "discretionary" character of political commitment: since no one can take concrete action in favor of every cause, choices are necessitated about where energy should be directed, and different people will have different conceptions of what the highest priority, given their particular circumstances, is. The logic of Zionists' argument would lead us to oppose, for instance, rescuing *any* refugees crossing the Mediterranean, on the grounds that we cannot rescue all of them. In this light, BDS opponents' attempt to discredit the boycott campaign as selective emerges as an authoritarian bid to impose a single hierarchy of political priorities on activists – one drawn up in their own image, with defense of Israeli apartheid at the top.

FREEDOM TO BOYCOTT

In the face of the challenge posed by BDS to the usual norms of intellectual work, many academics argue that, rather than BDS, the "most open" debate among academics possible is the way forward. According to David Newman, for instance, "the boycott lobby would have a far greater contribution to make to the cause of Israel-Palestinian conflict resolution were they to use their campuses and organizations as places in which to facilitate Israeli-Palestinian dialogue, as honest, third-party brokers."[25] International conferences and exchanges among academics must be allowed to proceed, so the argument goes, because universities are the most progressive sector of Israeli society. If those whose will for a solution for Palestinians is supposedly the greatest are severed from contact with the outside world, how can the dialogue allegedly necessary for a resolution proceed?

As Steven Salaita has noted, however, it is perfectly possible to argue that the call to boycott already counts as part of a "dialogue" – "one in which the Palestinian people are finally able to participate. Their contribution to this new dialogue is the announcement that they will never tolerate dispossession and will never accept their fate as expendable in the Zionist narrative."[26] This is not, however, the kind of dialogue that Zionists have in mind. The kind they are interested in is the one in which anti-Palestinian academic business, including the structural exclusion of Palestinians trapped in the West Bank or Gaza, continues as normal – a fact that vitiates Zionists' claims to favor "free" or "open" dialogue or debate. Moreover, the argument that the boycott quashes supposedly necessary dialogue among international scholars ignores the obvious fact that the vast majority of academic conferences have no direct bearing whatsoever on the question of Palestine. As a result – accepting for a moment Zionists' claims that a "dialogue" which Palestinians are not asking for might be necessary – the boycott of such conferences doesn't constitute *any* impediment to dialogue. Indeed, if the Israeli academic world were actually a "hotbed of the peace movement," as has sometimes been argued, then it should be *willing* to respond to Palestinians' boycott call.[27]

When BDS opponents complain that the boycott violates "academic freedom," what they seem to have in mind is the following minimal definition of that concept: *individual academics' right to teach, enquire and communicate their research freely – and, especially, their right not to be excluded from academic forums overseas*. Since, as we have already stressed, and contrary to a frequent misconception, the Palestinian Campaign for the Academic and Cultural Boycott of Israel's (PACBI) academic boycott guidelines state that "mere affiliation of Israeli scholars to an Israeli academic institution is . . . not grounds for applying the boycott," the extent to which academic exchange is actually limited by the boycott is far less than commonly supposed.[28] But as it stands, the minimal definition of academic freedom we've just entertained is silent on some essential questions, in particular the question of whether *all* academics are entitled to academic freedom, or whether a version of academic freedom exists which is compatible with the crushing of Palestinians' academic opportunities through the Israeli occupation.

There is another hole in this minimal definition of academic freedom: it ignores the surprising but crucial fact that, in the sense intended by boycott opponents, academic freedom simply isn't characteristic of the everyday activities of the academy *anywhere*. In their most ordinary forms, research and teaching, and indeed the working life of universities in general, are already *constituted* by violations of academic "freedom" as BDS opponents understand it. The reality is that *academic freedom in the sense intended by boycott opponents simply isn't a feature of universities' day-to-day activities*. As we'll see, the reason for this is that academic exchange is intrinsically bound up not with the free exchange of ideas but rather with their regulation, or, put differently, their restriction or perhaps their censorship, by others: and, in consequence, also by the exclusion, or "boycotting," of academics in various academic forums.

That conclusion may seem surprising, but, even in light of received definitions of academic freedom, it shouldn't be. Academic freedom, as traditionally understood, concerns not just individual academics' rights, even though that is the way boycott opponents typically construe it. Traditionally, academic freedom is just as much a matter of the *corporate* right of universities to self-governance, free of external interference, particularly from the state. The principle of academic freedom prohibits external, non-academic actors from controlling or regulating academic business: instead, academic life should be regulated, very closely, by academics alone. Traditionally, universities assert academic freedom in order to insist that the right to regulate the speech and other activities of their members is vested in universities themselves, not anyone else.

Giving full due to this standard definition of academic freedom has straightforward implications for the way supporters should argue for the academic boycott. While we can, and must, oppose the discrimination and physical oppression that deny Palestinians full access to higher education, we should do this without acquiescing to a fantasy of what academic "freedom" under non-oppressive conditions is like, and we should not allow anyone to get away with the claim that the academic boycott is a departure from the usual norms of supposedly free scholarly exchange. On the contrary, *BDS is consistent with academic freedom in the traditional sense since it is an instance, precisely, of the self-regulating activity of the academic sphere.*

Whether from boycott opponents or advocates, arguments about academic freedom and BDS too often fail to recognize the constraints on free exchange intrinsic to the academic arena. It is simply not the case that academic freedom "proscribes censorship and prohibits any attempt to limit what is and is not acceptable to research, to teach, to question, and to debate," as is sometimes claimed.[29] When Judith Butler defines "academic freedom" in traditional terms as "an entitlement that professional faculty have to engage in self-governance and the *free* exchange of ideas," she ignores the ways in which those two sides of academic freedom are in conflict: the self-governance of academia consists precisely in the restriction, on "academic" grounds, of the free exchange of ideas.[30] An equivalent tension is apparent in Conrad Russell's definition of academic freedom as universities' claim to both "free intellectual enquiry" and "control over their own teaching."[31]

Closer to the mark are those critics who, like Piya Chatterjee and Sunaina Maira, stress the extent to which "for academics, censorship and repression generally comes wrapped in a liberal mantle, and . . . is waged through the language of . . . academic freedom itself."[32] With its appeal to notions of professionalism,[33] scholarship, balance and civility as ways of limiting acceptable academic discourse, academic freedom emerges in this analysis as "a notion that is deeply bound up with academic containment,"[34] an intrusion into the academy of political imperatives from outside it, geared toward the "overt policing of knowledge production," often as part of wider cultural animosities.[35] That conclusion is often hard to avoid. But even this ignores the ways in which the academic arena is inherently not a sphere of freedom into which political imperatives intrude but one that operates instead through multiple systems of exclusion, justified as either the consequence or the condition of universities' autonomous self-governance.

What are some of these systems of exclusion? The most obvious affects not academics but students – those deemed insufficiently performing intellectually. Such students are never admitted to university in the first place, or ejected from it in the course of their studies or excluded from particular institutions, streams, courses or degrees. Among academics, too, regulation through exclusion is constitutive of the hierarchies which structure professional activity: academics are regularly excluded from jobs, conferences, research grants and publications, all through the ordinary processes of academic selection – appointment panels, peer review, the decisions of funding bodies and so on. Published scientific articles are, similarly, regularly retracted if their results are falsified or plagiarized:[36] Rodin and Yudkin even argue that professional malpractice by a researcher may constitute "entirely appropriate" grounds for boycott.[37] As this case shows, boycott-like exclusions are not simply tolerated as necessary evils: they are, mostly, celebrated as evidence of the rigor and intellectual legitimacy of the academic profession. We will discuss exclusions in academic life in more detail in the next chapter.

Universities' meritocratic ideology insists that intellectual attainment alone determines who gets excluded from what. But, in the context of debates over the academic boycott, it is crucial to recognize that individual academics routinely restrict academic exchange for reasons other than "purely" intellectual or meritocratic ones. Political boycotts, in particular, are at least as normal a feature of academic life as they are of life outside universities, though they are, as we will discuss in the next chapter, strongly disavowed. In fact, boycott played an important role in the prehistory of Israeli higher education itself: in 1914, Zionist teachers boycotted Palestinian schools run by the Hilfsverein der deutschen Juden (German Jews' Aid Society), the body sponsoring the establishment of Haifa's Technion, in order to force it to make Hebrew the principal language of instruction when classes started. A similar boycott was carried out in secondary education.[38]

The most famous case of political boycott is, of course, the academic boycott of South Africa, called for by the African National Congress (ANC) from 1958 onward and ratified by the UN in 1980 as part of a wider suite of boycott measures, on which the academic boycott of Israel is partly modeled.[39] As I have already mentioned, the South Africa boycott, unlike the academic boycott of Israel, targeted individual academics, not just South African institutions, and extended to refusing to include South African academics at conferences, publish papers by or with South Africans, mark South African theses and other measures.[40] The Association of University Teachers in the UK, for instance, recognized that some South African academics opposed racism and discrimination against black people. But, it resolved, "we must at the same time make clear the importance of maintaining the policy of total academic boycott."[41] The South African academic boycott was also explicitly presented, by the ANC at least, as one aspect of a wider *cultural* boycott – a framing which goes a long way to dispelling the mystique of the inviolability of academic exchange and the consequent taboo against obstructing it.[42] If academic exchange is simply "cultural," rather than a means of achieving the "fundamental human goods" of "advances in science and learning," then the stakes in boycotting it are lower.[43]

Russia's invasion of Ukraine in February 2022 elicited frequent calls for various kinds of academic boycotts. As in the South African case, these accompanied wider economic and cultural initiatives, including state-sponsored sanctions and divestment. Germany froze academic ties with Russia in order to examine Russian institutions' involvement with the invasion. The Australian National University broke off all institutional ties with Russian universities.[44] In a particularly telling instance of double standards, Glasgow University quickly suspended its ties with Russian institutions, even though it had recently taken the side of the Israeli occupiers of Palestine in censoring two cases of pro-Palestinian academic research.[45] No less than sixteen research bodies in Europe had also cut ties with Russia to a greater or lesser extent by mid-March 2022.[46]

The academic boycott of Israel is hardly exceptional, then, even if, as we will discuss in the next chapter, academics can be reluctant to admit the concrete ways in which their work might function politically. Nevertheless, boycotts are a recurrent aspect of academic life, even though it is only a minority of academics who participate in them. Just how recurrent they are can be gauged from the following further examples.

Publication boycotts. The extortionate subscription prices charged by the publisher Elsevier have led to over seventeen thousand researchers boycotting its academic journals.[47] For those researchers who refuse to undertake peer review or editorial work for Elsevier journals, this involves a direct obstruction of the academic freedom of those of their colleagues who choose to continue publishing with them, for the sake of the literally free exchange of ideas. In 2015, the entire editorial board of the Elsevier linguistics journal *Lingua* resigned en masse to protest against Elsevier's refusal to convert *Lingua* to open access. A number of the journal's editors encouraged their colleagues not to agree to take editorial board positions to replace them and even undertook to boycott the new editors if they were candidates for academic jobs for which they belonged to the selection panel.[48] Since 1989, at least thirty-two academic journals have been subject to similar resignations; at the time of writing, the mathematics journal, *Journal of Combinatorial Theory, Series A*, had become the latest to transition to a new, open-access formula.[49] So mainstream, in fact, is the Elsevier boycott that the University of California, Los Angeles (UCLA) officially encouraged its faculty in 2018 to consider refusing to undertake peer review work for the Dutch giant and to publish elsewhere where possible – an academic boycott in all but name.[50] As was soon noted, the possibility of an institutional boycott of Elsevier directly opens the door to a boycott of Israeli institutions.[51]

Research is sometimes also withdrawn or retracted for political reasons that go beyond academic politics. Such political dimensions of publication are often presented as a matter of "ethics." When a Stanford psychologist published an algorithm purporting to distinguish gay from straight people on the basis of their photographs in 2017, alarm bells rang about whether this could be used to discriminate against LGBTQ people. In response, the journal that had accepted the paper for publication initiated a further review into whether the photographs on which its research was based had been used ethically, effectively delaying publication.[52] This was, in other words, a temporary "boycott."

Conference and event boycotts. Conference boycotts have a prominent place in the history of intellectual politics. In 1986, the World Archaeological Congress was born as the result of a decision to boycott South African archaeologists as a protest against apartheid.[53] In 2012, Romanian researchers boycotted a "Diaspora" conference chaired by the prime minister, believing that attendance would have been tantamount to the de facto acceptance of his documented plagiarism.[54] In 2013, scientists boycotted a NASA conference that excluded Chinese researchers.[55] In 2014, over fifteen hundred researchers called for the boycott of the following year's International Congress of Quantum Chemistry to protest against its all-male program. A growing international movement, both in and outside academia, is boycotting panels and conferences which under-represent women.[56] Following the election of Donald Trump in 2016 and his notorious executive order banning citizens of seven Muslim-majority countries from entering the US, thousands of academics called for a boycott of international conferences held in the US as a means of exerting pressure on the new administration, and on those scientific associations whose meetings would not be shifted from the US so as to allow participation by Muslims.[57] Three conferences held in 2017 in Thailand were the subject of a boycott call on the grounds of the absence of academic freedom in that country.[58] In 2018, artificial intelligence researchers undertook to boycott KAIST (formerly the Korea Advanced Institute of

Science and Technology) in order to prevent it engaging in the development of autonomous weapons. The same year, UCLA declared a travel boycott of Oklahoma, preventing its employees going there on university business after that state passed anti-LGBTQ adoption laws.[59] When Kirstjen Nielsen, the secretary of the Department of Homeland Security under Trump, resigned in 2019, academics called for a boycott of any institution that gave her a position and pledged to boycott that institution's events, as well as any other event involving a member of the same institution.[60]

Teaching and whole-institution boycotts. Strikes and other forms of union interference with universities' business are directly comparable to boycotts, in that they restrict academic freedom in order to achieve a political goal, with strikes being regular features of university life in many places. In the UK, the University and College Union has initiated "full academic boycott" provisions against different institutions, including against London Metropolitan University and against the University of Leicester.[61] During the "Free Speech Week" declared by alt-right figurehead Milo Yiannopoulos at Berkeley in 2017, over one hundred faculty called for a boycott of all classes in order to counter what the signatories described as a "clear threat to public education."[62] In 2021, the World Health Organization signaled that it would not fund research at the University of Melbourne because of that institution's collaboration with the weapons manufacturer Lockheed Martin.[63]

Ranking boycotts. Many academics reject the ubiquitous rankings of institutions, programs and journals. The German Sociological Association and seven Indian Institutes of Technology, as well as many individuals, are among them.[64] Following the Russian invasion of Ukraine, *Times Higher Education* stated that it was taking steps "to ensure that Russian universities are given less prominence" in the ranking tables it publishes.[65]

Most telling, perhaps, as indications of the normality of boycott in the academy are boycotts within Israeli academia itself. Boycott opponents have argued that BDS only "serves to further weaken and delegitimize the pro-peace and pro-Human Rights lobbies within Israel as a whole," since the accusations of anti-Semitism regularly leveled against boycotters are generalized to anyone opposed to the occupation.[66] This argument, made, for instance, by David Newman, is already remarkable for its victim-blaming, making boycott supporters responsible for *being slandered* as anti-Semitic, as though it would be possible to choose a tactic that would *not* arouse exactly the same charge. Newman claims that the academic boycott "serves to create a constructed and somewhat artificial unity of grass roots feeling against any form of pro-peace and anti-occupation elements who may then be automatically associated with the pro-boycott polemic, regardless of the fact that few Israeli academics on the liberal left support boycott, while many are actively opposed to such actions."[67] Yet support for boycotts can even be found in

Israeli academia. "Under some circumstances," according to Ariel Rubinstein, an Israel Prize Economics laureate, "academic boycotts should not be rejected."[68] In 2010, the Israeli Sociological Society (ISS) vowed not to hold conferences or other educational gatherings at Ariel University, in the illegal West Bank settlement of the same name, a decision it reaffirmed in 2018.[69] The boycott, according to the ISS's chair, would be "a way of hoisting a black flag of immorality over the occupation."[70] Many Israeli scholars are reported to engage in a "soft boycott" of conferences at Ariel, with some applying further boycott actions.[71] In 2018, the Israeli Anthropological Association (IAA) also resolved not to cooperate with higher education establishments in Israeli settlements. The IAA's resolution is a boycott in all but name, since it commits the association to refusing to hold conferences, workshops or other academic occasions in any of the three settlement institutions.[72] A small number of Israeli academics even support the full academic boycott of their own institutions.[73]

Critics of BDS tend to forget that boycotters also restrict *their own* academic freedom: in refusing to collaborate with institutional Israeli actors, boycotters are also cutting themselves off from certain avenues of intellectual exchange. This has some interesting consequences for boycotters' moral position: the harm entailed by BDS – curtailing academic freedom – is not suffered solely by the boycott's target but also by its authors. BDS critics cannot therefore present the boycott as a wrong inflicted just on academics at Israeli universities by an unaffected third party: in cutting links with Israeli institutions, boycotters also constrain their own academic audience. This is particularly the case given the boycott's institutional character: under its terms, as we have seen, no ordinary Israeli scholar is excluded from international fora merely in virtue of their affiliation with an Israeli institution. Boycotters, on the other hand, cannot attend *any* conference in Israel officially sponsored by an Israeli university. Paradoxically, therefore, the harm to boycotters – exclusion from all official Israeli conferences – is arguably more consequential than that on the boycott targets, who are excluded from *none*, as long as they return to their non-official, original academic roles. This is even more the case given measures like the funds established by various bodies, including the Israeli government, to undo the effects of the academic boycott, for instance by compensating boycotted researchers for BDS-inflicted setbacks to their work.[74]

Why do academics restrict their own, and others', freedom as often as they do? Presumably, because they wish to exert an influence on the conditions in which their own professional activity is conducted. They want to ensure, in other words, that their profession is exercised justly – that the norms governing the academic profession are ethical. Despite university managements' obvious wishes, academics are not drones whose role is confined to generating and then dispensing knowledge within fixed political and intellectual parameters: essential to the liberal image of academics as creative and autonomous intellectuals is the idea that, as such, they have a responsibility to continually monitor, and if necessary to try to modify, the nature of their professional milieu. Academic work intrinsically depends on practitioners' judgments about which activities are consistent with the nature of the profession, and which are not. The continuing self-definition of the parameters of their activity is therefore an essential part of academics' role as intellectuals: as Tanya Reinhart put it in response to an Israeli academic reluctant to support the boycott, the idea that "intellectual responsibility includes the safeguarding of moral principles" is part of the traditional spirit of academia – a spirit, we might add, honored more in the breach than the observance.[75] When Italian academics refuse to participate in the national research assessment exercise,[76] when Australian ones exert pressure to prevent a climate-change-minimizer opening a research center,[77] or a right-wing organization sponsoring a racist "Western Civilization" program,[78] when US mathematicians refuse to collaborate with military research[79] or when Swedish academics boycott a racism and extremism center because they believe it is excessively politicized,[80] they are all taking a stand in order to explicitly shape the nature of their disciplines. For reasons we will explore in the next chapter, activity of this kind is usually engaged in only by a minority of academics. But it is nonetheless a recurrent feature of academics' professional life.

BOYCOTT OR COUNTER-BOYCOTT?

Collectively, all these considerations seriously undermine the academic freedom argument against BDS. Those who object to the Israel boycott on academic freedom grounds owe boycotters a reply to the following question: what is it about the situation in Palestine that disqualifies BDS as a legitimate political act and that would not also immediately disqualify *other* instances where academics restrict their colleagues' academic freedom on political or moral grounds? If respect for "academic freedom" rules out boycotts against Israel, what, if anything, rules them *in* for other attempts to practice academic activity ethically, like all those I have just described? All boycotts are intended to exert pressure on academic disciplines in what the boycotters judge to be morally justified directions – yet, as boycotts, they could all be denounced as violations of academic freedom. BDS opponents must tell us what principled reasons distinguish opposition to the Israel boycott from opposition to these others.

In responding, only two possible courses are available to boycott opponents: either (1) produce a credible reason or reasons to rule out the boycott of

Israeli institutions while reserving the right to boycott elsewhere or (2) accept that nothing substantive separates BDS from other boycott calls.

Each position brings uncomfortable consequences. The first, which accepts the legitimacy of other academic boycotts, entails abandoning the entire academic-freedom argument against boycotts – perhaps the heaviest weapon in BDS opponents' arsenal. Other academic boycotts violate academic freedom just as much as the boycott of Israel does – but if these other boycotts are acceptable, then academic freedom cannot be the decisive argument against BDS of Israel that boycott opponents apparently intend it as. If other academic boycotts are valid, that means that academic freedom *can*, after all, be violated in certain circumstances. BDS supporters then only need ask why academic freedom should not also be violated in the case of Israeli universities, given their well-documented collaboration with the oppression of the Palestinians.

The second option – acknowledging that the boycott of Israeli institutions is not substantively different from other academic boycotts – requires boycott opponents to condemn other boycotts equally. This is the attitude suggested by Martha Nussbaum, who rejects academic boycotts *in principle*.[81] This is an extreme position, which would also have ruled out, for example, the call for a boycott of Serbian academics and intellectuals for their support for Serbian war crimes and crimes against humanity in the 1990s, the academic boycott of South Africa, Carlos Fuentes' call for an academic boycott of the US during the Vietnam War, US physicists' call for a boycott of weapons research at the same time, the subsequent widely followed call to boycott Strategic Defense Initiative ("Star Wars") research, the boycott of Russian institutions complicit with the invasion of Ukraine as well as any number of other discretionary academic decisions to withdraw collaboration for political reasons,[82] including a decision by Jewish Studies academics, including some opposed to BDS, who undertook in 2017 not to visit Israel in protest at the new law denying entry to supporters of the boycott.[83]

Nussbaum's position, however, is a minority one. It is striking that vocal BDS opponents have often not hesitated to participate in violations of their colleagues' academic freedom for political purposes. The rector of Rome's La Sapienza University is just one of many BDS opponents calling for a "boycott of the boycotters": academic freedom, apparently, can be suspended for Israel critics but never for Israel supporters.[84] Writing about the economic boycott, prominent BDS opponent Alan Dershowitz has stated outright that "governors and legislatures are morally and politically right to counter-boycott BDS."[85] Academic BDS itself is, however, already exactly that – a *counter*-boycott. Israeli universities participate massively in the "boycotting" of Palestinians, excluding them not just from the free exchange of ideas but also from the conditions in which their basic rights can be respected. As

Magid Shihade has argued, the response through BDS should precisely be seen as a counter-boycott:

> The boycott against Palestinians in Palestine and elsewhere and against pro-Palestinian voices on US campuses is already in place, and the only way to counter the surveillance, repression, and silencing is by going further with more boycott resolutions against Israel in all academic associations, opening the space for more honest discussion, and increasing the numbers in the boycott movement to make it safe to stand for justice in Palestine.[86]

One of the most prominent anti-boycott voices in the US, Cary Nelson, is another example of an opponent of the Israel boycott who doesn't hesitate to engage in boycotts for other reasons. In 2006, Nelson committed himself to a "personal boycott" of New York University (NYU) in order to support the recognition of the NYU graduate student union by the university's administration. The fact that he later recanted and described this as a mistake[87] doesn't alter the fact that he has been a frequent participant in strikes – teaching and research "boycotts" – across the country.[88] Nelson makes a half-hearted attempt to differentiate between strikes and boycotts so as to support the former but not the latter, but the weakness of his argument is glaring: strikes and boycotts are parallel in that both involve restrictions to the "free flow of ideas" in the service of a higher political agenda.

Even BDS opponents, then, have regularly acted to restrict academic freedom while also arguing for the primacy of that value when they condemn the institutional Israel boycott. As I've been arguing, this shouldn't be surprising: the academic arena is not one of the unfettered interchange of ideas but is instead constituted through the regulation, and therefore the restriction of the ideas expressible within it, in order to serve various ends. Despite the generally disavowed character of academic politics, researchers regularly decide to exclude themselves and others from different academic fora on what are actually political grounds, understanding "political" in terms of both academic and non-academic politics. Attempts to demonize academic BDS as a departure from normal practice therefore fail.

Academia is no different in this regard from other areas. Politics, in general, can be seen, in part, as the project of shaping the norms of public discourse – the project, in short, of promoting some kinds of discourse and discouraging others.[89] There is nothing illiberal in this conception. Politicians should, for instance, act to make discourse promoting racism and sexism socially unacceptable, as one aspect of progress to a more just world. That is why BDS opponents, whether academic or not, regularly find themselves supporting other kinds of boycott activity while opposing BDS itself.[90] The question is thus not whether restrictions on academic exchange are valid – everyone thinks they sometimes are – but *which* ones are: which of universities' many counter-communities it is legitimate to boycott at any given time. We cannot adjudicate this question without asking what ends the academic profession should be serving. Reflecting on this important subject will allow us to see why Nussbaum's blanket opposition to *all* academic boycotts is untenable.

WHAT IS A UNIVERSITY FOR?

Academic freedom is a different right from the more general right that everyone should enjoy to participate in the free exchange of ideas. In order for there to be meaningfully *academic* freedom, a specifically academic arena, from which non-academic parties and practices are excluded, has to be delimited. Without the exclusion of non-academic parties and practices, *academic* freedom cannot exist.

That throws the spotlight onto the question of what makes academic freedom *academic* – what defines, or should define, the nature of academic exchange. For an answer, we can look to a common belief about higher education: that it both does and should serve social progress. This suggests that boycotts and other obstructions to academic freedom are justifiable if they serve the end of social progress – the very end to which the institution of the university is supposedly directed in the first place. However, among many academics, the belief that universities serve social progress provides grounds for skepticism about BDS: surely, BDS skeptics say, as a practice that should inherently serve social progress, academic exchange with Israel should not be boycotted; not only does boycotting Israeli academic institutions impose restrictions on an inherently beneficial activity (academic communication) but the path to reconciliation also surely lies in increasing, not restricting, the opportunity for the world's dialogue with Israeli institutions.[91]

The belief that higher education serves social progress actually contains in itself a rationale *for* BDS, and not, as BDS opponents would have us believe, against it. If the justification of academic exchange is that it leads to socially beneficial outcomes, then that suggests that it is not an end in itself, but a *means*: the only reason we think academic exchange is worth pursuing is not that it is intrinsically desirable in itself but that it leads to a better world for everyone, and not just its immediate participants.[92] A better world, then, is the desired goal. But there is no reason to believe that academic exchange is the *only* route to that goal: it may well be that there are means of achieving social progress which don't go via the seminar room but, for instance, via protest on the street. Indeed, the history of struggles for social progress suggests that it is exactly *not* academics who march in the vanguard of social change. BDS opponents whose commitment to the pursuit of social progress is genuine need to demonstrate why *their* favored method for attaining it, academic "dialogue," is more likely than BDS to succeed. And they need to show why the kind of social value to which they're committed – "dialogue," or the intrinsic value of scholarship – trumps the social good for which BDS aims – an end to a situation of oppression. At the very least, they have to give reasons why they are not even prepared to *try* BDS, for a limited, experimental period, to see whether, in fact, it proves a more effective instrument of social progress than the more idealistic mechanisms they prefer. Too many Zionist academics also owe us an explanation for why they will take every conceivable step to persecute BDS supporters, with the goal of stamping BDS out entirely – thereby making it impossible to know whether boycott tactics might in fact be effective.

This is even more the case given that the application of BDS tactics does not, in fact, reduce the amount of intellectual exchange that actually happens among academics: it merely redistributes it. Boycotters who reject institutional collaboration with Israel do not stop collaboration overall: they just collaborate with other partners, including with non-boycottable Israeli academics (those not in official leadership positions in their institutions). Nor do boycott targets excluded from participation in certain international fora stop *all* academic communication: they just engage in it elsewhere. Even if the boycott were universally applied, the amount of academic intercourse in the world would not actually *diminish*: boycotting Israeli academic officials would create opportunities for others. So critics like Nussbaum who consider academic exchange as the most important good cannot argue that BDS limits it in any *quantitative* sense. But perhaps it can be said to "impoverish" it qualitatively. Boycott opponent Russell Berman makes exactly that claim.[93] Yet, qualitatively, BDS tactics can only be said to impoverish academic exchange and limit academic freedom if the opportunities to include *others* that the exclusion of boycottable Israeli academic officials opens up (e.g., in conference schedules) are discounted.

COLLABORATION AND COMMUNITY

Boycott supporters have characteristically argued that, by promoting Palestinian rights, including academic freedom, BDS is a mechanism for universalizing knowledge. In a campaign aimed at securing wide-ranging Palestinian rights, suspension of academic freedom for a small number of Israeli academic officials is a reasonable price to pay. As Omar Barghouti has noted, "In situations of grave violation of human rights, the right to live and freedom from subjugation and colonial rule, to name a few, must be of more import than academic freedom. If the latter contributes in any way to suppression of the former, more fundamental rights, it must give way."[94]

But the status of academic interchange as a means to this end is not the only reason for which BDS is legitimate. Less obvious a reason is the political meaning of the very act of engaging in academic exchange. Academic interlocutors are chosen, not imposed. There are very few situations in which collaboration with a particular individual, and with them only, is academically necessary: mostly, academics have a choice of potential collaborators; often, especially outside the sciences, they have a real choice about whether to collaborate at all. Collaboration is a choice, and therefore a political act. To collaborate with someone is to admit them into one's community. This has immediate consequences for our understanding of the nature of intellectual exchange: communities are sites of political definition, and since academic exchange with someone is almost always discretionary and reflects an unforced choice, socio-political factors – factors of community selection – and not just intellectual ones, are inscribed into the very nature of academic cooperation.

The choice of collaborators is performative: it constitutes taking a position on the kind of academic community that should exist. In most cases, the political meaning of a collaboration will not be salient enough to warrant any form of boycott. But in the case of academics directly acountable for extremely serious crimes, whether through their individual activities as weapons researchers or war propagandists, or through their official ones as representatives of institutions that support those crimes, the political dimensions of collaboration cannot simply be ignored. The rationale for boycott in this situation has been well articulated by Igor Primoratz of the Hebrew University of Jerusalem, in the context of his own call for the boycott of Serbian intellectuals in the 1990s. He is worth quoting at some length:

> When the evil or injustice that is being committed is committed by someone who is associated with me in a significant way, and in particular when it is committed in the name of the group to which I too belong, I may protest the evil or injustice, and dissociate myself from it and from those perpetrating it, in order to show that it is not perpetrated in my name too, and thereby say something of critical importance about who and what I am. For "who one is" for moral purposes – e.g., a Nazi, a racist, a Christian, a humanist – is determined not simply by substantive contributions to various good and evil causes but to some extent by what and whom one associates oneself with, and in some contexts this depends importantly on the symbolic gestures one is prepared to make.[95]

Israeli academic officials' responsibility for Israeli universities' support for the occupation excludes them from the kind of intellectual community to which boycotters aspire – one that is, in fact, oriented toward the goal of social progress.

As we have seen, no academic has an *obligation* to include any other in collaborative ventures like conferences, grants and the other kinds of structures targeted by the boycott. Still less do they have an obligation to cooperate with the official representatives of the institutions of repressive states. Israeli academic officials therefore have no *special* right of access to these structures that is greater than anyone else's. Just as important, however, is the fact that the attempt to outlaw the academic boycott is, as we have seen, a violation of *boycotters'* academic freedom. The academic boycott is the refusal to be associated with a particular category of institution – Israeli ones. As such, it is an obvious exercise of academic freedom: academic freedom must include the freedom to *refuse* certain associations, or it is not freedom at all.

Academics, I have shown, regularly boycott one another, and it is right that they should do so, since regulation through exclusion is an intrinsic aspect of academic self-governance. This is, however, a largely disavowed aspect of academic life, and one which its practitioners have difficulty acknowledging. The fact that politics is ubiquitous in universities makes the myth of its absence even more essential to them. In their self-image, academics, whatever their disagreements, are united around independent scholarly and disciplinary norms; their imagined professional identity, and the work of research itself, remain untarnished either by the influence of external political blocs or by mundane disputes over the material conditions of employment.

In a world of structural proletarianization and the galloping exploitation of casual and precarious labor, this aristocratic self-image takes no small measure of willful blindness to maintain. Its continuing dominance – and, for the moment, it *is* still dominant – means that any fundamental discord over academia's own ground rules is largely absent from the terms in which the profession thinks about itself. To BDS opponents' typical accusation of "why just boycott Israel?" BDS supporters should therefore make the following rejoinder: "Why *exempt* officials of Israeli institutions from what are, in reality, commonplace acts of academic activity?" Actual boycotts are regular features of academic life; their possibility flows directly from the distinctive character of academia as a profession. Outlawing them, we've seen in this chapter, is tantamount to outlawing a constitutive feature of academic professionalism itself.

Chapter 3

Little Israels

The call for Boycott, Divestment and Sanctions (BDS) is made in universities that are under scrutiny from both left and right. On both sides, it is a commonplace to compare them to authoritarian regimes: the Soviet Union, Iran, even the bureaucracy of the Habsburg military.[1] For anyone willing to look properly, the analogies are in fact obvious – and nowhere more so than in universities' treatment of Palestine supporters. But unflattering comparisons between universities and repressive states are misleading in one basic way: many of the regimes to which universities are usually likened make no secret of their hostility to liberal values. In this respect, Israel provides a far better analogy. Israel's subjugation of Palestinians would let it hold its head high in any roll call of authoritarian states, but it is distinguished from many of them by the extent of its liberal posturing, its determination to assert itself, against all the evidence, as an enlightened haven of civil liberties: "the Middle East's only democracy," multicultural, tolerant, cosmopolitan, with Tel Aviv "the epitome of coexistence for all its accepting attitudes."[2] This posture makes Israel a far preferable analogy to Iran or the USSR for contemporary western universities, institutions that throw a similar liberal mantle over their own often authoritarian practices. So it's only fitting, from this perspective, that Israel's prowess in higher education forms such a major part of its international image. Israel is characterized by high levels of economic inequality.[3] But in its mythology of the "start-up nation," a society of educational high achievement with more PhDs per capita than anywhere else, it exemplifies, despite its high levels of economic injustice, not only the kind of authoritarian double standard amply on display on contemporary campuses but also the kind of knowledge society that neoliberal universities typically aspire to create.

If we want to understand what is at stake in the academic boycott in the west, and so to argue for it more effectively, controversies over BDS have to be put in the context of the politics of knowledge and the ideologies of higher education that are currently dominant in universities. As I will describe in this chapter, universities around the world are being increasingly "Israelized" – characterized by norms of physical and ideological "enclosure" supported by authoritarian and repressive practices that are turning them, more and more, into little Israels. University authorities, and the financial and commercial interests they largely serve, are typically either overt supporters of Israeli Zionism or complicitly silent in the face of Israeli apartheid. So it's not surprising that certain broad parallels can be identified between the conditions on higher education set by university authorities and the material and ideological characteristics of Israel's repression of Palestinians. Vastly different in the gravity of their human consequences and in the urgency of the political response they demand, universities and Israel are nevertheless sites of analogous enclosures: in Israel, the literal enclosure of Palestinian land and the brutal repression of Palestinian lives and freedom; on university campuses, managements' increasing enclosure of the conditions of education and academic independence, with the often ruthless suppression of Palestine advocacy as one of its most obvious aspects. This comparison is not at all intended to trivialize Palestinians' oppression in Gaza and the West Bank: the campaign for Palestine justice is of a different order of magnitude and must be a far higher priority for progressives than university reform. The point is to highlight structural similarities between what is happening in the very different registers of Palestine and neoliberal tertiary education. These similarities are, perhaps, one of the reasons that attitudes to Israel and its boycott and those to contemporary transformations of higher education so often align – why supporters of BDS are often among those calling most loudly for universities' liberation from market logics.

It is not just university managers who strongly resist BDS: ordinary academics often do so too. To see why, we need to analyze what it is about the nature of academic labor that has so often turned academic workplaces into little Israels. In the previous chapter, we touched on the ideologies of community and the role of regulation through exclusion that characterize the university milieu. In this chapter, we extend this analysis while also scrutinizing the numerous authoritarian tendencies of contemporary higher education and the dispositions of compliance embedded in the way it operates. As I hope will become clear, this will give us a better grasp of the resistance to Palestine justice campaigns, especially BDS, that is encountered on campus, among support staff, management and academics. If, as we'll shortly see, academics often won't even defend *themselves*, asking them to defend Palestinians becomes an even greater challenge – and the successful academic BDS initiatives that have been taken so far emerge as even greater achievements.

We begin by interrogating the role of academics' political agency in the university context, since many academics' disengagement from explicit politics plays a crucial part in the boycott's lack of large-scale uptake. We go on to consider another highly functional aspect of the institutional background to the academic boycott campaign, already suggested in the previous chapter: the overarching role of exclusion, whether physical, intellectual or temporal, in universities, which reinforces opposition to the boycott's politics of Palestinian inclusion. This leads us to a sketch of different mechanisms of enclosure and surveillance in contemporary universities, which I compare to the coercive colonial practices that Israel deploys against Palestinians. Finally, we discuss the particular, and paradoxical, role of the humanities as crucial theaters of boycott activism and resistance.

DENYING POLITICS

Academics who encourage their colleagues to implement the institutional boycott of Israel violate one of higher education's firmest commands: *never politicize*. In an academy often attacked as in thrall to dangerous "political correctness" – that is, politicized to the point of censorship – and riven, as we saw in the previous chapter, by endless "political" disputes, including over Palestine, the claim that politics is regularly taboo will seem ludicrous.[4] It is anything but. Just like any structured, professional activity, academia certainly has *its own* politics: as discussed in chapter two, academics seek power, strategize, form blocs and make professional choices in ways that they believe further their values or interests and that sometimes align with political choices they make outside the institution. This is not, however, the kind of politics that is relevant here: university workers are no more or less "political" in this – trivial – sense than are other comparable professionals. It is no more informative to conclude that universities are especially political places because they are the sites of *academic* or *intellectual* politics than it would be to conclude that offices are especially political because they are the sites of *office* politics. But if academia well and truly has its own politics, that is where politics in universities is supposed to stop. In the imagination of most academics, universities should be undistorted by *external* political agendas: the objection that supposedly purely academic topics have been "politicized" is one of the right's main complaints against the academic left.

That doesn't mean that politics isn't regularly *discussed* in universities. When prominent BDS opponent Cary Nelson claims that "all teaching and research is fundamentally and deeply political," especially in the humanities and social sciences, what he means, he tells us, is that it is in "dialogue with cultural values and norms that undergo continual change and that are sites of struggle, linked to assumptions about identity that are socially and politically constructed, engaged with social life and the public sphere and thus with the politics of culture, constrained and encouraged by discourses embedded in politics."[5] This claim of the distinctly political character of academic work amounts to the observation – an uncontroversial one – that universities abound in discussion of political topics: Nelson's claim that the humanities and social sciences are "in dialogue" with politically important themes means that academics and students often *relate* their teaching and research to political issues.

The crucial point, however, is that *talking about politics is not the same as participating in it*. If we understand politics as the effort "to share power or . . . to influence the distribution of power, either among states or among groups within a state," then, contrary to Nelson and others' belief, it plays almost no part in most academics' professional (as opposed to personal) lives, even when its "political" character is trumpeted.[6] "Academics look at the social world as something to be studied, to be researched, to be analyzed, even to be opined – but not to be acted on," according to Daniel W. Drezner in his study of the "ideas industry."[7] This is not to say that academics *never* act politically: "there comes a time," one US scholar is quoted as saying in the aftermath of Donald Trump's election in 2016, "when you have to take your head out of your books and your computers" and "try to come out, as some people say, on the right side of history."[8] Most of the time, however, books and computers are where academics' heads stay firmly planted: the distinguishing feature of many kinds of academic professionalism, especially in much of the humanities, is its aspiration to stand imperiously above, and therefore not immediately affect, worldly political matters. Universities are "non-partisan," without being "value-free," as one academic has described their own university's position.[9] To deal with "the broadly defined 'humanities,'" Said wrote in 1982, "is to deal with the non-political."[10]

The comment captures an important truth: while academics often debate or invoke politics, sometimes heatedly, academic work rarely *engages* it; even if academics' choice of problems to teach or research is informed by political considerations, and academics intend their teaching and research to contribute to advocacy for particular political positions, including Palestine justice, these goals are typically understood as derivative of their more essential academic features. Academic work can serve secondary political purposes only if it is, first and foremost, *academic*: the expression of political positions cannot, in conventional understandings, be allowed to escalate so far as to jeopardize scholarly objectivity, which is what guarantees universities' imagined status as independent, non-partisan institutions. One can teach a course on Middle Eastern politics with the intention of promoting students' appreciation of Palestinian calls for justice, but one cannot do so in a way that precludes students taking a pro-Israeli position. Academic merit must be assiduously distinguished from political acceptability: students must not be penalized for their political positions, nor research rejected or ignored because of the author's political views. Scholarship requires "disinterested reason," and students must be judged on the merits of their work, not their politics;[11] in Matthew Abraham's words, "to establish a strong political position is to be considered simplistic, lacking nuance, engaging in binary thinking, or advancing a politically motivated critique."[12] "A lectern should not serve as a soapbox, a classroom should not be a venue for indoctrination, a professor should not be the conveyer belt for a party/politically correct line," as Norman Finkelstein puts the point.[13]

It's therefore no surprise that the assertion of the political nature of academic work, especially in the humanities and social sciences, is rarely meant to suggest that it could bear any strong relevance, let alone constitute any real challenge, to *specific* political actors. Politics as a concrete practice – and, even more so, the politics of Palestine justice – is for the most part taboo in universities. Cary Nelson concludes as a result of four decades' observation that "the overwhelming majority of faculty members are reluctant to reveal their political views to their students"; "during my last six-year stint in the political science department at DePaul University in Chicago," Norman Finkelstein tells us, "the country passed through two presidential elections, September 11, and two major wars, yet I can count on the fingers of one hand the number of political conversations with my colleagues."[14] So while academics do from time to time use their professional personas to take a stand on questions of immediate political moment, they do so mostly in heavily qualified ways, and almost always with the reminder that their students or readers must decide for themselves where they stand. Cushioned in that very typical proviso, the divorce between scholarship and politics is consummated. Politics is constitutively insulated from academic authority. It is the domain of opinion, where participants must ultimately be free to make their own choices: scholarship, safely confined within the seminar room or academic article, is politically inert. Speech in universities simply does not usually aim to mobilize opinion in favor of a concrete political outcome. If humanities research and teaching is "*fundamentally* and *deeply* political," as Nelson suggests, it is because it is not *self-evidently* or *overtly* so: Nelson's adverbs are needed precisely because the political character of humanities disciplines is not obvious at first glance.

Given their general professional aversion to explicit politics, academics' reluctance to embrace BDS is wholly expected, but it becomes even less surprising when seen in light of the profession's general unwillingness to seriously defend its own professional milieus from the decades of higher education "reform" that have degraded it in many parts of the west. All around the English-speaking world, and in many places beyond it, neoliberalism in universities has largely won a crushing victory at students' and academics' expense. In that light, insistent claims of disciplines' "political" character stand out in bathetic relief against their inability to accomplish what should be, surely, among their most elementary "political" aims – safeguarding the institutional security of their own practitioners. In relation to an important mechanism of the neoliberalization of higher education, the rise of academic managers, one attentive observer even feels that "the colonization of higher education by management has *never* been openly discussed."[15] Another – a London politics academic – says he found his five-year experience as an official of the University and College Union "exhausting and demoralizing, because so few academics seemed willing to participate" in defense of pay, pensions and reforms of higher education governance.[16]

Any number of aspects of the professional culture of higher education support western academics' unwillingness to acknowledge or confront their own political agency, whether over BDS or over their more immediate self-interest. In *The Authoritarian Personality*, Adorno identified the tendency of educational systems "to discourage anything supposedly 'speculative,' or which cannot be corroborated by surface findings, and stated in terms of 'facts and figures.'"[17] The analysis is still germane after more than seventy years. As the very agents of the positivistic educational culture Adorno identified, and institutionally immersed in a highly quantified world of enrollment figures, citation counts, grant income, funding formulas and ranking positions, there is nothing surprising in academics' apparent inability to engage in "speculative" politics by grasping their own potential to act. The investment which academics typically bring to questions of disciplinary, intellectual politics – which field will a new position be created in? what subjects are to be compulsory for final-year students? – contrasts starkly with their frequent disengagement from the broader issues which set the parameters of their professional life, whether over the Israel boycott or many other macro-questions of institutional politics.[18] As we saw in the previous chapter, there is no lack of precedent for political activity by academics. But it is understood as exceptional, and often viewed with a certain degree of hesitation or embarrassment, even by its participants.

Palestinians cannot expect strong support from a profession that often cannot bring itself to defend its *own* members: resistance to the boycott is one especially obvious consequence of academics' general disengagement from politics. This resistance is mostly not, of course, of an active kind: when the Modern Language Association put a motion to its members in 2018 effectively *banning* future discussion of BDS, the disengagement of the membership was such that only fifteen per cent bothered voting, an abstentionism that handed a decisive victory to boycott opponents.[19] Yet the ubiquity of political disengagement and disavowal does not mean that academics are somehow unaware of their own politics: as Eyal Weizman has observed in the context of debates over Israel, the decision to avoid politics "requires an understanding of the logic of politics as much as evading the military requires understanding the logic of military action."[20] Nor does it mean that academics' preferences have no political consequences. The effect of scholarly political quietism is, of course, wholly political in its reinforcement of the status quo: in recent years, for instance, most academics have generally shown all too little opposition to state-sponsored attempts to outlaw BDS in universities, or to impose the International Holocaust Remembrance Alliance's definition of anti-Semitism, which includes criticism of Israel as an anti-Semitic act, and which has been adopted, without serious or influential critique, by a growing number of universities worldwide, and often used to repress speech on Palestinian rights. As we saw in the last chapter, real clashes of interest, with concrete implications for academics' immediate professional choices, still do arise from time to time: debates over BDS are one such case. But when they do, the very perception of "politicizing" a supposedly neutral terrain acts as a significant brake on their spread. Despite the fact that, in reality, there is nothing unprecedented about boycotts as a matter of political practice in academia, the complaint that the Israel boycott politicizes the supposedly apolitical domain of "scholarship" is one of the strongest threads running through the anti-BDS literature and acts as a powerful disincentive to engage in the academic boycott, even for those academics sympathetic to Palestine.[21] As the complaint exemplifies, whenever internal dissent breaks through to the surface of academia, it is typically understood as exceptional, a disturbance to the status quo, the resolution of which will restore the academic corporation to its previously fantasized, apolitical arcadia.

DEMOCRACY AND CAMPUS EXCLUSION

On the characteristic liberal interpretation of higher education, universities are supposed to lay the groundwork for social progress through public enlightenment. Intellectually, they are understood as contributing to the "extension and deepening of human understanding" in the sciences and humanities;[22] culturally, they are claimed to enrich the sphere of available expressive and artistic meanings; socially, they are supposed to spearhead a growing sensitivity to, and tolerance of, human difference, thereby driving a constant expansion of the horizon of social inclusion; politically, they are justified through their presumed capacity to foster the progressive improvement and autonomization of critical citizen-subjects, raising standards of democratic participation and removing barriers to social advancement. These grandiose ambitions make a stark contrast with the actual antidemocratic practices of exclusion found in today's universities. These practices are omnipresent in the contemporary academy and considerably reinforce Zionists' case against the democratic aspirations of BDS.

In short, attitudes to the academic boycott are closely bound up with attitudes to exclusion and enclosure in universities. Exclusion is, as we have already seen, both constitutive of higher education and, in a different and far more serious way, intrinsic to Israel's apartheid politics against Palestinians. Israel has the reputation of a pole of scholarly and scientific excellence at the service of a highly educated, inclusive society. This helps it "smartwash" the colonialist violence with which it encloses Palestinians, whether physically, politically or ideologically (this last through what Ramzy Baroud calls the "persisting information blockade" that the realities of life in Palestine regularly have difficulty penetrating).[23] On campus, knowledge and educational opportunity are also enclosed, this time by the constraints of the neoliberal economy and by the various management practices of the contemporary corporate university.[24] In the face of Israel's enclosure of Palestinian freedom, the academic boycott is part of Palestinian society's attempt to isolate Israel behind a compensatory financial, political and ideological enclosure or "picket line," taking the gamble that doing so will create sufficient pressure on the Israeli state and its allies to trigger policy change that will secure academic and other more basic freedoms for Palestinians.[25]

In addition to the kinds of antidemocratic enclosure achieved by putting proper higher education out of reach of the economically disadvantaged, enclosure of an entirely literal kind has become an even more obvious feature of universities' physical environments. Universities around the world sustain a discourse of civic engagement and celebrate – in large part for marketing purposes – their "public intellectuals" while, at the same time, acting against the dissemination of knowledge by intensifying the policing of their external and internal boundaries. In occupied Palestine, this obstruction and policing are blatant, with checkpoints and Israel Defense Forces (IDF) patrols regularly preventing students' access to university. In the west, campuses are usually accessible, but other types of obstruction are in place: no presence on campus without identification, no access to libraries' holdings without a student card, restricted entry to university buildings, obstacles to non-enrolled students auditing classes, encouraged or obligatory RSVPs to academic talks, paying entry to public lectures and politically motivated restrictions on use of or access to campus venues. Measures like these will be well known to anyone familiar with how modern universities work. As the built environment of higher learning is transformed into the "hubs," "pods," "nodes" and "resource" and "engagement" centers of contemporary campus urbanism, more and more of university life is closed, reserved and policed.[26]

These kinds of measures embed the expectation that higher learning is a restricted privilege, access to which should not be universal. If this is the default expectation, the obstacles to Palestinians' access to university can only seem less serious, and the call to take steps through the boycott to remove them only more outlandish. This is particularly true of those university systems, as in the US, UK or Australia, with traditionally high numbers of carefully controlled fee-paying international students. Strict limits on the time available to complete degrees, the transfer to universities of responsibility for ensuring students not overstay visas or, in some UK universities, the use of regular fingerprinting to confirm lecture attendance, all blur the lines between education and the border control apparatuses of the security state.[27] The difficulties Palestinian students experience coming to study in the west are just one manifestation of the enclosure of academic opportunity so characteristic of contemporary academic culture.

Corresponding to the physical enclosure of academic spaces is the enclosure of academic time. In the occupied West Bank, the university day is severely shortened by the hours students take to pass through checkpoints on the way to campus; Palestinian students would be fortunate if their study time was eaten up only by the demands of paid work, as is the case for students in many other parts of the world. For academics, overwork is one of the most frequently denounced problems of professional life, particularly for the low- or often effectively *un*paid, precarious workforce on which universities now depend for large amounts of their teaching. Yet academics' frequent unwillingness to seriously challenge their escalating workloads often rests on a peculiar masochism, also characteristic of other white-collar professionals: the tendency to take each new demand on one's time, each subsequent encroachment of "work" on "life," as just the next opportunity to showcase individual resilience. The willingness to surmount, through puritanical discipline, whatever punishment the institution next inflicts becomes a perverse mark of superiority in a competitive professional milieu deeply marked by Darwinian logic. For academics, the profession's vocational nature – academics often think of themselves as "called" to their disciplines by a driving inner "passion" – means that "work" and "life" are, in any case, hard to tease apart, and the enclosure of their "personal" lives by professional responsibilities consequently more surreptitious.[28]

This has a direct relevance to the question of the boycott. In a context of institutional pressure continually to absorb, and indeed to seek out, new demands on time as a token of professional validity, the call to boycott – that is, to decide *not* to take part in – certain avenues of often prestigious international (Israeli) collaboration is highly counter-cultural. It is even more so when the entrepreneurial ideology of academia gives rise to a significant fear of opportunity refusal and pushes academics to constantly maximize the number of fora at which they market their research. The pressure is greatest on recently minted doctoral graduates, a point in an academic career when competition for opportunities is most intense. As one Italian postdoctoral researcher has put it in the context of her decision to support the boycott, "In Italy today, as in most of Southern Europe, a researcher's hopes of obtaining paid work are distant mirages. In consequence, an academic who [offers a postdoctoral fellowship] isn't prepared for getting no as an answer. Refusal is considered a luxury."[29] With these pressures, blacklisting Israeli-sponsored jobs or conferences is, given the prestige of the Israeli academy in many fields, nonsensical on the usual criteria of professional success, as well as when judged by the typical norms governing academic use of time.

STATES OF ENCLOSURE

Attitudes to the academic boycott are also conditioned by the general norms of control and surveillance that universities maintain against their staff and students. Palestine supporters risk the full force of campus repression. The relatively small but very public number of cases of university staff being dismissed or expelled, denied tenure, dragged through the courts, harassed, bullied or intimidated serves as a major disincentive for academics to engage in Palestine advocacy. Palestine activism in universities is generally policed more intensely than any other cause both by university administrations and pressure groups like Canary Mission or UK Lawyers for Israel, which fight campus Palestine advocates. This situation is facilitated and normalized by the general expectation of repression that obtains on campus. By temperament, academics are often cautious, so even the merest possibility of following Norman Finkelstein, Steven Salaita, Valentina Azarova, Cornel West or David Miller, all of whom lost or were denied academic positions as a result of their advocacy for Palestine, is frequently enough to scotch any impetus to boycott.[30]

Aside from celebrated cases of Zionist interference like these, one of the most flagrant current manifestations of campus repression, and one where universities' general policing culture intervenes most explicitly against Palestine justice, is the UK's "Prevent" scheme, which, as such, merits particular attention.[31] Prevent is an "anti-radicalization" initiative introduced by the UK government in 2011 to identify students vulnerable to "extreme" ideas, including "non-violent" varieties of extremism, which, the government explains, "can create an atmosphere conducive to terrorism and can popularize views which terrorists can exploit."³² Nothing is immune from Prevent's mandate, and especially not support for Palestine: members of Palestine societies in UK universities have been particularly subjected to scrutiny and repression.³³ In one assessment, Prevent extends "an infantilising model of securitised child protection" to students, with the goal of installing a culture of surveillance of students by staff and of staff's own self-censorship – a generalization of the climate of distrust and (self-)monitoring already characteristic of academic workplaces under New Public Management regimes.³⁴ It is remarkable how willing university authorities have been to "cooperate" with security agencies in the surveillance, and hence the intimidation, of students in the Prevent framework. This cooperation considerably heightens the risk of taking a political stand on Palestine. In a 2011 report, Universities UK stated that even "*potentially* aberrant behaviour" among students must be "challenged and communicated to the police where appropriate."³⁵ One UK university reports a "direct linkage between Special Branch and Registrar," a "generic data-sharing protocol" as well as "informal channels of communications" between the university authorities and specialist security police; another is reported as having provided the police with "a room on campus so that better communication with staff and students can take place."³⁶ The effects on academic exchange have been as intended: the authors of the 2017 *Rethinking Prevent* report conclude that a "policing culture" now exists in UK universities, leading academics "to be extra vigilant about how they articulate themselves," a situation which "quite often translates into a form of self-censorship."³⁷ The politics of Palestine justice is not the only area in which debate has been stifled.³⁸ In such a context of the overwhelming assertion of state-backed institutional authority, adopting an oppositional stance like support for BDS pits academics against their universities acutely, especially given the equivalence that Zionists typically try to establish between support for Palestine and terrorism.

Prevent is an extreme manifestation of far more banal techniques of campus governmentality like the codes of staff and student conduct found in many universities. Sometimes, including at my own institution, these codes have been used to sanction BDS initiatives.³⁹ Whether through Prevent or other legislative constraints, or through their own local regulations, such restrictions on academics' and students' autonomy as agents with the freedom to adopt oppositional stances to their institutions' prevailing biases are a counterpart to the limitations that increasingly characterize universities physically. These practices reinforce, on the scale of the campus, the very norms of physical and ideological enclosure that many states, including Israel, defend on the national scale. As a state of enclosure *par excellence*, Israel justifies the brutality of its coercive practices as necessary for the flourishing of liberal social values and sanitizes them for the consumption of a "civilized" public.

The structural parallel with the modern university's enclosure of education and dissent is obvious.[40]

Readers inclined to dismiss this comparison as tenuous should hesitate before doing so: university vice-chancellors and presidents, tasked with enforcing often arbitrary differentials of power on campus, resort, often willingly, to ultimately coercive practices, as Finkelstein, Salaita and others can attest. Given the characteristic high interchangeability between the most senior leaders of universities and the functionaries of modern governments, the dispositions and responsibilities of power in the two roles cannot ultimately be so different – if they were, we would not see figures like Larry Summers, Glyn Davis, Richard Descoings, Michael Ignatieff, Baroness Amos, Rami Hamdallah or Menahem Ben-Sasson make the transition between the upper echelons of politics and the leadership of top universities in, respectively, the US, Australia, France, Canada, the UK, Palestine or Israel.[41] In Israel itself, the military and Shin Bet are frequent sources of universities' leaderships: to give just two examples, Ami Ayalon, former director of the Shin Bet, a decorated former navy commander and ex-cabinet minister, was executive chairman of the University of Haifa for the six years until 2017; another ex-Shin Bet head, Carmi Gillon, became vice president for external relations at the Hebrew University of Jerusalem in 2007.[42] Whether in Israel or outside it, there is, fundamentally, no deep difference of kind, though there is an obvious and extreme difference of magnitude, between advocating reforms that would cripple students with debt, colluding with the police to intimidate Palestine sympathizers, preventing pro-Palestine events taking place on campus or fingerprinting international students when entering lectures, on the one hand, and, on the other, approving draconian border security measures, consenting to the illegal detention of refugees or political prisoners or any of the other abuses that nation-states regularly license, Israel among them. Whether in the management of states or universities, coercion can be justified and rationalized in the name of necessity, pragmatism or precedent, with the decision-makers regularly sheltered from unpleasant proximity to the implementation or the effects of their decisions. The dispositions of abstract, bureaucratic violence involved are qualitatively similar. The parallels are most clear when the heads of western universities take on the role of agents of Israeli policy and repress staff and students' pro-Palestinian and BDS activities.[43] In this light, we can understand one aspect of university leaders' near-universal support for Israel and hostility to BDS: quite aside from the strong motivation provided by Israel's academic capital, university heads may recognize somewhere in the back of their minds that, in the relevant respects, their own institutions in the age of neoliberalism have much in common with Israel itself.

It is unsurprising, then, that attitudes to BDS largely align with attitudes to the transformation of higher education under neoliberalism: supporters of

BDS are typically counted among the most vocal critics of the "totalitarianism of the private sector" to which universities aspire, while, on the other side, university authorities and the financial and corporate interests that sponsor them have hardly distinguished themselves as being at the vanguard of opposition to Israeli crimes.[44] This is not to say that no Zionists oppose "managerialism" in universities – Cary Nelson, an important figurehead of the anti-boycott movement, is a major critic of the neoliberal university – or that all BDS supporters contest it; nevertheless, as a general rule, the correlation stands.[45] University executives are particularly consistent in their hostility to the boycott call.[46] Larry Summers, former president of Harvard following stints as treasury secretary in the Clinton administration and chief economist at the World Bank, is both a prominent opponent of the academic boycott ("deplorable," "near anti-Semitism," "morally insensate," "racist") and a pharaoh of neoliberalism.[47] While Harvard and other top institutions in the US are generally, thanks to the tenure system and a rigorous conception of academic freedom, partial hold-outs against the "McKinsey Stalinism" of universities in much of the rest of the English-speaking world, Summers' reign in Cambridge was notorious for its centralizing, authoritarian and chauvinistic bent: properties easily recognizable by any observer of the neoliberal university.[48]

DISCRETION AND THE INSTITUTION OF CRITIQUE

Any attempt to understand the institutional context of BDS in universities must pay special attention to the humanities, a domain in which the call for the boycott of Israel has been particularly strong, especially in the English-speaking world. Thanks to their frequent investment in a certain kind of skepticism and critique, humanities disciplines can often be sympathetic to counter-hegemonic politics: as their comparative receptivity to the boycott call exemplifies, the humanities largely conform to their popular reputation as fertile ground for critique and political radicalism.[49] But the danger that the humanities' institutionalization of critical analysis carries with it is often neglected. While validating intellectual dissent, the argumentative moves and the critical habits of mind associated with the humanities also play a particular – and particularly unrecognized – role in legitimating and reproducing the forms of domination, including Zionism, which characterize the contemporary world.

The majority of humanities scholars are not, of course, explicit Zionists, but their prevailing resistance to the boycott aligns with Zionism admirably. In order to understand this resistance better, the humanities' broader role in the reproduction of domination needs careful analysis. One fruitful starting point is offered by what I will call the humanities' *discretionary* character: the fact that humanities disciplines are, as fields, extremely open, with the arguments that can be sustained in them depending crucially on the individual preferences and imagination of the participants. What counts as a viable intellectual position in philosophy, literary studies or history is contested, and positions come and go with changing intellectual fashions and personal sensibilities. This means that participants' own discretion plays a large role in shaping the knowledge that a discipline produces and the authority its proponents enjoy.[50] This discretionary character is obvious from students' first engagement with the humanities. Students are encouraged to "follow their hearts, to choose the specializations and research interests to which they are most deeply drawn," in Cary Nelson's words, and are often recruited into humanities subjects on the basis that they are following their "dream" or "passion" – a framing which construes university education as a sophisticated form of (sometimes deep) personal gratification.[51] In learning to theorize about the human world and in continually being invited to elaborate new generalizations about it, students quickly discover that, in the pursuit of this gratification, intellectual success is to no small extent the result of their own discretionary self-confidence, verve and force of will – qualities of mind that, in mature scholars, become what Hamid Dabashi describes as "that self-confidence, that self-consciousness, that audacity to think oneself the agent of history that enables a thinker to believe his particular thinking is 'Thinking' in universal terms."[52] Intellectual originality and independence are highly prized: students are rewarded for finding ways of asserting their individuality, whether through the novelty of their analyses and observations, their pursuit of an original question or the imaginative framing of an established topic. Whatever the particular means chosen, the point for the student is to demarcate themselves from their peers by highlighting their own intellectual distinctiveness.

The consequences of this "discretionary" character of the humanities are wide-ranging. On the one hand, discretion provides an opening for progressive shifts in intellectual practice, sometimes driven by social movements outside the university, such as efforts to decolonize disciplines and restore subaltern and non-European knowledges to their rightful place. What receptivity the humanities show to BDS is, in part, a consequence of this progressive discretionary mindset. On the other hand, the centrality of discretion empowers participants to pursue intellectual practices that support various forms of domination, Zionism included. Regardless of the political valency of their results, habits of discretionary intellectual adventurousness are frequently encouraged among both students and academics, necessarily accompanied, if they are to succeed, by the projection of confident certainty in the intellectual positions they involve.[53] In her fascinating study of academics serving on grant-funding peer review panels in the US, the sociologist

Michèle Lamont quotes a remark whose validity holds for the humanities quite generally: "anyone who's ever written [a proposal]," Lamont was told by one of her interviewees, "knows that you [have to] sound convincing even about things you're not sure about." "A convincing proposal does not guarantee that the applicant really knows what he or she will be doing," Lamont concludes, "panelists understand that proposal writing requires a certain amount of 'impression management' or 'bullshit.'"[54] First experienced as students, the truth of this description holds for all stages of the academic life cycle. Institutional life in the humanities is, in a sense, the emergent product of the creative individual risk-taking and intellectual daring of its participants, constituted by discretionary choices, personal interpretations and subjective intellectual styles: in that setting, the boundary between scholarship and opinion ("judgment") is often fluid. In some contexts, students and academics are required to cultivate their own capacities of discretionary choice, elsewhere, to comply with the choices of others. This is true both in the expression of disciplinary knowledge in ordinary academic work and at the level on which claims between different disciplines need to be adjudicated for the purposes of attributing university resources.

For all the emphasis on intellectual rigor and seriousness, and for all the insistence on the need to complexify universal categories, thought in this regime becomes a voluntaristic expression of personal interest, fueled by an individual's originality, determination and talent. The complexity of the world is subordinated to a conceptual matrix selected and adjudicated on a highly personal basis by whoever holds the authority in a particular academic context: the lecturer in the lecture theater, the peer reviewer, the plenary speaker. This creates an environment in which Zionism is no more than one – particularly strong – strand among the many threads of institutionalized discretion, all of them serving particular interests, that together make up the fabric of academic life. This is true not just of the most openly hermeneutic disciplines like literary studies, in which the role of personal sensibility and opinion is self-evident. It is true even of more apparently "scientific" humanities fields like linguistics, as I have explored elsewhere.[55] Lamont documents how peer reviewers maintain their belief in the supposedly meritocratic character of their funding decisions "by seamlessly folding their idiosyncratic preferences and tastes into the formal criteria of evaluation."[56] As one of her interviewees puts it, "Excellence is in some ways . . . what looks most like you" – a situation that they describe as "always a bit of a problem."[57] "It is impossible," Lamont observes, "to eliminate the effect of interpersonal relationships, including clientelism, on the evaluation process," but "discussions proceed as though panelists were free of these influences. Their individual preferences are usually construed in universalistic terms, despite the particularistic aspects introduced by real-world considerations."[58] In the case of

Zionists within the overall clientelism of the academic system, "excellence" looks like hostility to BDS.

Lamont's conclusions speak volumes about the ideological environment in which humanities scholars make the call for boycott. Prima facie, one would have expected her study seriously to challenge the practice of panel peer review and to throw a spotlight onto questions of equity and bias in humanities research funding. In many other domains, the admission of the intrinsic role of subjective criteria would prompt calls for urgent reform. Yet not once do Lamont or her reviewers in major journals call for a socialization of research funds, or their allocation on a less prejudicial basis – by lot, rotation, or a vote of a much larger pool of assessors, themselves democratically elected. There is no reason that these mechanisms are impossible; far from their being harmful, most individual academics would benefit from them. The fact that no one calls for them reveals much about the profession's complicity with, and investment in, arbitrary regimes of unjustified power.[59] In such an environment of normalized – indeed, celebrated – arbitrariness and inequity, it is little wonder how few academics are calling for efforts to be made to support educational justice for Palestinians. The hegemony of Zionism rapidly dissolves into the background of institutional life, worthy of as little protest as the other constitutive injustices of the university: Zionists are just another powerful lobby pursuing the discretionary self-interest to which humanities academics are habituated as a founding condition of their membership of the profession.

ZIONIST UNIVERSALS

Lamont's reviewers deploy categories like "excellence" and "originality" to rank grant proposals. The use of general categories like these to capture specific details of the world – the subsumption of a "particular" under a "universal" – is *the* basic move of intellectual analysis, whether in philosophy, history or cultural studies. From their very first year in humanities disciplines, students are encouraged to deal in general categories – *subjectivity, nature, the west, ethics, the unconscious, justice, cinema* – and to use these categories to impose order on the variety of the empirical world. Sometimes the task is to master the categories imposed by a discipline or an individual authority; often, however, students are also supposed to invent their own. Universalizing categories persist as study becomes more advanced. The lesson is clear: the greatest rewards will go to those most adept at reconciling the twin demands of fidelity to the discipline's received categories – always as interpreted by particular authorities – and the expression of appropriate originality in devising their own purportedly new ones.

Little Israels   73

This leveling of the diversity of experience into the fixity of abstract categories is an inescapable aspect of intellectual life, but it is still an act of symbolic force that can be justified only by its results. That point is not lost on participants in debates on Palestine, the stock-in-trade of which is supplied, as Saree Makdisi notes, by disputes over the validity of categories like *racism, genocide, apartheid, colonialism, refugee* or *democracy* for the particulars of life in Israel and occupied Palestine.[60] We will return to this question in chapter six. For now, let's note how one BDS critic, Cary Nelson, has explicitly recognized the emancipatory political objective of the abstractions deployed by the Palestine solidarity movement and criticized Judith Butler, in particular, for her use of them:

> While gender and justice are concepts that operate in different registers, both are socially and historically constructed. An abstract notion of justice can serve as a social good and can hail people's sense of identity and patterns of behavior, but it has no place in discussions of the Middle East without historically-based qualifications. Like other BDS advocates, Butler takes political self-determination as an unqualified good for Palestinians, an end result that then becomes a sine qua non for any acceptable resolution of the conflict. Anything less than that, she believes, will not constitute justice.[61]

Beyond the clear implication that something less than Palestinian political self-determination *might* be a just solution, what is striking in Nelson's position is the selectivity of his demand for the "historically-based qualification" of abstraction. "We thus get nowhere," he continues, "by holding aloft a lantern called justice and letting it blind us to complexities of culture, history and national desire, along with the realities of economic and social integration." In Nelson's view, "justice" for Palestinians demands such qualification – but the abstract notion of Israeli "academic freedom" apparently has no corresponding need to be related to the concrete historical situation in which it is invoked. Nelson's maneuver is exemplary of the discretionary and preference-guided nature of the deployment of general categories in humanities disciplines: the aspects of the world singled out for categorization, and the choice of the categories with which they are captured, are always a function of particular epistemological and (micro)-political interests. In such a situation, there are many kinds of institutional force which outrank the force of reason as guarantor of the disciplinary success of a particular set of abstract categories. The current entrenchment of Zionists' preferred categories – Israel as a democracy, not an apartheid state; Palestinians as *extremists* or *fanatics* (terrorist, backward, etc.); BDS as *anti-Semitic* rather than *liberatory* – emerges as just one more instance of the discretionary character of humanities work.

The particular modes of reasoning and discursive practice into which students are inducted in humanities subjects always represent, as we have seen, discretionary selections from among the many alternatives that could equally have been adopted instead. Any curriculum entails choice – of theories, emphases, texts, schools, methods and so on. In the humanities above all, this selection is shaped in an obvious way by the ideological hegemonies at play, all grounded and justified in the classroom by the rationalizing authority of the academic in charge. Through assessment, students' facility in accepting this authority – including creatively – is made the criterion for the measure of their "excellence," "originality," "intelligence," "capability" or "talent," and hence for their credentialization for the purposes of entry into the labor market.[62] In this way, the humanities classroom becomes an elementary site for education in the exercise of discretionary power – the kind to which students must learn to submit if they are to go on to assume a role in the economy, and which is on show everywhere in world affairs, including over Palestine. The practices of assessment and examination inherent in higher education, which bury students' intellectual demonstrations in often oppressive bureaucratic constraints (word limits, formatting prescriptions, citation conventions, due dates, etc.), are an especially concrete manifestation of the "discretionary" power of academic authorities and "prepare students both to undergo and, no doubt, also to exercise and impose the modes of population administration and the practices of new [public] management," as Muriel Darmon has noted in her study of French higher education.[63]

The authority invested in the lecturer to evaluate students' work, and to dismiss competing theoretical claims in the classroom on a discretionary basis, encourages an acceptance of arbitrary symbolic authority which is soon re-engaged outside the lecture theater. The problem was noted decades ago by Paulo Freire: "the teacher," Freire observed, "confuses the authority of knowledge with his or her own professional authority, which she [or] he sets in opposition to the freedom of the students."[64] The symbolic power to which young people are subject in the humanities classroom, and which they also learn to deploy for themselves, offers a foretaste of the arbitrary dispensations to which they are subject as citizens of modern states or as job seekers in employment markets. Given that academic study is directed toward the conferring of a degree, and that, in theory, the better the degree, the more attractive the employment options, interpretations of the intellectual qualities of students' work translate directly into evaluations of their suitability for material and other rewards. Work judged as "original," "sophisticated," "imaginative" or "well argued" contributes to a student's prospects of economic success or social prestige after graduation; work judged to embody the opposite qualities undermines it. As Lamont's study confirms, and as any humanities academic will acknowledge at some point, these judgments are highly subjective. The intellectual *Realpolitik* exerted in the world of ideas prepares students for the material *Realpolitik* they endure, exert and observe as graduated wage earners.

For all their overt ideology of critique, the humanities therefore inculcate in students an acceptance of the lines of discretionary academic authority parallel to the ones that cohere the structures of contemporary societies. The humanities thereby play their part in reconciling students to the world and to its current imbalances of power and contribute to the ideological grooming of the next generation of the economy's generalist labor force – the administrators, teachers and technocrats, as well as the pool of precariously employed service-industry, knowledge and creative workers, one of whose functions is to help maintain the stability of the status quo, including over Palestine. This ideological work is a crucial social function of humanities education, equally obscured by the cliché of the humanities' irrelevance to the "real-world" as by the counter-claim of their "deeply" or "fundamentally" political (understand, "progressive") character. Philosophy departments that typically graduated full-blown revolutionaries would not survive long. Instead, philosophy and other humanities disciplines – like the pure sciences – prepare graduates to join a large and mainly compliant labor force in sectors of the economy for which they are often significantly over-qualified, and which are unlikely to satisfy any intellectual or cultural sensibility that their degree may have cultivated. The writer Germaine Greer was unusually explicit on this point in an address to graduating Arts students at Sydney University in 2005: "When things get bad," she told the audience, "when you're bored shifting around enormous hedge funds or when you're pole dancing, you've still got . . . your critical ability" – a "critical ability" which, in Greer's vision, is evidently cultivated only in order to be suppressed for all practical purposes.[65]

Israel and Palestine will not, of course, even be at issue in the majority of humanities courses. But the discretionary nature of the theoretical generalizations taught and examined in humanities departments nonetheless helps us understand a puzzling feature of the debate in universities over BDS: the immunity of Israel's liberal image from public contestation by many academics. As the resistance to the boycott demonstrates, academics have often been reluctant to treat the facts about Palestinians with the seriousness they deserve or to question the Israeli narrative about its own commitment to "peace." It is easy, as well as accurate, to account for this in general terms as simply another instance of dominant ideas serving dominant social forces, but without an analysis of the particular mechanisms that produce this result in the academic sphere, we miss something about the distinctiveness and entrenchment of campus Zionism. I have suggested that in a climate as habituated as the humanities to the acceptance of discretionary categorizations and interpretations enforced essentially on the basis of authority, the dominance of anti-Palestinianism is nothing novel.

The point is perhaps clearest with regard to a crucial element of the ideological structure of the BDS debate and one of Zionists' most effective weapons against boycotters: the accusation of anti-Semitism. In the humanities, one of the reasons for academics' acute sensitivity to this talismanic charge is precisely the performative and discretionary character of the evaluations that typically are made in their disciplines. In a discursive environment habituated to the performative authority of subjective evaluations, the mere leveling of the accusation of anti-Semitism by an authority figure is enough to make it stick. This displays in miniature a deeper feature of the politics of BDS in universities: in a milieu so traversed by dispositions of compliance, and simultaneously so satisfied in its own intrinsic embodiment of critique, a heavily contested political position like support for the boycott will take exceptional impetus to generalize.

The humanities have often been the object of ideological critique from the left, drawing attention to the political import of disciplines' received ideas and contesting their perpetuation of diverse forms of oppression under the cover of disinterested scholarship. But perhaps it is not generalizing too far to suggest that critics have characteristically been less sensitive to the ways in which, regardless of the particular content of a discipline, the mental habits that the humanities foster in students contribute to the social relations that support domination. The forms in which knowledge and the activity of thinking are presented in the seminar room play a crucial role in accustoming students and the academics that some of them go on to become, to the arbitrary exercise of power. In that context, Israel's power over Palestinians is just part of the mix.

Chapter 4

Disruption, Protest, Democracy

Boycott, Divestment and Sanctions (BDS) in universities advances when academics are persuaded to withdraw from various kinds of ordinary scholarly activity. But this is not the only way in which BDS activists try to influence how debate about Palestine on campus unfolds, and certainly not the best known. In contrast to the passive withdrawal of participation, the active disruption of Zionists invited to speak in public, including at universities, is probably the aspect of BDS and wider Palestine activism which gains the most public attention.[1] Just as academics engaged in the boycott are accused of compromising academic freedom, activists engaging in disruptive protest are regularly criticized for their supposed hostility to "free speech" – another of those apparently indisputable formulas meant to end all discussion the minute it is invoked, disguising the social, political and economic interests at work in its exercise.[2] In a parallel to the defenses offered of boycotting, activists often claim that they are behaving democratically and that the disruption is, in itself, an exercise of free expression aimed at promoting Palestinians' own liberties.[3] Palestine supporters regularly find themselves having to justify protest and disruption tactics against Zionist criticism in this way: on campus especially, there is, in David Estlund's words, an "enormous moral presumption, which seems to be widely accepted, against speech-interfering protests."[4]

Disruptions happen, and will continue to happen, for a good reason: as the history of social movements and grassroots activism in Palestine and elsewhere amply attests, disruptive protest has regularly been an instrument of social progress, and activists are confident in its political productivity.[5] That confidence does not need any theoretical foundation, any more than do the innumerable other political activities in which we engage simply because we have confidence in them – attending a meeting, holding a placard or banner at a protest, making arguments for different positions. Like disruptive protests, these are all practices whose existence we mostly just accept. Just as we don't need a theory of placard-holding in order to hold a placard, so too we have no need for a theory of disruption in general to justify engaging in it: in many circumstances, its political utility – sometimes necessity – is self-evident, at least to activists. Nevertheless, disruption can be highly problematic to others, and the controversies it generates are often heated, with possibly serious disciplinary consequences for participants: sometimes, as at the University of California, Irvine, in 2010, or at Humboldt University in Berlin in 2017, activists are even prosecuted criminally for disrupting invited speakers.[6] In an academic political culture based on speech and marked, as we saw in chapter three, by high levels of conformity and low levels of "material" contestation (e.g., strikes), the arena of speech and disruption is one in which questions of power and coercion can be keenly felt. This is all the more the case since there is probably no area in which mainstream liberal premises have been so widely internalized as in debates about "free speech." So how should activists understand and intervene in these debates? The issues matter: disruption raises questions that are crucial for grassroots politics beyond BDS, and it is important for activists' approach to it to be grounded in realism about what speech events are actually like, not in an idealist (and idealist*ic*) fantasy of them.

"Language and politics are inseparable in the Israeli-Palestinian conflict," Saree Makdisi writes, and their interplay "has a special, almost unique importance" to issues of Palestine justice.[7] Disruption of speech events is a key manifestation of this inseparability, but it is striking how little serious attention in the free expression literature has been devoted to it. The existing literature, including on free expression over Palestine, mostly assumes a strongly non-interactive context of speech production: the center of gravity of most discussions of free speech lies in the relation between finished, single-author texts or blocks of "speech" (speeches, books, cartoons, webpages, talks at conferences, etc.) and the state or other sovereign authority (such as a university). Discussions of this kind crystallize around questions of censorship: when, if ever, is it right to prohibit or punish speech or writing? That is, of course, no minor issue.[8] But there is less discussion of free speech questions as they apply to "interactive" contexts in which the issue is not the suppression or punishment of an already finished text but the kind of *response*, including possibly a disruptive one, that a listener should make *during* the initial production or "performance" of a piece of speech which has not been prevented from going ahead. For most activists and university authorities, this is a far more relevant issue.

SPEECH AND SOCIAL CONFLICT

The aspiration for equal, democratic communication rights for everyone flows naturally from the wider aspiration for an end to exploitation and injustice in general. In this light, disrupting speakers, especially in the kind of staged ways we will discuss here, is likely to strike many people as self-evidently wrong. Worse, it seems to violate basic tactical common sense: if Palestine supporters interrupt others, how can we demand that our own public events not be disrupted in return? Disrupting speakers in official contexts like talks at universities also infringes deeply entrenched principles of social behavior – conventions of politeness that are so ingrained that many people have difficulty seeing them as *just conventions* and not the *only feasible way* to act in public. These conventions are particularly embedded in universities, which are structured by hierarchical relations between experts and learners. Despite the existence of participatory formats of academic communication like the seminar or the tutorial, public speech in universities is modeled predominantly on the lecture – a non-participatory address delivered to a silent, respectful audience by a single authoritative speaker. Even outside a strictly pedagogical context, disrupting a speaker like this flies in the face of the way people have generally been socialized to behave on campus. This is especially so in light of universities' particular commitment to enforcing a stultifying "civility" that represses the slightest hint of dissent, as Steven Salaita, dismissed for an "uncivil" tweet, and any number of other cases illustrate.[9]

When protesters stage a disruption at an official event, the predictable complaints about "free speech" being violated give the impression that speaking has simply been shut down in toto. This is, of course, misleading: it is crucial to recognize that in situations of disruption, it is a particular *speaker*, not some notional "speech-in-itself," that has been interrupted. Instances of disruption differ from each other in many ways: whether they prevent the speaker from even beginning to talk (rare) or interrupt him or her in midstream (common); whether the interruption takes the form of questions to the speaker or the statement of a counter-position; whether the interrupters are part of the rest of the audience or demarcate themselves from it; whether the interruption is protracted or momentary. Regardless of these differences, it's an inconvenient fact for the usual complaints about protest that people who disrupt an invited speaker typically do so *by speaking* – by exercising, that is, their *own* free speech. Speech, in this situation, isn't therefore stopped but, as it were, changes hands: the authorized, official speaker is replaced by the unauthorized disrupter, or, more frequently, disrupter*s*, who try to seize the floor.

This throws the focus onto the conditions that govern the original speech event and the distribution of roles within them – the reasons why some individuals and political positions are typically "cast" in the role of authorized speaker, while others are cast in that of the disrupter. Social conflictuality must be at the heart of any answer to this question: decisions about who gets to speak, with what kinds of audience and what guarantees of being able to finish without interruption, are all settled by the history of competing interests that shape the balance of forces in the public sphere at any given time. In this context, it's important to note that, in our era, "free speech" has come to be strongly identified as a demand of the political right – almost always, it is invoked defensively by conservatives to express their outrage when the speech prerogatives to which they have become accustomed are challenged, including when their speakers are interrupted, usually fleetingly, by progressives. The fact that the greatest public outrage about violations of "free speech" comes when right-wing gurus, official spokespeople or conservative syndicated newspaper columnists furiously denounce affronts to *their* freedom of speech already offers grounds for considerable skepticism about the way "free speech" as a political value is used.[10]

What is at issue, then, when considering speech and conflict, is not so much freedom of speech as control over what we can call, for want of a better word, *communication* (a notion I'll say more about shortly). Questions of who gets to speak, on what platform, with what kind of audience and what guarantees of non-interruption concern the circumstances of communication, not of speech. Freedom of speech and freedom of communication are different beasts: in public parks, plane toilets or solitary confinement, speech may be perfectly free, but since no one is there to listen and nothing is therefore communicated, it is of limited political interest. It is opportunities to *communicate* to others, opportunities to hold a platform, that are the real object of political claims to speech rights, since it is these that are not evenly distributed but the results of a history of social and political conflict with designated winners and losers.

In most places, freedom of political communication – the ability to hold a genuine public platform for one's views – is the preserve of a tiny coterie of powerful political and media figures. As a consequence of the ubiquitous ideology of social homogeneity that surrounds most mainstream political discussion, that fact is not as appreciated as it should be. This ideology trades on discourses – at best aspirational, at worst cynical – of the "community," "national values" and similar fictions, in order to obscure the omnipresence of domination and the merciless realities of social difference that it engenders, including in communication. The strength of this ideology means that claims that speech is, in fact, far from free in the west (including in western universities) are bound to raise hackles. Surely that can't be right, critics immediately object: people can more or less express themselves freely on social or alternative media, in comments sections on online media sites, on blogs and so on, and they even have a chance to attract audiences by doing so. But even if it is easier to get a platform *of some kind* than it once was, there is no right to an *audience* gathered in front of it – no prospect of free political *communication* for everyone. No one can (or indeed should) be forced to listen to the speaker on a platform, whether a physical or online one: whether or not a speaker is heard must remain the choice of potential audience members themselves. That simple truth brings us to the heart of why communication can't be considered free: the idea that freedom to *communicate* exists in any genuine sense in modern societies ignores the fact that the possibility of attracting an audience depends on the speaker's ability to inform potential listeners that the speech is happening in the first place. People cannot decide to listen to communication which they do not even know is taking place: for this purpose, it is the ability to *advertise* or *broadcast* one's communication widely that matters. But this ability is, clearly, far from evenly distributed. The social geography over which information about speakers and platforms is transmitted is not smooth and open: rather than offering equal resonance for all voices, it is structurally warped into a variable topography of baffles, sinks and echo chambers that amplify some speakers and mute others. When an Israeli dignitary delivers an official address at a university, the occasion is widely publicized. When Palestine solidarity activists put on events and are lucky enough for them to go ahead unhindered, they typically have far fewer means to advertise that any speech is happening.[11]

These struggles over platforms are central to what it means to be engaged in politics. Speech is not just the medium in which political struggle is conducted: it is an object of contention in its own right, with competing political actors vying over control of opportunities and channels of communication. Crucial to politics is the effort, within a social space constituted by players with conflicting interests, to shape and regulate the channels of communication through which those interests can be served and to establish norms over the content those channels transmit. This is exactly what is happening when protesters disrupt a speaker or stage a mass walkout, but it is also seen in many other contexts – the tactic of no platforming and struggles over access to the mainstream media and other forums for the wide circulation of speech, as well as the academic boycott itself, which aims to reduce the audience and thereby the reach of the platforms available to certain Israeli institutional leaders.[12] Political actors, both states and individuals, regularly act – in ways that may be legitimate or not – to shape the terrain over which speech is broadcast; to open, close and structure the platforms that are available for speech in the domains they control. This is the context in which the varied forms of disruption explored here should be understood.

Placing conflict at the heart of an analysis of speech situations entails an important shift in the way that questions of speech rights, and hence of disruptive protest, should be conceived. Traditional liberal conceptions of speech rights make most sense if it assumed that speech is originally or fundamentally free – that no one who wishes to speak is prevented from doing so, that there are no intrinsic or systemic barriers to anybody freely expressing what they want to say, and that speech, especially in universities, enables the open discussion, free from domination, that must underlie any democratic process of deliberative decision-making. The presumption, according to this conception, is that any violation of speech is illegitimate: since there are no inequities in the original distribution of speech opportunities, there is no call for any correction, whether through disruption or other means, aimed at resetting the balance of speakers that already exists. "Negative" freedom of speech – the right of whoever happens to be speaking not to be prevented from doing so – trumps "positive" freedom of speech – the right of *everyone*, including those currently excluded from speaking positions, to gain access to platforms from which they can communicate freely. Disruptive protest against Zionist speakers by Palestine solidarity activists is typically justified, by contrast, as aimed both at promoting Palestinians' own *positive* freedom of speech, which is violently suppressed in Gaza and the occupied West Bank, and at compensating Palestine advocates' exclusion from the most powerful platforms.

In universities, one major bias in the distribution of speech opportunities lies in the greater access Zionists have to university platforms: Zionists and their spokespeople are frequent visitors at the world's universities, whereas Palestinian advocates are regularly excluded, by the universities directly, by governments or by digital platforms like Zoom, YouTube or Facebook.[13] Even the discussion of the Palestinian cause is open to exceptional censorship, as any number of attempts to muzzle it internationally – for example, in France, Germany, Italy, the UK, the Netherlands or Canada – show. In France, pro-Palestine events that were prevented by university authorities from going ahead include Stéphane Hessel's talk at the École normale supérieure in 2011, Palestine conferences at the University of Paris 8 and Sciences Po (Institut des Études Politiques) Lyon and a public meeting at Toulouse 2 Le Mitrail in 2012, another talk at Sciences Po Lyon in 2014, a talk at Sciences Po Nancy, an exhibition at the University of Aix-en-Provence and a talk/debate at Paris 1 in 2015, a public meeting on Palestine at the University Jean Jaurès in Toulouse in 2017, a lecture at the same institution in 2018 and a talk and film screenings at the University Paul Valéry in Montpellier in 2019.[14] In 2022, the French government was even seeking – unsuccessfully – to ban several Palestine solidarity organizations outright.[15] In the US, the Trump administration's legislation purportedly aimed at combating anti-Semitism, and anti-boycott laws in over thirty states, have deprived, or threaten to deprive, the Palestine solidarity movement of numerous platforms.[16] In several European countries, acceptance by different bodies, including many universities, of the flawed definition of anti-Semitism by the International Holocaust Remembrance Alliance (IHRA), which counts criticism of Israel as an anti-Semitic act, has led to a similar severe crackdown.[17] In 2022, Sheffield Hallam University used the IHRA definition to suspend the Palestinian lecturer Shahd Abusalama.[18] In 2021, the University of Glasgow, which has also adopted the IHRA definition, apologized for a 2017 article on Zionist influence in British politics in a university-run postgraduate journal and obstructed a scholarly talk on "Decolonizing Palestine" on ludicrous anti-terror grounds.[19] The same year, the University of Santiago de Compostela in Spain canceled a course called "Auschwitz/Gaza: A Testing Ground for Comparative Literature" under pressure from Jewish organizations on the grounds of anti-Semitism.[20] According to Jonathan Cook, "Israel, and anything related to it, has become such a combustible subject – one that can ruin careers in an instant – that most political, academic and cultural figures in Germany now choose to avoid it entirely":[21] in 2020, for instance, the Weißensee Kunsthochschule Berlin withdrew funding and closed the website of a program on "Unlearning Zionism" as a result of Zionist pressure;[22] in 2021, the Goethe University, Frankfurt, denied the group "Students against Right-Wing Hate" the use of a room for screening a film about the discussion of Palestine in Germany.[23]

Among the most telling rationalizations offered for the obstruction of Palestine-related speech is the accusation that it is "contentious" or "a source of conflict." This was the rationale for the banning of a 2014 talk at Sciences Po in Lyon – a striking illustration of how even the stated liberal purpose of free speech, allowing controversial ideas to be debated, ceases to apply when it treads on Zionist toes.[24] In her monumental account of the obstacles she faced in mounting a conference on the one-state solution in 2013, Susan Drummond has illustrated how the academy "has been structured to limit the kinds of arguments that can be successfully made and understood about the Israel-Palestine conflict."[25] In the US, the legal advocacy organization Palestine Legal responded to almost two thousand incidents involving suppression of pro-Palestinian activity in the eight years from 2014 to 2021.[26] If Palestinians and Zionists were equally matched forces and if Palestinian points of view could be freely expressed in the same forums as Zionist ones, disruption would be less necessary. But since Palestinian perspectives are so systematically censored, Palestine solidarity activists find themselves in a zero-sum game: when it is impossible to win an independent platform for Palestinians, exposure can only come at the expense of one for Zionists.

The structural limitations on debate about Palestine in academia go beyond simply who is allowed to participate in it: the very terms in which discussion is conducted are frequently weighted in favor of the Zionist status quo, including through anti-boycott measures and laws punishing criticism of Israel as anti-Semitic. The dominance of a given social group entails not just physical control over the means of communication but also ideological control over the limits of acceptable content. The difficulty that academics experience in trying to normalize talk of Israeli "apartheid" and "racism" are cases in point. When a Zionist scholar describes mass Palestinian dispossession in 1948 as a "social revolution of land ownership,"[27] the very possibility of that description illustrates how the norms governing the framing of historical and political facts about the history of 1948 can entrench an anti-Palestinian perspective. In a similar vein, Zionists' intense policing of pro-Palestine discourse induces among many academics high levels of self-censorship and reluctance even to address the topic, constituting another major obstacle to debate. This climate of repression can also prevent anti-Zionism from gaining a foothold in institutional structures and curriculum: for over a decade, San Francisco State University obstructed the overtly pro-Palestinian Arab and Muslim Ethnicities and Diasporas Studies program by refusing to appoint sufficient faculty to it.[28] If university authorities "need to throw you under the bus, they will do that as well," a Dutch academic states, "This has led to self-censorship on a high level."[29]

WHAT IS SPEECH?

Once the illusion is abandoned that speech is not an object of social conflict, and that public speech events are somehow exempted from political struggle, the existence of disruption, as a bid to conquer the right to speech by force, becomes far less remarkable. But what exactly is it about "speech" that makes it an appropriate object of political struggle and that might justify disruption of one kind of speaker in order to promote other speakers' positive freedom to communicate? Even asking the question highlights the extraordinarily high level of abstraction on which discussions about language use as a political category take place. Just as no one defends an absolute "freedom of movement" – one which would authorize you, for example, to go wherever you wanted, whenever you wanted, regardless of who was in your way – no one, or almost no one, is prepared to defend a freedom of speech that applies *absolutely*, to *all* speech regardless of its context. Even dogged free speech proponents draw a line somewhere, often, for instance, in cases of incitement to violence or hate speech, which are exempted from broader freedom of speech protections by at least some free speech proponents.

Progressive participants in free speech debates have often pointed out the inadequacies of the liberal conceptions of freedom operative in them, which are undermined by an "under-theorization of the ways in which power itself structures and shapes what is experienced as 'freedom.'"[30] Less often appreciated is the inadequacy of the prevailing conception of speech itself. The intuitions that lead people to discuss "free speech" as something desirable or dangerous are, after all, various and imply different understandings of what speech is, what it does and what, so to speak, it is "for." We might, for instance, believe that free speech is intrinsically valuable – that speech should be free because the opportunity to express oneself in language is a central aspect of our identity as people (our "human nature") and therefore something that should not be restricted or that should be restricted as little as possible.[31] Or we might think that the value of free speech is largely instrumental – that free speech is desirable because of the effects it has: that only if speech is maximally free can we have the kinds of open public debate that allow the truth to be discovered and the right political decisions to be taken (this is, of course, the essential rationale of Mill's classic advocacy of free speech in *On Liberty*). Both these ideas imply a broader understanding of what speech is like, how it functions socially and individually and how it relates to the participants in the situations in which it occurs. To argue that speech can inherently harm, and that it should therefore be subject to restrictions, involves taking a position on exactly the same questions.

A voluminous literature is dedicated to the subject of free speech. But only a small minority of it analyzes speech in a way that looks beyond intuitive and usually inexplicit ideas about what speech, as an aspect of people's behavior, is actually like. Most political debates about free speech, especially but not just in the media, are strikingly lacking in any kind of critical or even informed stance toward the category "speech" itself – a stance, in other words, that goes beyond common preconceptions and is informed by the large body of empirical and theoretical work now available on the subject. This body of work, I'll suggest, can throw some light onto questions that any politics of free speech or disruption needs to consider: What actually happens in speech situations? Whom does speech affect and how? How can we tell what the "content" or effect of speech is? What happens when someone's speech is disrupted?

In mentioning the existence of specialist work on these topics, my intention isn't to cast myself as an authority on "speech" or to presume to enforce scholarly conclusions about it in a way that puts an end to debate. Even if this *were* my aim, I wouldn't be able to honestly achieve it, since the nature of language and communication has always been a highly contested question in which no one can claim to be the mouthpiece for a single set of unanimously accepted and "scientific" answers. Anyone familiar with the discipline of linguistics can attest to the fact that no consensus exists among academic specialists about what the right analysis of language, speech and communication actually is. Rather, then, than charging into the debate atop the white steed of academic objectivity, my aim is to show how questions about speech rights and disruption *can be thought about differently*, once we are prepared to be a little critical about the assumptions on which the usual framings of the issue rest. Speech is, in many – but not, of course, all – ways, what we make it. That means it is both intellectually and politically productive to suggest how the usual premises of discussions about speech rights could reasonably be altered. Once we accept that there is a variety of ways in which the nature of speech and speech events can be conceived, we have freed up some elbow room in which non-hegemonic actors, including Palestinians and their solidarity advocates, can assert their claims and deploy their methods.

SPEECH, COMMUNICATION, EMOTION

What are the usual premises and assumptions of discussions about speech rights? One particular assumption continually resurfaces which needs to be questioned if we're accurately to gauge the options available to activists trying to bring about political change. This is, to put it simply, the assumption that *speech is essentially communication*: freedom of "communication," indeed, often serves as a synonym for "freedom of speech." David Estlund is typical in stating that "there is no denying that obstructive protests intentionally interfere with certain communicative acts of others." "Certain *communicative* acts": for Estlund as for most contributors to these debates, speech can be unproblematically construed as communication. Even if we've already seen that speech and communication are different, the identification of the two will still probably strike most readers as unobjectionable: surely there is nothing wrong, for the purposes of discussing free speech, with concentrating on the communicative power of language?

Discussions of speech and politics would benefit, however, from recognizing the ideological quality of the claim that speech is mainly a matter of communication. Ideological concepts are, on Slavoj Žižek's description, those that are "functional with regard to some relation of social domination ('power', 'exploitation') in an inherently non-transparent way."[32] It's a hallmark of such concepts that they seem both utterly obvious and unchallengeable – "How could speech be anything other than communication?! Aren't you communicating to me right now?!" – and, when you scratch their surface, remarkably hard to specify in any detail. This is exactly the situation with the concept of "communication." This isn't the place to embark on a full-scale analysis of the view of speech-as-communication. But since the conclusions of such an analysis are of considerable utility to radical politics, and since the communicative view of speech is often presupposed in otherwise critical discussions of the topic, let's take a brief detour into the subject.

It's easy to agree that two people can "communicate" – share – things with each other in a debate or conversation. But what does this actually mean? What are the "things" that get communicated? Many answers would be likely to identify "ideas," "information," "opinions," "facts" or something similar: at the moment, for example, we could say, uncontroversially enough for everyday purposes, that I am communicating – in writing – certain ideas that I have about speech and protest. I'm doing so by stringing together words which have meanings (if we wanted to press the point, we could say mostly "literal meanings") that correspond to the ideas that I'm wanting to communicate, and, if you're following me, it's because, as someone who understands English, you're understanding the same meanings when you read my words as the ones I understood in writing them. Language emerges, on this picture, as a kind of shared *code*. For many everyday purposes, this way of conceiving of language as a code for the communication of ideas has a lot to be said for it.

If we are to recognize the ideological dimensions of the code/communication model of speech, and so to undermine it in intellectually and politically productive ways, it will help to appreciate its historical specificity. For the code/communication model is, precisely, historical – the contingent product of a specific set of social and intellectual developments. It reflects a heavily ethnocentric understanding of language that developed in European modernity, and it is certainly not universally shared today.[33] This understanding is not politically innocent but, in Richard Bauman and Charles L. Briggs' description, turned language into "a perfect vehicle for constructing and naturalizing social inequality," "stripped of ties to particular social locations and interests and freed of all forms of social difference and conflict."[34] We will see how this might be the case as we consider how linguistic issues play out in Palestine solidarity activism.

In the context of public addresses of the kind that BDS supporters might interrupt, an immediate shortcoming of the communication model of speech is that many of the ideas conveyed to the audience on such occasions are typically already known to many of its members. When a Zionist guest (or a pro-Palestinian one, for that matter) speaks publicly at a university, much of what they say consists in contextualization, reminders and reiterations of common talking points. The amount of information communicated – transferred from speaker to hearer – is often therefore far outstripped by the quantity of ideas with which the audience is already familiar. For a model of speech predicated on the idea that speech events consist in the *transfer* of information from one consciousness to another, it is something of a problem if, in fact, much of the information is already there: if that is the case, no *transfer* is needed, and communication becomes a heavily redundant exercise. All the other motives that bring people to public addresses – satisfying their curiosity about what the speaker *is like* in order to gain insights into how politics might connect to life, reinforcing their existing convictions by giving them authoritative validation and so on – outstrip the narrow communicational view of language. In particular, the "validation" function of a public address, aimed at boosting the audience's confidence in their beliefs, quintessentially targets not communicated thoughts but whatever the non-rational psychological factors are that constitute confidence. This is something that the standard justifications of free speech, which only consider speech as communication and condemn interruption as the violation of a bloodless, rational protocol of information transfer, simply fail to take into account.

Yet another problem with the view of speech as fundamentally geared to neutral communication is that it is strikingly incomplete. In particular, recent work in philosophy, linguistics and cognitive science requires us to acknowledge the major role of emotions in language – the extent to which language is *not* just rational, the extent to which it cannot just be seen as a mechanism for the transmission of stable informational content. Traditionally, linguists believed that (to borrow the influential phrasing due to Edward Sapir in 1921) "ideation" – propositional thought – "reigns supreme in language." Sapir acknowledged that emotion and volition "are, strictly speaking, never absent from normal speech," but he went on to claim that, despite this, their expression "is not of a truly linguistic nature."[35] On the face of it, that's a surprising conclusion: if emotion and volition are *never absent*, it seems a bold decision to exclude them, by simple fiat, from the empirical study of language – but this is exactly the effect of the bias Sapir expressed, which has been shared by the vast majority of the discipline of linguistics until comparatively recently.

These days, however, many specialists increasingly take the role of *embodiment* and *emotion* in thought and language seriously: the fact that we don't just speak with our minds but with our bodies and our feelings too. What they are discovering is that it is not simply "reason" that governs thought and language: we are not *just* the vessels of a cold rationality, not *just* in what William James called "a cold and neutral state of intellectual perception," elevating us out of our emotion-ridden corporeality into the enlightenment of objective, disinterested reason.[36] The cognitive psychologist Luiz Pessoa, for instance, argues that cognition and emotion should be viewed "as complementary pairs that mutually define each other and, critically, do not exclude each other."[37] Emotion is, on this view, front and center in the operation of language (Jesse Prinz argues that it is central to morality, as well).[38] This is even the case in what we might have thought to have been the stronghold of dispassionate, non-emotional reason: abstract thought. Work in psychology suggests that "emotional content . . . plays a crucial role in the processing and representation of abstract concepts."[39] Speech is not, on this picture, "dispassionate": even when talk is abstract – for instance, when it concerns questions of "justice" or "human rights" – it does not provide us with a neutral arena in which a transcendent reason can work itself out in a way that frees us from our natural bias and interestedness. Instead, speech essentially engages the non-rational, emotional, embodied dimensions of our psychology, at the same time as the rational ones. Yet these dimensions are completely missing from standard discussions of freedom of speech, which abound in references to knowledge, opinions, ideas, beliefs, agreement and disagreement and other essentially conceptual, rationalist and intellectual constructs – as though speech was amputated of the rest of its life.[40]

The words of a campus speaker do not, then, just convey ideas which trigger agreement or disagreement: they also arouse emotions – enthusiasm or aversion, anger or admiration, sometimes disgust, relief or any number of others. The effort to ignore the irrational, non-cognitive dimensions of speech is, however, central both to modern conceptions of language as the instrument of reason and objectivity and to many liberal justifications of free speech. But if speech is just as much about emotion as it is about ideas, then it is far from the supposedly ideal instrument of deliberation that many liberal rationales for free speech presuppose, and a challenge arises for the usual arguments against disruption. A particular challenge derives from the temporality of emotions. Emotions have an immediacy that the rational logic of ideas lacks. An idea or argument is not closely tied to the circumstances of its delivery and so can be effectively refuted well after it has been expressed. Emotions, by contrast, are far more context-specific: they fade and so cannot be reacted to post hoc to anything like the same extent: instead, they call for an on-the-spot response. Someone who has just been deeply insulted or outraged cannot realistically be told to hold their anger and keep it for later, any more than a stand-up comic's audience can be asked to hold back their laughter so as not to interrupt the next gag. In both cases, the audience's reaction cries out to be expressed. This has an interesting implication for disruptive protest. A classic liberal argument for free speech is that our nature as linguistic creatures gives us the right to express ourselves freely. As Erwin Chemerinsky and Howard Gillman put it in their *Free Speech on Campus*, "to hide who you are and what you believe, for fear that the mere act of expressing yourself risks punishment, is an exceedingly cruel and oppressive circumstance."[41] From that point of view, the recognition that speech both involves emotion in the speaker and triggers it in the audience leads us to the following conclusion: since emotions call for immediate expression, an outraged audience has *just as much intrinsic right to express that outrage* as a speaker has a right to speak. In a speech context set up as a monologue, like a campus lecture or speech, this can only mean taking the floor away from the original speaker.

In most cases, the confiscation of the floor is fleeting – the speaker's delivery is temporarily punctuated by the audience's outburst of shock, horrified gasp, acclamations or brief cries of denunciation. In some cases, however, a more sustained confiscation of the floor is needed to properly express the listener's reaction, and the interruption is more enduring. Activist disruptions are, of course, premeditated and so have a strategic element as well as a reactive, emotional one. But they are, nevertheless, authentic expressions of often deeply felt emotional reactions, and so, on Chemerinsky and Gillman's argument, they have every right to be expressed.

Once we take the problems with speech-as-communication seriously, there is a whole literature in linguistics and philosophy of language, which can help us to fashion an alternative account of what speech is. These alternative accounts, associated with figures like the Russian linguist Valentin Voloshinov, place an emphasis on *contextual* over *literal* meaning, on the grounds that the purportedly stable, self-identical information that is transmitted on the standard picture of communication is exquisitely prone to contextual modification.[42] The speech whose freedom is in question becomes not a neutral medium for the broadcast of unchanging quanta of information but is fragmented into a multitude of situated events, each with their own political and emotional valences and effects. The same words cannot be assumed to carry the same "message" on every occurrence they are uttered, since the very notion of "message" functions precisely to strip language of its situated, interpersonal dimension – to throw the focus away from speech as an act by a *particular* speaker in a *particular* context directed to a *particular* audience, onto a view of it as communication of an unchanging, context-neutral "message" resting on the bedrock of words' "literal meaning."

The notion of literal meaning itself is politically significant and demands particular scrutiny. As the linguist Michael Toolan puts it, literal meaning is "a cultural and ideological construct very much designed to characterize some language practices as orderly, authorized and authoritative (and others as not so)," and which is "therefore well suited to and reflective of societal interests in literacy, order, and authority."[43] Palestine supporters experience exactly the effects of this social interest in authority whenever debates about the justifiability of disruptive protest of Zionists turn on the ostensible "literal content," rather than the clear political intent and situated interpersonal effect, of Zionists' speech. In one such controversy in which I was involved, protesters disrupted a talk entitled "Ethical dilemmas of military tactics in relation to recent conflicts in the ME" by a British supporter of the Israel Defense Forces (IDF). In the past, this speaker has described Israel as "world leaders in actions to minimise civilian casualties" and reiterated the belief, originally expressed in the context of the 2008–2009 Gaza War, that "no army in the history of warfare had taken greater steps than the IDF to minimise harm to civilians in a combat zone."[44] On the implicit "communication/code" philosophy of language, these are, first and foremost, propositions with literal meanings which, right or wrong, communicate ideas that contribute to a broader, rational debate about the Middle East. Of themselves, they are purely informational: they are "only words," not "words that wound." On the revised view being advanced here, in contrast, the words become many other things besides components of a communicated message, and their role as conduits of information no longer enjoys the same privilege. They become slurs against Palestinian people, the expression – because they are so patently inaccurate – of disrespect for the audience, facets of a bid for authority on the part of the speaker, an instance of political organizing, community affirmation or institutional legitimation and so on. Thinking of speech as a medium that does more than simply or even mainly communicate means that the question of the justifiability and intensity of objection, including by disruption, is reset: when students briefly disrupted this speaker's talk, they were doing more than violating the sober, rational unity of a "message" being communicated, even though this was, of course, the main way in which their actions were subsequently framed by their critics. If speech is more than simply communication, then there is no reason – for example, when thinking about the justifiability of disruptive protest – for it to be treated as if it were simply that alone.

SPEECH AS INTERPELLATION

The very conception of speech's communicative or referential function has, then, undergone significant revision in recent decades. Under the new picture, language is not just a conduit for conceptual meanings that can be transferred between sender and receiver. Far from this hyper-rational, ascetic and aseptic vision – one more suited to machines than to people – speech becomes, as it were, a "whole-body" event, which engages far more dimensions of personhood than rationality alone.

If we are to develop a conception of speech adequate to a politics of emancipation and justice, we have to attend to all the things that speech does other than "communicate," however we precisely interpret that. We have already discussed speech's role in arousing and expressing emotions, but what other functions does it perform? We could give many answers. What functions speech can perform is a matter of interpretation on which opinions can legitimately differ. The more attention is directed to speech events, the more we should expect to become aware of different ways to describe what speech does (how it "functions"), and the more likely we are to encounter disagreement about what the dominant "functions" of this or that piece of speech actually are.

Nevertheless, we can look to the linguist Roman Jakobson for one useful taxonomy of linguistic functions. Jakobson identified six functions of language, only one of which, the "referential function" (also called the "denotational" or "cognitive" function), corresponds to what we've been calling "communication."[45] In addition to this communicative, "referential" function, speech functions, in Jakobson's scheme, to express or suggest emotions (Jakobson's "emotive function"); to engage or influence the addressee (the "conative" function); and to perform a variety of closely related tasks united by Jakobson under the label of the "phatic function": "establishing, prolonging, or discontinuing communication" (as when we say, on the phone, "I really have to go now"), "attracting the attention of the interlocutor or to confirm their continued attention" ("are you listening?") or checking whether the "line of communication" itself is working ("can you hear me?"). Jakobson also identified a "metalinguistic" or "metalingual" function, in play whenever we turn language back on itself and use words to explain what other words mean, and a "poetic" function, which he described as the "focus on the message for its own sake."[46] For Jakobson, true to the received philosophy of language we've been discussing, it was the communicational "referential function" that dominates, but it cannot be separated from the others: no instance of speech is purely referential or, indeed, a pure instantiation of any one of the functions alone.

Attending to Jakobson's functions allows us immediately to pinpoint ways in which the purpose of Zionists' public addresses at universities goes well beyond either communicative or emotive functions. For one thing, such addresses are clearly aimed at attracting and holding the attention of the public, thereby boosting the social prestige of the speaker and their hosts through association with an institution of higher learning. This is related to Jakobson's "phatic" function, and it is entirely independent of what is communicated in the course of the address. Campus talks are also clearly aimed at fulfilling the "conative" function of "engaging" or "influencing" the addressees. The metalinguistic function of language, in which words are used to explain the meaning of other words, is also strongly in play in addresses about Palestine or Zionism, which are replete with attempts to define the terms of the debate. This kind of self-referential language use is an unavoidable part of all speech: we regularly find ourselves, in all sorts of context, needing to explain or define what we mean. In contexts of political struggle, however, it has a clearly ideological role, aimed at imposing politically favorable definitions of contested terms.

Speech has, then, far more dimensions than we commonly acknowledge, and it should not be treated in politics as though it didn't. But for present purposes, if we're to properly consider what speech is like in contexts of oppressed groups' struggles for justice, Jakobson's list needs to be supplemented by at least one other function, which we'll call the *interpellative* function of language. Recognizing this function will allow us to go beyond the narrow view of speech as informational transfer between two minds and properly analyze its embeddedness in and connection to social practices, including those of Israeli apartheid.

The term "interpellation" was introduced by the philosopher Louis Althusser in 1970 as a contribution to a Marxist analysis of the reproduction of social structures of modern capitalism. Interpellation is a hypothesis about what we might call the "identity-forming" or "social-engineering" aspects of social practices (including speech) and the ideologies they embody – how particular combinations of practice and ideology induce people to take on different kinds of identities or subject positions.[47] The identities we take on are multiple: as bearers of a particular nationality, as citizens of a particular polity and as gendered and racialized subjects, to name only a few especially high-level, often consciously held ones. They are also frequently contradictory: many people today, for instance, find themselves torn between the subject positions of "consumer" and "polluter," depending on the relative force of the interpellations of the market economy and environment movements. As this case illustrates, different political forces want different types of subject. Because their existence constitutes an obstacle to Zionism, Palestinians are the objects of a permanent interpellative battle. Zionists try to cast them as dispensable, backward, anti-Semitic extremists, an interpellation answered by Palestinians' self-perception as the holders of a national identity with political claims distinct from other Arabs.[48] Similarly, the Palestine solidarity movement interpellates Zionists as colonizers, dispossessors and racists, while Zionists interpellate themselves as progressive and peace-loving, the deserving subjects of an ethno-state, and so on.

Highlighting speech's interpellative function goes well beyond the obvious claim that people use language to say things about themselves and their political opponents, but captures two essential facts. The first is the fact that, in Lorna Finlayson's words, "there can be no sharp disconnect between i) what is said about us, ii) who we are, and iii) what we are able to say" – or, we might add, do.[49] Central to the theory of interpellation is the idea that individual identities or subject positions are not the autonomous expressions of people's independent nature, organically coming to fruition within a neutral social environment. Rather, identity is an *effect*, and identities are, in important ways, *prompted, constructed* or *induced* from outside, by social structures and practices from which the exercise of power is never absent and for which the kinds of identity produced have major political consequences: this kind of conception of identity, as Judith Butler notes, "establishes as political the very terms through which identity is articulated."[50] The kind of subject we are is a result of the mix of different "interpellations" which have been imposed on us – the different ways in which the social practices in which we participate have "called out" to us, the ways we have been able (or had) to respond to them, and the dispositions, beliefs and expectations about ourselves that we have internalized as a result. When Shlomo Sand describes how "history lessons, civics classes, the educational system, national holidays, memorial days and anniversaries, state ceremonies," religious festivals and children's songs contributed "a central component of his self-identity," his "sense of being a descendant of the ancient Jewish people," he is describing the process of interpellation within social practices that Althusser theorized.[51]

The second important fact highlighted by the concept of interpellation is that speech, and speech about politics in particular, is not a transcendent activity floating freely above the world of social bonds, antagonisms and interests. Speech is a practice in its own right and takes place in a web of other practices: its roots plunge deep into the social world and its conflicts, to which it contributes via the various interpellations that it enacts. The politically relevant meaning of speech for speakers and hearers lies not just in an abstract content that is notionally transferred from one mind to another but also in the role speech plays with respect to practices which it reinforces, undermines or transforms.

An Israeli dignitary's campus speech performs multiple interpellations that reinforce the murderous practices of Israeli apartheid. But it does more than just reinforce: in fact, the speech is a *necessary accompaniment* of these practices, because it is inconceivable that Israel would maintain its apartheid policies without the effort to justify and excuse them before public audiences, as well as to obscure their real nature. The subjugation of Palestinians rests not just on direct exploitation, oppression and violence but is also maintained through the interpellations of Palestinian and Israeli identities which Israel effects in order to win acceptance for its policies – Israelis as civilized, western and moral; Palestinians as violent and uncivilized fanatics. Given the kind of relations Israel wants to entertain with the rest of the world, especially the west, propagandizing of this kind is integral and necessary to Israeli apartheid: without a diplomatic effort to produce the appropriate interpellations, Israel would risk aggravating the status of pariah that it is determined to avoid. Appreciating this necessary complementarity between speech and apartheid in the Israeli case lets us sidestep the usual debates about whether speech plays a minor or a major role in sustaining racist oppression.[52] In the case of Israeli anti-Palestinianism, the practice of apartheid and the practice of speech about it on the part of Israeli dignitaries simply cannot be dissociated.

Interpellation is one of the functions of speech which Jakobson, who belonged to rather a different intellectual tradition from Althusser, did not even consider. As well as its other functions, language plays an interpellative role through its centrality to the practices that fashion our subject positions, constituting and reinforcing the presuppositions we have about who we are and shaping the kind of loyalties and animosities we experience toward different aspects of our world. It is important to appreciate that the interpellative potential of speech is most fully activated when words' bond to collective social practices is tightest. Rashid Khalidi charts the role of institutions like the press, schools, religious establishments, clubs, libraries, charities and political groups in shaping emerging Palestinian identity in the late Ottoman period. The interpellative power of speech is central to all of these and unfolds in the context of organized social institutions.[53]

As many of these institutions exemplify, the collective practices in which interpellations are activated often have a coercive dimension. The interpellations exerted through institutions like schools, which aim to produce subjects well-adjusted to the prevailing economic and socio-political conditions, have a coercive element at their base, in that failure to conform to their requirements opens students up not only to various forms of stigmatization but also to actual punishment (detention after class, suspension, expulsion, etc.). It is when words have an obvious link to practices – real or plausible – of non-verbal coercion that their interpellative power is the strongest. Speech is, for instance, often central to the highly coercive process of crossing checkpoints in the occupied West Bank, which involves questioning and the production of documents. David A. McDonald describes how the "actions necessary to successfully traverse an Israeli check point . . . instantiate a prescribed Israeli discourse of Palestinian subjugation and criminality," seen, for instance, when a Palestinian is forced at gunpoint to refer to Al-Quds as "Jerusalem" – a powerful interpellation which can prompt either subjection or resistance. McDonald observes that "reiterations of such banal activities as producing a state issued identification card, removing bags and articles of clothing for inspection, and waiting patiently in endless lines, can over time have the same constitutive meaning as more inflammatory measures such as arrest and harassment. State imposed identities become stabilized, sedimented in everyday practice, through such banal rituals and engagements."[54] This is a perfect description of interpellation. Verbal abuse of Palestinians, likewise, takes on a more menacing quality when it is dispensed by armed settlers under the protection of Israeli troops, or by IDF troops themselves at checkpoints or elsewhere;[55] declarations of the legitimacy of Israeli dispossession and ethnic cleansing are all the more chilling when articulated by an official of the very government responsible for those practices.[56] This connection between interpellative speech and coercive practice is important to discussions of disruptive protest, for reasons we'll see later.[57]

Through interpellation, speech and the social practices in which it is embedded play a role in forming subjects.[58] Identity is social: who I am and who I see myself as being are as much to do with my place in the world, my social position, the possibilities available to me, the social "move space" which I occupy, as they are about my "inherent" or "independent" nature, whatever exactly that might mean. Yet, for all its individual significance, the "subjectivating" role language plays in forming identities through interpellation functions *collectively*. Subjects are not interpellated as unique, stand-alone individuals but as *members of a broader class* (Palestinians, Israelis, refugees, victims, freedom fighters). The collective identity conferred on and experienced by subjects is also never fixed but is continually fashioned by the ongoing work of interpellation and the individual's responses to it. There is a sense, indeed, in which identity itself is a *practice* – something one does, not something one has. In reference to the recent political history of Palestine, Khalidi stresses "how rapidly views of self and other, of history, and of time and space, [can] shift in situations of extreme political stress, which [can] be seen as watersheds in terms of identity." He observes that "constructs of identity and of political preference, and understandings of history, which appeared long-lasting and persistent in certain circumstances, could crumble or evolve almost overnight."[59] This is a description of the intense interpellative power of practices, including linguistic ones, in moments of political crisis.

For attempts to understand disruptive protest, an important consequence of the collective nature of interpellation is that, as Judith Butler points out in her 1997 book *Excitable Speech*, subjects can be interpellated even by language with which they have no immediate connection – language that isn't directly addressed to or heard by them and that doesn't refer to them.[60] This is an aspect of speech that Jakobson's analysis, confined to the individualized speaker-hearer pair, misses completely. Discourses, ways of using language within particular institutional practices, contribute to constituting subjects of certain kinds even in those subjects' absence and even without reference to the subjects in question. Speech harms or benefits collectives, not just individuals. When a prominent Israeli politician denounces Palestinians collectively, framing them as violent, uncivilized, anti-Semitic fanatics, the speech, inserted as it is within the coercive practices of Israeli anti-Palestinianism, has significant political force and will disproportionately influence (though not, of course, fully determine) the way Palestinians *in general* are perceived and hence treated in the community in question. When settlers claim to be the "founding family" of a settlement on Palestinian land, no Palestinian is addressed or referred to, but the claim is a bid to impose a highly detrimental identity on the true Palestinian owners precisely by *failing* to mention them and thereby symbolically dispossessing them of their land.[61] Whether or not these interpellations were directed at or heard by any Palestinians personally, they enter into circulation nonetheless, helping define what is sayable about Palestinians, influencing subsequent discourse and reappearing in their own right whenever the original speakers are quoted. As a result, they help shape expectations about what practices toward Palestinians are normal, expected and reasonable. Linguistic interpellation has, in other words, precedent-setting and normalizing effects that extend well beyond words' immediate audience. No Palestinian needed to hear either interpellation in order to be – indirectly – interpellated by them. On the purely subjective level, hearing that someone has denied your rights behind your back, as it were, can have an even more powerful effect than in person.

An understanding of speech-as-communication makes it much harder to recognize these effects. Communication is a resolutely individual linguistic function in which any link to social practices is broken: I cannot communicate with someone if they are not listening to me (or reading my words), and I cannot communicate *about* something to which I do not refer. Whether I'm speaking to one person or to a thousand, communication has occurred to the extent that the ideas "in my head" succeed, via language, in entering every other head. Communication is measured on the scale of the individual, and it fails to the extent that the speech's "content" – the ideas that the speaker (or writer) has in mind – is not faithfully transferred to each and every listener (reader). When an Israeli dignitary uses a university platform to spread anti-Palestinianism, the communication/code ideology of speech sees them as simply *speaking about* or *referring to* Palestinians and Israelis. This relationship of "aboutness" (often called "reference") is a cornerstone of the communication/code view, and it makes the ties between speech and power completely invisible: the Israeli dignitary, on this account, is entirely equivalent to the Palestine-justice advocate, since, even though their perspectives are vastly different, both are "simply" speaking about, or referring to, the same things. The communication/code view is therefore consistent with a rejection of disruption, on the grounds that *all the speaker is doing is talking about Palestinians*. What could possibly be the harm in that? Even if a proponent of the communication/code view can acknowledge that, of course, the speaker is talking about Palestinians in a way that is intended to advance their own clear political interests, this is seen not as the *most politically relevant* fact about the speech but as a secondary and incidental property that should not shape any political response. Most discussions of speech rights, protest and free expression operate with a communicative, individualizing understanding of speech. Acknowledging interpellation as central to speech, by contrast, means releasing speech from the idealist absolutization of communication as its only function, and recognizing it as a component of material practices that need to be considered in collective, political terms.[62]

This turns the rights and wrongs of disruptive protest on their head. Focusing on speech's interpellative function leads us to consider speech as, inherently and essentially, a medium for the pursuit of interests and agendas. This means it is just as important to assess its political properties in terms of what it is *for* – why the speaker is articulating it – as of what it *says* – what its "content" is. The fact that, unlike communication, interpellation is not tethered to the narrow circuit of speaker and hearer, but is bound up with collective practices and disperses itself throughout an entire political community, means that the individual and the code/communication view of language that goes with it cannot be the right frame of reference for considering the question of disruptive protest: as Jodi Dean has explored at length, mistakenly "capturing" social phenomena in the restrictive ambit of the individual is a hallmark of the ideology of bourgeois modernity.[63] On the interpellative view, the politics of speech is no longer just about safeguarding *my* right to say what I want but about the *systemic, collective* effect of the interpellative speech and the practices with which it is connected. The legitimacy of disrupting an invited Zionist speaker on campus should not therefore be assessed in the only way the liberal free speech tradition assesses it – individualistically, as if the affront it presents to a single individual's right to self-expression is its only politically salient property. It should, instead, be assessed collectively, as an aspect of a collective struggle for political goals where what is at stake is not just an individual's right to speak but Palestinian society's conditions of *collective identity* and the legitimacy of the practices that oppress them. Phrased in this way, the rationale for disruptive anti-Zionist protest can immediately be appreciated. A powerful Zionist speaker's words do not just communicate a message but effect interpellations which consolidate and justify, and therefore contribute to maintaining, practices of serious injustice. Without the work of interpellation, these practices would be politically inconceivable for an Israel that poses as committed to human rights. Once this is acknowledged, disruption ceases to be an unjustifiable violence against a neutral order of communicated ideas, understood as inherently innocent of action. Instead, it becomes an intervention into a field where speech and the most damaging kinds of material practices are intimately bound together.

REDISTRIBUTING SPEECH

As well as instances of communication, Zionists' speeches at universities are charismatic performances, displays of political power, motivational addresses and racist interpellations of Palestinians. In none of these guises does speech possess the rationalistic virtues that traditional defenses of free expression are designed to protect. When Palestine activists disrupt a Zionist speaker engaged in these activities, they are stepping out of the role conventionally assigned to the audience, that of the mute recipients of a speaker's words. But listener passivity is not a baseline norm of all public speech events (e.g., think of the frequency of interruption of speakers in parliaments, or at jovial social occasions like birthdays and anniversaries).[64] Rather, it is an act of *deference* to the speaker, the organizers or the other members of the audience: to stay silent before an official speaker is an active affirmation of the speaker's (and/ or their host's) authority which, in universities, often ultimately rests on the availability of campus security to eject anyone who tries to confiscate the floor.

As simply a convention, the audience's silence is something that should be considered as discretionary. When a talk is open to the public, there is no pre-existing contract that mandates non-interruption: indeed, interruptions that affirm the speaker, like applause, are entirely acceptable. The public character of invited talks at universities has important consequences for the legitimacy of disruption. Sponsors of Zionist guests at a university can put on private, invitation-only events, vet attendees by calling for RSVPs to the talk or ask the speaker to deliver a guest lecture in a politics course, the academic character of which would legitimately preclude disruption. In any one of these speech contexts, organizers are justified in not tolerating disruption (which does not mean, however, that protesters would necessarily be wrong to disrupt). But when the speaker is hosted in a public venue, it is up to the public to determine if the usual conventions should be followed or not. Who gets to hold the floor in a public appearance is a matter to be negotiated by the speaker and the audience: the speaker has a right to the floor only for as long as the audience tolerates them. Speakers clearly view their ability to address an audience without interruption as a mark of the audience's acquiescence to their authority. The German far-right politician and philosopher Marc Jongen, for instance, wrote of his successful participation in an event at Bard College in the US in 2017 as a victory for his politics, noting that "the fact that the event took place at all – and I have not been shouted down – is already a great success – for political debate culture and for our cause."[65]

Nothing requires the audience to respect the authority of a speaker like Jongen. The possibility of violating the convention of audience passivity is as much an expression of freedom and autonomy as is the ability to express oneself in language. There are, in fact, some speakers whose authority must not be respected, since doing so reinforces the illiberal and antidemocratic interpellations their speech contains. This is most obviously the case of Zionist dignitaries invited to prestigious public speaking occasions on university campuses. The natural conclusion, for an anti-authoritarian politics that intends to challenge power where it is exercised, is that disruption is a necessary political response. While the audience has many ways to suggest their distance from a speaker – body language, muffled commentary, brief exclamations – interruption and counter-speech is the only way in which disagreement can be made fully overt, and the only way the hierarchies of power operative in a public lecture situation can be explicitly overturned. Most fundamentally, interruption is an act of discursive redistribution in which a subaltern actor confiscates the context of communication for their own purposes – in this case, the defense of equal rights for Palestinians. Speech is, indeed, one of the only domains in which this democratic redistribution is possible. Disruption of speakers is not justifiable simply because they are making hostile interpellations. But when those interpellations are understood as the necessary complements of the war crimes and genocidal violence they seek to justify, and therefore as an inevitable part of the same web of practices, disruption is an act of resistance – an act of "civil disobedience" against the speech conventions that contribute to the maintenance of apartheid – which does not fall victim to the conveniently idealist illusions of dominant views of speech.

Interrupting Zionists is, then, an attempt to undermine the nexus of practices and ideologies on which Zionist power rests. But it has a further important property, paradoxically contrary to the usual imputations of authoritarianism and coercion with which protesters are met: it performs a democratizing role, in that by creating a public scandal, it opens up the rights and wrongs of speaker and disrupter to the possibility of public debate. Typically, the existence of a disruption at a campus address attracts, through word of mouth and (social) media reports, far greater public attention than the address would have garnered in its own right. In this, disruption serves rather than obstructs the cause of greater public education about the issues in question, since it typically broadens the public to whom the broad outlines of the topic of the address and the protest against it are communicated. Speaking about the boycott in general, Nadia Abu El-Haj comments that "the effects of the strategic choice of academic boycott have been remarkable" since "it has brought critical conversation into the U.S. public domain in a way [she has] never seen before."[66] A similar assessment applies to instances of disruption. For an ideology of speech-as-communication, it is therefore far from clear that disruption impedes communication. Conventional liberal denunciations of disruptive protest, intent on preserving the existing monopolies over speech, are completely incapable of recognizing this obvious fact.

THE HECKLER'S VETO AND THE TACTICS OF DISRUPTION

Before leaving the topic of disruptive protest, we'll briefly consider two last arguments against it. The first criticizes disruptive protest on the grounds that there is a sense in which protesters are coercing an audience, who have come to listen to the speaker, not to them. In confiscating the floor from the speaker, protesters are, so this objection goes, exercising a "heckler's veto," inflicting themselves on an *involuntary* audience. It is certainly true that disruptive protest is a coercive intervention into a speech situation in which other audience members' preferences simply do not matter. Audiences are, however, always "involuntary," in the sense that they have no control over what they are going to hear; any number of contingencies can mean that a listener's expectations are disappointed. Since hecklers are exactly that, they have almost no capacity to impose an outright *veto* on the speech going ahead: they disrupt the speaker, but they are not usually able to shut them down. This is exactly where the usual assimilation of protest to censorship is so misleading.[67] And even if they *did* completely prevent the advertised speech going ahead, there is an obvious argument that the harm inflicted on the rest of the audience is far outweighed by the benefit to the struggle for Palestinian rights.

The second argument against disruptive protest is that the freedom of speech principle is most valuable exactly to supporters of minority or dissident views, like Palestine supporters, since they're the ones whose avenues for public expression are most likely to be blocked. Given the difficulty of making pro-Palestine arguments publicly, this argument states, activists simply can't afford to violate others' freedom of expression through, for instance, disruptive protest: doing so would mean undermining the strongest principle to which they themselves can appeal in favor of their own right not to be censored.[68]

Despite a certain intuitive attractiveness, this argument is not compelling either. The idea that Palestinians and their supporters have to endorse Zionists' freedom of speech since doing so sets a "precedent" that they themselves depend on is one of those powerful illusions that so many are mesmerized by. It rests on a Pollyannaish conception of the way that political interests get played out in society. If forces of progress have to rely on "precedent" to guarantee their speech rights, we are in even more trouble than we thought. Precedent doesn't count for much when politics intervenes. A platform for progressives is won and maintained through political organization, not bestowed by the grace of legal or social precedents. War criminals, invader-settlers and their apologists should not be excused from contestation when they justify ethnic cleansing, slur Palestinians and throw discursive sand in the audience's face: freedom for their speech means ongoing oppression for their victims. The most imperative realization for a materialistic politics of speech is the understanding that "speech" is not a magic garden miraculously exempted from the antagonisms and power imbalances of real politics. A docile world does not put itself into suspension outside the gates of discourse, obediently waiting for reasoned argument to settle all differences inside. Power does not respect reason. Political speech, speech by political actors, is material and should be treated as such. Palestine supporters should defend their speech rights on the grounds of the speech's content, not by appealing to an abstract procedural commitment to precedents for speech going ahead. And they should not hesitate to disrupt the interpellations by which powerful Zionists consolidate material anti-Palestinianism: disruption is not an unwarranted violation of the sanctity of a realm of pure ideas or debate but a concrete riposte to practices in which the force of words goes hand in hand with the force of lethal weapons, checkpoints, walls and armored bulldozers.

Some might worry that the present endorsement of disruptive protest opens the door to chaos in public political meetings. The opposite is the case. Once abandoned the artificial and repressive idea that the speaker's right to the floor is inviolable and that audiences must never interrupt or answer back, a more rational and democratic public political debate is immediately encouraged, in which *both* speaker and disrupters are accountable to each other and to the rest of the audience for their interventions, and never immune from the need for justification. If Zionists appeal to arguments like those made here to justify their own disruptions of Palestine solidarity events, that is, of course, entirely their prerogative. But it is morally unjustifiable since, unlike in the case of pro-Palestine activists, the interruption serves the cause of ongoing violent dispossession. This basic fact, not procedural questions about freedom of speech, is what Palestine solidarity activists should continually bring their arguments against Zionists back to. If "the whole point of rational discussion," as Said argues, "is to attempt to change the terms and the perspectives in which insoluble-appearing problems are understood," then disruption of the kind defended here has everything to contribute to it, by setting the conditions for a far more transparent, collectively regulated and ultimately productive political debate than the propagandistic, set-piece performances by Zionist apologists that universities currently host.[69]

Appendix: Speech, Practices, Power

It's worthwhile exploring the interpellative function of speech a little further, since it leads us into some subtle and important debates about how language works politically. Readers who feel they don't need to venture this far can safely skip this appendix and go straight to the next chapter.

As we have seen, talking of language's interpellative function forces us to concentrate on speech's connections to the social world and its power to shape collective and individual subjectivities. This power is hardly invisible, unknown or even particularly controversial, but, thanks to the ideology of language as communication, it is still often absent even from serious discussions of speech rights and disruptive protest. If interpellative effects are considered at all, it is usually through the frame of the concept of "performativity," originally introduced by the philosopher J. L. Austin in his classic lectures *How to Do Things with Words* and significantly developed and extended by Judith Butler and others. In various versions, the concept of performativity has become the dominant understanding of language's political power in many academic disciplines, and it has exerted considerable influence outside the university. While interpellation is not commonly evoked in mainstream academic discussions of language and power, performativity enjoys significant currency.[70] As we will see, however, at least in its most common guise, the presumption that speech is fundamentally performative poses an obstacle to analyzing its interpellative force in the context of speech rights and disruptive protest. Since the performative presumption is so influential, it is useful to show why it is, in some ways, unhelpful.

For Austin, performativity was a property of certain utterances: expressions like "you are sentenced to five years without parole," as spoken by an Israeli judge to a Palestinian prisoner; "This settlement is named 'Ariel,'" as spoken by the settlers establishing the West Bank settlement; or

"I condemn Hamas," as spoken by a western politician. The essential property of performative utterances is that they *bring about a change of affairs in the world simply in virtue of being spoken*: the utterances just mentioned *constitute* sentencing, naming and condemning, respectively, and transform the status of the defendant, of the settlement (at least for its settlers) and of Hamas – from defendant to sentenced prisoner, from unnamed to named, from uncondemned (by the speaker) to condemned. To the extent that it is performative, an utterance does not just communicate but *accomplishes an action* – rather than just "saying something," it "does something," as Austin described it.

In line with the received speech-as-communication ideology, Austin and much of the tradition he inaugurated assume that performatives are the exception in language: most utterances are not performative but communicative (Austin called them "constative"). More recent thinkers, by contrast, understand performativity not as a property of certain utterances but of certain kinds of *discourse*. Performativity becomes, on Judith Butler's description, the "power of discourse to produce the phenomena that it regulates and constrains," with hate speech and pornography the two kinds of discourse that have received most attention.[71] On the account of hate speech and pornography developed by scholars like Rae Langton and Catharine MacKinnon, hate speech directed against minorities *degrades those minorities simply in virtue of being spoken*.[72] In the case of racist discourse like speech directed against Muslims or Palestinians, the idea would be that racist discourse *accomplishes, by its very expression, the subordination of racially oppressed groups*. It does this, for instance, by discrediting Muslims or Palestinians and thereby robbing them of the social legitimacy and confidence they need in order to enter the public sphere as effective actors or by undermining their social standing to such an extent that any defense they might make of themselves will not be taken seriously.[73] The thoroughly political character of speech derives, for many thinkers, from its supposedly performative character.

For Mill and for the mainstream liberal free speech tradition anterior to the hypothesis of performativity, speech's real-world effects justify silencing only when they are *immediate*: only at the moment that a speaker's words incite an audience into on-the-spot action is language considered dangerous, and regulation or repression of it therefore countenanced. It was always striking that no thought was given to the possibility of deferred effects: as long as it did not cause any harm *now*, speech was tolerated – little matter if it caused serious harm later. The performative analysis considers speech's real-world effects on a deeper temporal horizon. Its recognition of discourse as a domain of social and political action in its own right, with its own cascading real-world effects, was a significant breakthrough, since it helped open up the details of particular discourses and speech acts to the possibility of a concrete politics, the particulars of which are highly controversial and still being worked out.[74]

The performativity analysis explains the harmful effect of hate speech and pornography by categorizing them as a form of *action*: when a Zionist denies Palestinians their status as a people and paints them collectively as backward, hate-filled terrorists, they are, on the performative account, *enacting* or *creating* oppression against Palestinians. But a well-known shortcoming of this analysis, pointed out by Judith Butler, is that it fails to capture the gap between the speech and its intended effect: the extent to which subordination of Palestinians is achieved by the speech depends on the circumstances in which it is uttered.[75] Not all utterances of anti-Palestinian speech succeed in wounding Palestinians, depriving them of social legitimacy and confidence or undermining their social standing – any number of other factors, including especially how much the speech is contested during its articulation, can cancel out its harmful effect. If language is often experienced as wounding – if its performative status as action is frequently all too real for its political targets – it is also sometimes not. Instead of wounding, words can stimulate defiance, contestation, incredulity or ridicule. But if speech's power to act doesn't depend on the words but on something about the context – put differently, something about the practice in which the speech is embedded – then there is a sense in which it is not speech itself which should be credited with power. This is exactly the situation with anti-Palestinian speech: as we saw in the previous section, the interpellative power of anti-Palestinian speech depends, in part at least, on how tightly it is bound to the real practices of violent anti-Palestinian coercion which it ideologically justifies, and so is not an inherent result of its performative character.

According to Austin's original formulation of performativity, performative utterances work because they follow certain rules: they are the "effects of a rule-bound discourse that inserts itself in the pervasive and mundane signifying acts of linguistic life," as Butler has put it.[76] If performatives work because they conform to certain *rules* of language use, then the power of speech is fundamentally a matter of *convention* (rules being things which depend on convention to be followed), and performatives are effective if they adhere to the appropriate conventions, as embodied in particular rules, in any given instance.[77] Anti-Palestinian speech would, on this model, be understood as exerting its harmful effects by invoking racist "conventions" and precedents which reinforce anti-Palestinian beliefs and practices. This framing can suggest that change is simply a matter of altering or disrupting those conventions – ultimately, perhaps, of entering into a new "contract" about how speech is to be regulated, for example, by changing the kinds of talk we find acceptable about racial or political minorities. For Rae Langton, accordingly, "the space for potential speech acts can be built by speakers, as can the limits on that space."[78] If we accept this analysis, we will be inclined to look for solutions to linguistically mediated oppression on the level of language and meaning. We might, for instance, as Butler and others suggest, try to turn hostile speech against the oppressor, to "resignify" it in a way that empties it of its original harmful effect, as in situations of linguistic reclamation (e.g., the reclamation of the slur "queer" as a mark of gay identity).

It is, however, exactly by conceiving of words' power as "conventional," and hence as open to being repaired simply by a "resignification" of this kind, that the underlying violence of the social order risks being mystified.[79] Just like the traditional idea, much beloved by the ideology of communication, that the proper response to bad "arguments" is to offer good ones, the proposal to counter hate speech by resignifying or reclaiming it does not get beyond consideration of words and meanings. As such, it displaces the focus from the social practices with which it is in fact bound and which must be taken into account in any attempt to develop an antiracist politics that goes beyond discourse to engage with the entirety of the social world – one that construes the fundamental adversary as people and practices, not words and ideas.[80] Judith Butler, accordingly, stresses the fact that the "sphere of political performativity includes and exceeds verbal and written utterances."[81]

What does this mean for disruptive protest? It does not mean that the remedy for harmful interpellations is never resignification, counter-interpellation or simply counterargument: there are situations, usually when the two sides of a dispute are otherwise equal, in which the force of language *can* be countered linguistically, on its own terms. Disruption of a speaker is not always the right response to hostile interpellations. But resignification, counter-interpellation and counterargument are of limited use when the opposed parties are not simply at odds in argument, in a way which can theoretically be settled by the "force of reason" alone, but where the opposition fundamentally involves unequal material forces, as it does in the case of Palestine, where harmful speech is the flip side of Israeli practices of war crimes and genocidal violence. This embeddedness of speech in material practices is central to the interpellative account, which, true to its thoroughly materialist lineage, sees the subject-forming capacities of speech and ideology as bound to social practices that exceed the domain of discourse.[82] The real-world effects of language are not, therefore, effects of speech alone but of speech as a component of social practices.[83]

Most current discussions of speech harms and speech rights operate with the alternatives of counterargument or reclamation/resignification of speech, on the one hand, and simple prohibition or censorship of speech, on the other. Actual contestation and disruption of the original speech act rarely enter the frame. This is remarkable, especially since reclamation and counterargument have serious shortcomings as a political response to harmful speech.

Reclamation affects words or phrases, and it therefore offers no answer to the adaptability of interpellation – the fact that the dispensers of hostile interpellations do not care about which particular expressions are used. When one slur is reclaimed by its targets, there is always another that can be produced. And once reclamation has been attempted, as Anshuman Mondal points out, dominant groups can argue that oppressed ones no longer have the right to be offended when the reclaimed word is used in its original, hostile sense.[84] Counterargument, too, is a politically weak response for Palestine solidarity activists, since it simply actualizes what was always a premise of Zionists' public justifications of their policies: the fact that no policy speaks for itself, the fact that there is always *someone* to whom it needs to be justified. In merely offering arguments against Zionist speakers in the usually brief question period at university talks, Palestine solidarity activists are, in one sense, playing into their opponents' hands: even if some points can be scored against the Zionist speaker, they will claim credit for their willingness to enter into supposedly "open" debate.

Chapter 5

The Politics of Regressive Research

Creating a "laboratory of ideas" in the service of national development: this is how Gabi Baramki described his aspiration in founding Birzeit University, Palestine's first.[1] Baramki's description of the purpose of a university is entirely conventional: the development of ideas and thinking is at the heart of higher education's self-conception. So debating the academic boycott of Israel means debating the nature and purpose of thinking in universities: the kinds of thinking that exist there, the kinds that universities should be laboratories for and the purposes that academic thinking does and should serve.

When we refer to "thinking," "thought" or "intellectual activity," we mainly have something individual in mind. But saying that someone has thought hard about something often means more than that they have reflected on it intensely on their own. Particularly if we are talking about academics, researchers or other "intellectuals," it is also likely to mean that they have involved others in the development of their ideas – by talking with them, by informing themselves of others' thoughts, by inviting reactions to what they have written. Laboratories, whether literal ones or Baramki's "laboratories of ideas," are collective places. Contrary to a frequent stereotype, then, what we call "thinking," especially in universities, is a communal activity at least as much as a solitary one. The academic does not, as sometimes might be believed, resemble Rodin's "Thinker" statue, heroically wracked in solitary meditation. They are, often far more, the orator before a crowd, adjusting the presentation of their ideas in response to the agreement, heckling or indifference their words provoke, the public an active partner in the elaboration of their thought, not its passive recipient.

For academics, then, thinking means dialogue – conferences, seminars, informal conversations, feedback on written work – not the solipsistic generation of a line of reasoning and its dogged pursuit to its ultimate logical conclusions. In fact, the very *formulation* of new ideas is impossible without considering the prospective audience for whom they are intended. Far from being an accessory, after-the-fact dimension of intellectual work, questions of audience shape the character of a theoretical analysis or intellectual position at its origin. In developing her ideas, an academic thinker engages in a process of imaginative projection in which she continually assesses the likely reception of her words by the readership or the audience to which they will be presented. Considerations of how this implicit public will respond, what objections the author will encounter and what claims she can reasonably make with different audiences all play a role in the development of her thought.

But when thinkers engage in the academic boycott, they suspend their input to this dialogue – and so, in a certain sense, they choose, with certain participants and in particular institutional contexts, to *stop thinking*. As we have seen, the decision often provokes indignation: surely progressive change, for Palestinians or for anyone, is impossible if its intellectual foundations are undermined. Isn't a lapse into anti-intellectual philistinism a well-known danger for the left? How can academic defenders of Palestine possibly advance their cause by *avoiding*, even just partially, intellectual exchange with Zionists and Zionism? If we praise Palestinians in Gaza or the West Bank for physically confronting the Israeli occupation, aren't we hypocritical if we abandon or undermine any of the debates, conferences and other academic forums in which dialogue and the confrontation of ideas could take place?

Questions like these express powerful anxieties, which earlier chapters have tried to allay. But they ignore the simple fact that, as Steven Salaita points out, "*Palestinians have not asked for dialogue as a form of solidarity.*"[2] Indeed, as is often noted, the very failure of the political "dialogue" culminating in the Oslo talks and the creation of the Palestinian Authority lies at the origins of Palestinian society's call for Boycott, Divestment and Sanctions (BDS). Nevertheless, the belief that maximizing academic dialogue is essential is, as we have seen, widespread. In a political culture corrupted by ubiquitous short-termism and other impediments to deliberative thought – fake news, the short-term media cycle, the sound bite – universities' responsibility to resist an anti-intellectual refusal of discussion seems especially serious. In previous chapters, we have considered objections to the boycott predicated on academics' obligation to privilege dialogue, intellectual exchange and reflection. In this chapter, we will first discuss some general connections between scholarship and political quietism, before considering two case studies of recent debates about the political stakes of intellectual analysis in contexts unrelated to BDS, Palestine or Israel. As these case studies demonstrate, even ostensibly progressive intellectual work is not necessarily socially beneficial and does not intrinsically advance public enlightenment. As a result, there can be no inherent objection to the boycott on the grounds that intellectual work in universities *necessarily* contributes to progress and therefore should never be obstructed.

INHERENTLY PROGRESSIVE?

The conviction that academic work and intellectual exchange are intrinsically progressive, and that dialogue involving them is always desirable, is pervasive. In the humanities, which often lack immediately obvious "real-world" applications, the idea may appear less absurd than it should. Outside the humanities, vast tracts of intellectual activity serve clearly harmful ends: nuclear and conventional weapons research, research designed to bolster the security and surveillance state, research contributing to the spoliation and degradation of the environment. Here, no one tries to argue that enquiry or the exchange of its results is inherently progressive. In cases like these, it is not just conferences or collaborations with *Israeli* institutions that should be boycotted: this research should not be conducted at all, wherever it is happening, and people of conscience have an obligation to obstruct it by whatever means they have at their disposal, including boycott.[3] With respect to this research, a certain "anti-intellectualism" is therefore called for.

To anyone outside the humanities and social sciences, the suggestion that research and academic exchange are necessarily socially beneficial no doubt seems ridiculous. That is, nevertheless, the presupposition of many arguments against the academic boycott, so it is the one we have to address here, if always with a certain amount of incredulity that it could ever be seriously offered. It should be obvious that research in the humanities can be conducted or harnessed for socially harmful purposes: even ethics, as James Eastwood has demonstrated in his study of the Israel Defense Forces' (IDF) use of that subject, can support military violence.[4] In cases like the (now closed) Human Terrain System or the Minerva initiative – social-science research designed to support US military intervention and strategy – the politically retrograde character of enquiry is clear.[5] With research like this, there is no sense in which ongoing academic exchange is desirable in itself.

There is, however, a more subtle sense in which thought in the humanities and social sciences might be considered as politically regressive: the mystifying way in which it can suggest that political questions are beyond the reach of ordinary people and confined to a privileged domain of qualified experts. Decades ago, Edward Said criticized the use by Middle East "experts" of "social science jargon and ideological clichés masked as knowledge" to sustain anti-Palestinianism.[6] Noam Chomsky, too, has made a critique over many years of the reactionary role played by academic expertise in political science.[7] Chomsky begins his well-known 1966 essay "Objectivity and

Liberal Scholarship" with the following generalization about the role of intellectuals, including – or especially – those in universities:

> If it is plausible that ideology will in general serve as a mask for self-interest, then it is a natural presumption that intellectuals, in interpreting history or formulating policy, will tend to adopt an elitist position, condemning popular movements and mass participation in decision-making, and emphasizing rather the necessity for supervision by those who possess the knowledge and understanding that is required (so they claim) to manage society and control social change.[8]

The consequence, for Chomsky, is that academic experts' monopolization of decisions over public policy must urgently be reversed: "there is no body of theory or significant body of relevant information, beyond the comprehension of the layman, which makes policy immune from criticism," Chomsky believes. "To the extent that 'expert knowledge' is applied to world affairs," he concludes, "it is surely appropriate – for a person of any integrity, quite necessary – to question its quality and the goals it serves."[9] In *The Question of Palestine*, Said explicitly refused to propose an "expert view": the intellectual, as he put the same point elsewhere, "ought to be an amateur."[10] The consequence is obvious: in "enclosing" political questions behind a claim to an expertise supposedly out of the reach of ordinary actors, academic research and its communication can perform an antidemocratic function. This function is on regular display when opponents criticize BDS supporters for adopting a position over Palestine and Zionism without being experts in the topic.[11]

Part of Chomsky's classic broader critique of academics is that their complicity with power and their frequent closeness to the political establishment quarantine them from the democratic forms of political engagement which make progress possible: the hostility with which academics often greet BDS, a popular participatory movement initiated by Palestinian civil society that directly challenges academics' prerogatives, is just one of the many factors that support this critique. Israel itself offers copious exemplification of intellectuals' compliance with and instrumentalization by power, as Said, Ilan Pappé and Shlomo Sand in particular have documented, but the phenomenon is a constant of the political history of intellectual work.[12] The French Communist Party sought out the most highly qualified graduates to work on its widely circulated intellectual periodical, *La nouvelle critique*, because they supposed, according to Frédérique Matonti, that advanced "academic capabilities could be conducive to political docility."[13] Miklós Haraszti relates the satisfaction with which Hungarian writers and artists in the Soviet era discussed the details of their "problems" with state censorship of their works. In their mouths, Haraszti observes, being censored "became a sort of homage to the artist's importance, a sign of their proximity to power."[14] It was not just behind the Iron Curtain that intellectual workers derived a perverse affirmation from the state's control of their ideas. In the context of the dependence of American science funding on the cold war arms race, "the feeling," one researcher is reported as admitting, "was that if the memos and reports you wrote weren't stamped 'secret,' they just weren't important."[15]

Pierre Bourdieu emphasizes the disengagement from reality that is a constitutive element of academics' professional games: in a sense, he says, scholars feel "entitled to perceive the world as a representation, a spectacle, to survey it from above and from afar and organize it as a whole designed for knowledge alone."[16] The etymology of "scholarship" in the Greek word for "leisure," *skholē*, highlights the status of theoretical work as what Bourdieu calls "serious play" – a moment of "social weightlessness" produced by the "neutralization of practical urgencies" that "implies (active or passive) ignorance not only of what happens in the world of practice . . . and, more precisely, in the order of the *polis* and politics, but also of what it is to exist, quite simply, in the world." "It also and especially implies," he notes, "more or less triumphant ignorance of that ignorance and of the economic and social conditions that make it possible."[17] For Bourdieu, a break with the world and the demands of action in it are therefore constitutive of the "scholastic disposition" itself. "Most cultivated people," he says, "especially in the social sciences, have a dichotomy in their heads which strikes me as completely deadly: the dichotomy between scholarship and commitment – between those who devote themselves to scientific work, which is done on the basis of academic methods and intended for other academics, and those who are engaged and take their knowledge outside."[18]

The common misconceptions about the intrinsic progressiveness of academic work Chomsky, Said, Bourdieu and others call into question need to be challenged again today for the purposes of advancing the academic boycott. I will do so here by examining two cases in which ostensibly progressive intellectual activity and exchange in the humanities and social sciences were *not* suspended, but where, I will claim, they should have been. If even research with an overtly socially beneficial rationale can turn out to be politically regressive despite itself, we have to abandon any claim that the academic exchange of research is an intrinsic social good, and the onus shifts onto Zionists to detail exactly *what* progressive effect boycotting compromises and why they think the academic boycott of Israel is always to be rejected. Recognition that academic thought is sometimes politically regressive helps undermine BDS opponents' assumption of the inherently progressive character of scholarship and academic exchange and supports the case that suspending research and scholarly dialogue can be a necessary political response in certain – carefully delineated – circumstances.

Chapter 5

BOYCOTTING THE NON-GOVERNMENTAL ORGANIZATIONS

The generation of ideas in academic research is, I noted earlier, hard to tease apart from the process of their exchange and dissemination. Since these processes are social, questions of who is engaged in them inevitably have implications for what knowledge is generated. There is no idea which is not to some extent engendered collectively: knowledge production is a social phenomenon, even (or especially) in the hard sciences. The objections and observations an academic will take into account when revising a research paper depend crucially on the audience to which earlier versions have been exposed: different audiences mean that different intellectual backgrounds and priorities have been brought to bear in the course of the ideas' development.

This introduces a political dimension into the very definition of academic work. In particular, questions of access to academic institutions are, as we have seen, inescapably political in nature. This is why the academic boycott aims to reverse Israel's structural obstruction of higher learning in Palestine and so to diversify and enrich the audience in which research circulates and by which it is shaped. The first case study we will consider in this chapter starkly throws into relief issues of who is included in, or excluded from, the dialogue of academic research and the implications this has for the necessity that the research take place.

In 2014, Australian, Nepalese and Sri Lankan human rights researchers sponsored a conference in Bangkok, "Enhancing Human Rights and Security in the Asia Pacific." The conference had an unimpeachable – and overtly political – goal: to contribute to torture-eradication efforts in the region. To do this, a novel methodology was adopted. Rather than going on an antagonistic footing toward torture-perpetrators like state security services, human rights researchers would try to work non-adversarially with them, operating "with the grain" of agencies like the Sri Lankan military. The project aimed "to bring about authentic security sector reform by working from the inside," in a bid to eliminate the socio-cultural factors which normalize torture.[19] Danielle Celermajer, the conference director, said that since human rights organizations have failed to stamp out or even reduce torture, "some of us have to get down from the stands of naming and shaming and onto the field of engagement with those who perpetrate it."[20] The conference was to be attended by over one hundred participants from across the region, including members of both the Sri Lankan security services and anti-torture non-governmental organizations (NGOs). But shortly before the conference was to begin, the Sri Lankan authorities presented the conference organizers with a highly unwelcome ultimatum: retract the invitations of certain NGOs, or the military representatives would not attend. In other words, the conference organizers had to "boycott" the NGOs, or the Sri Lankan authorities would boycott the conference. Neither option was acceptable. Collaboration with security forces was at the heart of the conference's intellectual rationale, yet disinviting the NGOs was something that, the organizers said, "we found repellent and that we were well aware contravened principles that we and others in the human rights world hold dear."[21] It was a "tragic choice" in which there was no course of action without undesirable consequences.[22]

Originally, the Sri Lankan authorities had demanded the exclusion of four NGOs. But after protests from the conference organizers, they insisted that only two, Right to Life and Rights Now, be disinvited. The organizers ended up reluctantly complying with this request. The conference director explained that the two organizations' exclusion was necessary if collaborators in the project at the Centre for the Study of Human Rights at the University of Colombo were to be able to continue their anti-torture work:

> Our local partner leading the project in Sri Lanka advised that it was crucial for them to sustain a relationship of engagement with the security forces. To refuse to accede to this admittedly strong armed and unreasonable request would be the end of any ability on their part to critically engage the forces and would likely result in serious repercussions for them personally and organisationally. It also risked having the other security organisations that had committed to attend pull out.[23]

The reasoning invoked to exclude the NGOs was parallel with the reasoning often invoked against BDS. Just as BDS opponents emphasize the necessity of dialogue with Israeli academia despite the structural exclusion ("boycott") of Palestinians, in the present case "critical engagement with security forces in order to get in to transform their cultures and everyday understandings and practices" was felt to be the most important consideration.[24] Translated to the Israeli context, this methodology would have entailed excluding Palestinian organizations in order to pursue with the IDF a dialogue aimed at transformation of culture and practices.[25] The conference director felt that maintaining dialogue with state perpetrators of torture was so crucial that she wrote to the remaining conference participants urging them to mute their criticisms of Sri Lankan police and military while at the conference itself.[26] Celermajer wrote that "while we will all no doubt find ourselves on occasion wishing to question the legitimacy of claims being made by Sri Lankan authorities, I would ask us to keep in mind the minimal positive impact that such confrontations would in fact have and their potentially deleterious effect on the conference . . . The stark reality is that if the Sri Lankan authorities feel themselves under attack, they will leave. They have made this clear to us."[27]

As in the case of resistance to the academic boycott, the organizers' decisions were a clear realization of the principle that academic exchange must be allowed to continue at almost any cost – in this case, even if it meant excluding two NGO participants, rewarding what they themselves acknowledged to be "strong armed and unreasonable" tactics and compromising the possibility of a frank "confrontation" over the honesty of claims made by torturers. Having set out to avoid "naming and shaming" torture *perpetrators*, the organizers' actions shamed two torture *opponents* through the humiliation of disinvitation from a forum which might have offered them some ideological and political legitimation. In the case of Israel, the decision to maintain dialogue by not implementing the academic boycott is the uncontroversial, default position. Here, by contrast, the decision to keep talking provoked vocal criticism from many quarters. The Sri Lanka Campaign for Peace and Justice, the Asian Human Rights Commission, the Asian Forum for Human Rights and Development, the Association for the Prevention of Torture and Human Rights Watch were among the bodies that criticized the conference's decision.[28] The NGOs Janasansadaya, Amnesty International, the Asian Human Rights Commission, the Commonwealth Human Rights Initiative, the Justice for Peace Foundation and the Open Society Justice Initiative all withdrew their own participation from the conference in protest.[29]

The conference organizers were mostly not criticized for the belief that collaboration with perpetrators could be a reasonable methodology in torture prevention work in some circumstances. Instead, critics focused on the political cover and international legitimation that the conference would provide for the Sri Lankan government's human rights abuses by welcoming its agencies to a high-profile event working to eliminate torture – an analogous objection to the one that can be made against international cooperation with Israeli universities. The conference was accused of complicity in the intimidation and silencing to which critics of the Sri Lankan regime are subject and of perpetuating "the imbalance of power that the Sri Lankan government has sought to impose at every turn whenever and wherever its human rights record has come under scrutiny."[30] As the secretary general of the Association for the Prevention of Torture argued,

> The preventive approach is often at its most powerful when the State engages with stakeholders in an informal or closed-door setting, away from the public spotlight where interlocutors can be frank and develop relationships of trust. In the case of this conference, discussions of prevention are occurring at a highly public international forum. In this setting it is important to remain true to the spirit of prevention and not let external forces dominate the terms of engagement.[31]

"The Sri Lankan government has been persistent in its intolerance of dissent, its attacks on human rights defenders and journalists and its assaults on academic freedom," Amnesty International wrote.

> The climate of impunity that exists in Sri Lanka has been devastating to civil society and to the rule of law. Brave individuals still able and willing to speak out openly against this trajectory of abuse deserve our respect and support. The organizers' retraction of their invitations sends a message that the sentiments of the officials who have been invited matter more than those of civil society participants. But in fact change in Sri Lanka, as anywhere, depends on individuals having the freedom to challenge state authorities to be accountable and to uphold human right and the rule of law. It is our duty to help them do that.[32]

For most observers, the political legitimation conferred on torture-perpetrators by their inclusion in the conference far outweighed the positive benefits the conference might otherwise have had. As this case shows, the advancement of intellectual exchange, even exchange sincerely and explicitly directed at the most laudable of political goals, the abolition of torture, cannot be argued to be *necessarily* indispensable to social progress: questions of who is included or excluded from academic exchange are crucial. Rather than insisting on the necessity of torture-perpetrators' presence, the conference's organizers could have chosen either to cancel the conference overall or, perhaps, to simply accept the Sri Lankan authorities' withdrawal, using the scandal this would have inevitably provoked to showcase and support the work of the forces fighting torture on the ground in Sri Lanka.

Excluding the security forces' representatives would not have earned the organizers any general opprobrium. In contrast to the accusations of anti-Semitism regularly incurred by those upholding the academic boycott of Israel, the organizers would not have had to endure accusations of discrimination or racism against Sinhalese. Nor would there have been any protests that, just as keeping talking with Israeli academic officials in public conferences is supposedly crucial to peace, so keeping talking to the Sri Lankan military was the sine qua non of efforts to eliminate torture in that country: none of the actors on the ground, indeed, appear to have believed that to be the case. On both points, the contrast with BDS supporters, regularly accused of racism and of obstructing the only conceivable avenue for progress, is flagrant. If engaging with torturers at an international conference is not indispensable to the elimination of torture, then engaging with Israeli anthropologists, historians, philosophers or physicists can hardly be a requirement of justice for Palestine.

Whether academic research should be pursued on a given occasion depends on multiple factors. The need to keep talking is not always the most important priority. In this case, suspending the ordinary course of academic business by refusing to allow the military's participation at the conference would have voided the conference of its stated intellectual purpose but would still, in many actors' judgment, have been the preferable decision. A conference in which victims' advocates and torturers are brought together on an equal footing is intrinsically a blow against the torturer, whom it forces into accountability before former victims and their supporters, stripping him of the absolute power he wields in his cells. Acceding to the torturer's demand to exclude even some advocates for the sake of allowing the conference to go ahead does the opposite, validating perpetrators over torture opponents as the principal agents of reform. In the 2018 book describing the research project of which the conference was a part, Celermajer candidly admits that the overall project did not meet its goals, failing "to touch or affect the factors that significantly contributed to the use of torture."[33] The gains in understanding promised by engagement with security forces did not, then, compensate for the concrete political setback caused to the human rights NGOs by their exclusion from the conference, the resulting legitimation of the army at their expense and the inevitable perception that other NGO participants were only there under sufferance. With less commitment to dialogue, and less investment in the necessity of academic exchange on the part of the conference, the promotion of anti-torture ideology in Sri Lanka would arguably have been better served. Identical conclusions obtain in the case of the academic boycott of Israel.

FOOTNOTES AGAINST HATE

The second case we will examine – the publication of a scholarly edition of Hitler's *Mein Kampf* in Germany in 2015 – is a particularly telling instance of the reactionary potential of supposedly progressive research and a second situation in which it is implausible to argue that the ordinary course of academic business must never be disrupted. The edition's publication amounted to the *lifting* of a powerful boycott, in the form of a state-sponsored publication ban, that had previously been in place, in the name of the importance of fostering wider public understanding about the origins of Nazism. Just as BDS opponents argue against the boycott on the grounds that academic contact with Israel must be maintained for the sake of intellectual and political progress, so German historians appealed to those very values to argue why the previous "boycott" on publishing *Mein Kampf* had to be reversed. The removal of the *Mein Kampf* ban reveals the regressive political potential of academic research and has many lessons for those who presuppose that the circulation of academic ideas is *always* and *necessarily* the most desirable political course.

The growing influence of the far right in Europe in recent decades has had a striking intellectual counterpart: numerous scholarly and culture-industry efforts to reanimate texts of the golden age of European fascism. In France, the works of notorious anti-Semites Lucien Rebatet and Charles Maurras were reissued by major imprints.[34] The *doyen* of French publishing, Gallimard, announced a handsome re-edition of Céline's overtly anti-Semitic pamphlets from the late 1930s and early 1940s. (The ensuing outcry led to the project's abandonment – a temporary one only, as Gallimard's managing director made clear.[35]) In the UK, the BBC provoked a minor scandal with a 2018 broadcast of Enoch Powell's chilling "rivers of blood" speech, interspersed with contextualizing commentary. In Germany, scholars from the Institute for Contemporary History (IfZ) in Munich published twenty-nine volumes of Goebbels' diaries;[36] Himmler's private correspondence was also published by Piper. Surrounded by resurgent far-right movements, publishers suddenly discovered a need not for prestige new editions of important *anti*fascist literature by figures like Trotsky, Brecht, Ludwig Renn, Daniel Guérin and others but for modern editions of texts by racists and fascists that had long been gathering dust in libraries, with the stated motivation of contributing to public "understanding" of the true nature of a dangerous, newly relevant political tradition.[37] The controversy that accompanied these efforts played out along similar lines everywhere. But nowhere were the stakes and contours of the debate more obvious than in the case that concerns us here – the publication at the end of 2015, by the IfZ, of a new critical edition of Hitler's 1925 manifesto, *Mein Kampf*, the "bible of Nazism."

Prima facie, the idea that in an era marked by the pan-European upsurge of the far right, academic research can best serve public debate by republishing, with great fanfare, a new edition of *the* iconic work of European fascism hardly bears scrutiny. The dangerous potential of *Mein Kampf*'s political rehabilitation had long been recognized. A ban on republication had effectively been in place in Germany since the end of World War II, when existing copies had been seized and warehoused by the allies, and copyright over the text vested in the state of Bavaria to ensure that reprints would be prevented. The Bavarian authorities refused to allow republication in Germany and frequently even launched lawsuits against attempts to republish the book in other countries, sometimes successfully. Bavaria's copyright expired at the end of 2015, seventy years after Hitler's death, and *Mein Kampf* entered the public domain, raising fears that right-wing publishers would lose no time in making it available to a new readership.

Anxiety about the possible effect of a re-edition was informed by contemporary political developments in Germany: in 2015, the far-right Patriotic Europeans against the Islamization of the West (PEGIDA) movement brought tens of thousands of people onto the streets, especially in the former

East Germany, on a virulently Islamophobic basis. The far-right Alternative for Germany (AfD) party was also making considerable political waves: from 2017 to 2021, it would be the third-largest party in the Bundestag. Neither PEGIDA nor the AfD is overtly neo-Nazi, and both publicly distance themselves from any association with Nazism, but they are both open to indisputably neo-Nazi elements.[38]

Like PEGIDA and the AfD, most mainstream modern European far-right movements also generally distance themselves from their historical predecessors. Nevertheless, Nazism in general, and *Mein Kampf* in particular, still exert a powerful hold over the neofascist imagination in Germany and elsewhere.[39] The German far right has frequently used *Mein Kampf* to justify political violence.[40] The phenomenon is by no means limited to Germany. Anders Breivik, who assassinated seventy-seven left-leaning Norwegians – mostly teenagers – in 2011, claimed in his trial that Hitler's manifesto was the only thing keeping him alive.[41] Another Scandinavian fascist, Anton Lundin Pettersson, who killed a student and a teacher at a school in Sweden in 2015, was a known Nazi enthusiast.[42] *Mein Kampf* itself regularly resurfaces in connection with far-right violence.[43] With anti-Semitism often reported to be on the rise in Europe,[44] the prospect of the book suddenly going on sale throughout Germany was, to say the least, troubling. In Bavaria, concerns had already been expressed in 2012 that directly studying part of *Mein Kampf* at school could raise the stocks of the small neo-Nazi NPD party.[45] Even Andreas Wirsching, the head of the IfZ, which produced the new edition, had said that he didn't want to exclude the possibility that "extracts from *Mein Kampf* could be instrumentalized for radical right thinking."[46] Russian authorities had banned *Mein Kampf* in 2010 out of fears it encouraged right-wing activity: perhaps, it was not hard to ask, Germany should do the same.[47]

In an attempt to counter what it saw as the likely political consequences of the book's reappearance on the market, in 2012 the Bavarian state commissioned the IfZ to prepare an annotated, critical edition for publication. The Bavarian government initially contributed half a million euros to the project but later withdrew the funding following controversy, including from Jewish community figures.[48] The new commentary on the book would contextualize Hitler's ideas in the history of European right-wing thought and provide a historical corrective to the numerous falsities conveyed in the text. In order to facilitate wide distribution and compete favorably with any projected commercial editions, the book was to be sold at an affordable price.[49] Despite – or, rather, because of – *Mein Kampf*'s strong market potential, the IfZ did not collaborate with any commercial publisher but published the edition in-house, thereby retaining control over sales as much as possible.[50]

At the end of 2015, the two volumes of the IfZ's handsome and austerely produced edition, containing almost two thousand pages of text, including eleven pages of full-color plates, were launched, and Germany's boycott of *Mein Kampf* officially broken. The edition encloses Hitler's text, printed in bold face, in a padding of copious editorial commentary in a lighter font, aiming, as the preface puts it, to "debunk the false information spread by Hitler, as well as his open lies, but most of all to reveal the countless half truths which achieved their ruinous propagandistic effect."[51] Andreas Wirsching, the IfZ director, justified the new edition on the thoroughly academic grounds that *Mein Kampf* is "a source of the first order for the history of Hitler and National Socialism." The IfZ's decision to produce the edition was based on the view that "it would be academically, politically and morally irresponsible to allow this bundle of inhumanity to roam without commentary in the public domain, without opposing a critical reference edition to it, which, so to speak, cuts the text and its author down to size."

The editors saw their critical edition as a way of countering *Mein Kampf*'s noxious ideological effect. But neither copyright law nor hate speech provisions had ever prevented Germans from acquiring Hitler's book from booksellers outside Germany, and the text had been circulating free online for years. Nevertheless, the expiry of the original copyright and the risk of an influx onto the market of brand-new copies in 2015 were central to the IfZ's case for a critical edition. While the institute's scholars were at work on the project, however, a legal development changed everything. In 2014, the conference of German justice ministers decided that *Mein Kampf* would remain banned in Germany and that legal action would be taken against any unannotated edition that was published after the copyright expired. Even though copyright law could no longer be used to control dissemination of the book, Germany's strict hate speech laws and prohibitions on far-right propaganda could take over – as, indeed, they did.[52] Bavaria's loss of copyright over *Mein Kampf* therefore made little difference to the status quo, and the major rationale for the new annotated edition had largely disappeared. The IfZ's republication project continued nonetheless.

The critical edition was a textbook application of the most traditional liberal beliefs about the role of free expression in democracies, identical to those constantly invoked by opponents of BDS. "He who knows only his own side of the case," J. S. Mill wrote in his celebrated defense of freedom of speech in *On Liberty*, "knows little of that. His reasons may be good, and no one may have been able to refute them. But if he is equally unable to refute the reasons on the opposite side; if he does not so much as know what they are, he has no ground for preferring either opinion."[53] Perfectly in accord with this traditional thinking, the commentary's editors stated in their introduction that since (so they thought) *Mein Kampf* would once again be available for anyone who wanted to buy it, "only one strategy appears reasonable: open, intensive and critical analysis":[54] "point[ing] out where Hitler's ideas came from, how much truth they do or don't contain, and what significance they had for the Nazis' ideologies and policies," as the project leader, Christian Hartmann, described it.[55] These are exactly the same terms in which opposition to BDS is often justified. Just as, for the IfZ, contemporary Nazism must be defeated through exacting critique and debunking of its canonical texts, so too, it is often claimed, the objective critical scrutiny on Israel that arises as a by-product of academic dialogue is essential to the effort for justice. Israel's lies and half-truths about the occupation must be confronted at the rigorous tribunal of science, the protocols of which must not be tampered with.

For all the importance of objective research, *Mein Kampf*'s editors emphasized that their work was not intended to be politically neutral – that it could not "limit itself to a purely passive presentation of a historical source." Constructed on scholarly principles of "rationality, verifiability and universal validity," the polar opposites of the spirit of Hitler's book, the commentary needed to offer, the editors said, a "comprehensively critical and . . . confident confrontation with Hitler's text, and . . . a form of presentation which puts an end to the potential impact of the symbol once and for all."[56] The edition was, in other words, intended as antifascist political action in its own right. This ambition appeared rather grandiose: because of the edition's length and scholarly nature, historians were certainly the only likely serious readership of the text,[57] yet the editors saw themselves as doing the work of a "bomb-disposal team." "The idea," Christian Hartmann said, "is to defuse the book with a new introduction and especially with a thorough scholarly commentary. This removes the book's symbolic value and makes it what it essentially is: a historical record, and nothing more."[58]

The edition provoked unprecedented discussion and controversy in Germany and abroad. The press conference presenting it to the public in January 2016 was attended by over one hundred journalists, including twelve TV teams.[59] This can only have amplified the book's success: initially a print-run of only four thousand, *Mein Kampf* went through six reprints and eighty-five thousand copies in a year.[60] The edition even made it to the top place in the *Spiegel* bestseller list – in, as it happened, the very week in April 2016 in which neo-Nazis were commemorating Hitler's birthday.[61] Originally intended to counteract the political effect of *Mein Kampf*'s reappearance, the IfZ edition created a *cause célèbre* in its own right, securing a visibility, currency and, arguably, social legitimacy for Hitler's text that republication by fringe far-right publishers could never have achieved. The editorial team's wish to "reach as large a circle of readers as possible"[62] had been satisfied in trumps: once a shunned document of hate speech or a far-right fetish object, the book had been elevated into a respectable literary commodity, the object of legitimate curiosity and consumer appetite.[63] The distinction between counteracting Nazi ideology and spreading it had been seriously muddied.

The public controversy on the ethics of the republication had resonance well beyond Germany itself. "The main purpose of critical editions is to preserve an original for all time," Jeremy Adler argued in a much-discussed essay. "This new edition," he wrote, "may have been produced with the best will in the world, but the reprinting of any questionable text can have only one outcome: to disseminate the author's views. No editor can determine whether these will meet with public approval or rejection – and responsible editors must not direct their readers."[64] In Adler's view, devoting a lavish critical edition to any text inevitably endorsed it as a classic – an impression reinforced by the published book's look and feel, likened by one commentator to "that of a canonical text of Western civilization."[65]

Press reports described the republication as *controversial* – a term free of any political or ethical condemnation, which suggested that in the official view of the media, the case for the wide dissemination of Hitler's book should at least be heard. This is parallel to arguments against boycott activists who disrupt Zionist speakers: just as *Mein Kampf* supposedly had to be republished to allow its lies to be exposed, so, it is often argued, Zionist defenders of Israeli apartheid should be allowed to enter the public sphere without disruption by protesters, in order to facilitate open scrutiny and critical debate with and about them. Often, however, the media's framing of the IfZ edition suggested actual *enthusiasm* for *Mein Kampf*'s reappearance in the public domain. A selection of headlines suggests the tenor of the coverage: "Hitler Has the Floor" (*Frankfurter Allgemeine Zeitung*); "Mein Kampf Edition Becomes Bestseller" (*DW*); "Mein Kampf a Bestseller Again" (*Zeit Online*); "Hitler's Racist Manifesto Is a Bestseller in Germany Now. That's Actually Good News" (*Washington Post*); "Hitler Is Back – Even Historians Think So" (*Die Welt*); "Adolf Hitler's 'Mein Kampf': The Unintentional Bestseller" (*Stern*); "Hitler's Rabble-Rousing Is Only Historical" (*Tagesspiegel*).[66] Through headlines like these, the media frequently served to rehabilitate *Mein Kampf* as an object of appropriate public value, interest and even entertainment: Hitler now "had the floor" or "was back," as the latest object of public spectacle. *Mein Kampf*'s bestseller status, frequently mentioned in headlines, was therefore to be welcomed. Roman Töppel, one of *Mein Kampf*'s academic editors, even participated in a public reading of excerpts from the book by the famous actor Götz Otto. The event, arranged by a foundation close to the liberal Free Democratic Party (FDP), the Thuringian branch of which did a deal with the far-right AfD to form government in 2020, was called "*Mein Kampf* is back!"[67]

Palestinian supporters often argue that there are cases where even *debating* the ethics of Israel's policies with their proponents can be politically counterproductive, since doing so concedes the possibility that fundamental and obvious violations of Palestinian rights *might* be justifiable. In a similar way, republication of *Mein Kampf* straightforwardly raised the question of whether a new critical edition, intended not only to undermine far-right ideology but also to reach as wide an audience as possible, could in fact strengthen it. Sensitive to the argument that an ascendant far right should not be enabled, some bookshops simply refused to stock the new edition.[68]

The project's full ambiguity and the strength of the possibility that it would simply rehabilitate fascist ideas under the cover of critical intellectual engagement with them are brought out by a disturbing parallel between the arguments for publication advanced by the IfZ and those put forward by *Mein Kampf*'s original Nazi publisher, Eher, which made much of the "know thine enemy" argument later also used by the publisher of the new edition. "Every German interested in politics should know their enemy," Eher's 1925 publicity for *Mein Kampf* ran: "Only then are they justified in reaching a judgement on him."[69] Similarly, Angelo Treves, a fascist activist and Hitler's contemporary Italian translator, used the argument of needing to know Hitler as justification for his role in bringing the book before the Italian public in 1934.[70] The idea has lost none of its currency on the right. Just as the IfZ explicitly presented the re-edition as an exercise in Enlightenment intellectualism, Der Schelm, the small far-right publisher, recommended its own unannotated reprint of *Mein Kampf* to "mature" citizens as an "academic source text," under the Kantian motto "Dare to think," and explicitly distanced itself from the book's hate-speech aspects. Clearly, the right does not believe that either academic trappings or invocation of Enlightenment independence of mind compromises the political benefit to it of Hitler's text.[71]

More than making the book's content once more available, now with commentary, the publication of the annotated critical edition created a new Hitler phenomenon largely independent of anything either the original text or the editorial commentary actually said, fueled by a media spectacle that followed its own logic, remote from the critical historical one advocated by the IfZ. From its inception, the editors had failed to break out of a narrow intellectualist framing of what it meant to reintroduce Hitler's manifesto to a fresh readership. Unable to conceive of the re-edition in any other terms than idealist ones – those of the enlightening educational effect they wished it to have – the IfZ team never distinguished between the book's notional content – the text and commentary – and the material event of its publication. The IfZ was guilty of the same fallacy as any number of critics of the academic boycott: the idea that the intrinsic content of research and its supposed promotion of progressive attitudes exhaust the politics of academic work. Just as BDS critics refuse to see that the material, political effect of collaboration with Israeli universities is independent of the content of the research conducted in them, so the IfZ team, trapped in an intellectualist conception of political action, failed to notice that the political ramifications of the publication might have nothing to do with the intellectual contribution their commentary made. They had, in short, no regard for the *actual* politics of academic work: exactly like BDS opponents, advocates of republication assumed that an intellectual justification of the edition was all that mattered and that scholarly and political value coincided.

Perhaps the most harmful effect of the re-edition, however, was its intellectualization of far-right ideology. The attention that the edition drew to questions of the accuracy and sources of Hitler's ideas served to erect an intellectual obstacle in the way of contemporary antiracism and antifascism. The journalist Antoine Vitkine summed up the point perfectly: "Do Germans really need," he asked, "to have proven to them the lack of rigor, the conceptual errors, the logical faults of an ideology which sent millions of people to their deaths?"[72] If "3700 footnotes" could constitute effective opposition to "Hitler's hate," as a *Spiegel* headline suggested, then the struggle against a resurgence of the far right took on a very different complexion from what is often believed.[73] The publicity generated by the *Mein Kampf* republication gave the impression that fighting neo-Nazism was not principally a political task – to which straightforward participation in, for example, demonstrations against the AfD could contribute – but a cultural or intellectual one, consisting in identifying and debunking Hitler's lies. The problem with that, as Götz Aly put it, was that the idea that Hitler was "a thoroughly bad criminal liar and a racist" was already "commonplace" and not in need of any scholarly demonstration: it is, arguably, no practical help to antifascists to take a political *axiom*, the falsity of Nazism, and turn it into an object of scholarly *debate*.[74] IfZ members often argued that republication contributed to the "demystification" of the text; in fact, however, the re-edition arguably performed a significant mystification of its own, by suggesting that the road towards defeat of a newly ascendant neofascist movement passed not through activism but through scholarship – a perfect instance of the mystifications of expertise, denounced by Chomsky and Said, that we discussed earlier. An equivalent mystification lies in the claim that the road to justice for Palestine necessarily passes through open academic dialogue.

There were many other ways in which the IfZ could have responded to the expiry of *Mein Kampf*'s copyright. A commentary could have been published in a *series* of annotated editions of Nazi-era texts and given a title that would not have traded on the mystique attaching to a banned book. *Sources of European Fascism: A Critical Edition*, with *Mein Kampf* appearing only as a subtitle for one volume, would have created a much smaller public spectacle than stand-alone republication of the text in its own right. The French critical edition that appeared in 2021, titled *Historicizing Evil – A Critical Edition of Mein Kampf*, went some way to adopting this strategy.[75] Even better, critical editions of *antifascist* literature from the Weimar and Nazi periods would have had considerably more potential political utility than republication of Nazi texts today. In any case, the debunking, demystifying effect sought by the IfZ could have been achieved without republishing Hitler's actual words. Claims can be debunked without republishing the text in which they appear in toto. Had the IfZ team published a popular book titled *Exposing Hitler's Racist Myths*, the public notoriety of *Mein Kampf* would not have experienced the same surge the edition gave it.

It was entirely characteristic of the debate over republication, as over the academic boycott, that refusing to engage with *Mein Kampf* (in this case by republishing it) was assimilated to *banning* it. Andreas Wirsching warned of the danger of creating a "ban" or "taboo" over Hitler's manifesto. "To try to prevent any sort of critical engagement with it would be tantamount to a short-sighted cover-up," he wrote. "It could give the (re)mystification of Hitler a dangerous boost, and might create the impression that even after death, Hitler exerts a sort of demonic power. It would prevent any historical classification, contextualization, and explanation of his impact. To make a taboo of it is therefore the opposite of having a mature debate."[76] The argument is curious. Choosing not to republish *Mein Kampf* or any other book does not constitute a *cover-up* of it, any more than refusing to disseminate *any* work fallen out of public interest does: it is always open to someone else to publish the work instead. In the same way, implementing academic BDS by refusing participation, whether one's own or that of Israeli academic officials, in conferences, does not constitute "banning" anything, since the unincluded participants can present their work in other academic fora elsewhere. Since no legal obstacle to an annotated edition of *Mein Kampf* remained, it was open to anyone to publish a commentary on the book, though it was certainly not anyone's *responsibility* or *duty* to do so.[77]

Construing the decision not to reissue Hitler's text as an endorsement of a ban on *all* historical analysis, as Wirsching did, had an obvious ideological utility: it completely erased the question of editorial discretion and responsibility. Confronted with a choice between *banning* discussion of Nazi politics and conducting a "mature debate" over it, no one would choose the former. In this light, the IfZ team's decision to publish the commentary was cast as the only reasonable one possible. Yet a choice between banning and allowing was not at all the one that the team faced. No one had ever thought to demand that a ban be placed on discussion of the accuracy of *Mein Kampf*'s claims: instead, the IfZ editors had just been asked not to prosecute that debate through a noisy republication of the work itself. The question confronting the historians, then, was about *how* to engage in intellectual debate on *Mein Kampf*, not *whether* to do so. Presentation of the choice as between censoring or permitting discussion of Hitler's ideas served to justify republication of the book by falsely construing it as the *only* intellectually responsible option.

The *Mein Kampf* commentary was the realization of a thoroughly intellectualist vision of political debate – one cut from exactly the same cloth that BDS opponents use to assert the all-importance of academic exchange. Implicit in its very rationale was the assumption that it could have only a politically progressive effect on its educated, presumably middle-class readership. Despite the often-demonstrated role of social elites as a vector of far-right politics, the IfZ team apparently saw no serious risk of a political boost to fascism through the publication of their edition.[78] Nor did they consider the even more likely possibility that by reintroducing *Mein Kampf* onto the contemporary German cultural scene, they instantly extended the boundaries of acceptable political discourse, casting somewhat less extreme ideologies like that of the AfD, sometimes claimed to have recently welcomed many ex-Nazi members, in a more moderate light, and allowing it to pose as more responsible and more centrist than would have been possible when the archtext of German fascism was still taboo in the public sphere.[79]

In launching the edition, the editors' intention had been to "fight Hitler's hate with footnotes." But it was not their critical footnotes which dominated the headlines: entirely predictably, it was *Mein Kampf* itself, triumphantly now declared, as we have seen, to "be back." In the period following publication, Nazi elements of AfD ideology gained greater political attention.[80] Some time after the republication of *Mein Kampf*, Björn Höcke, the Thuringian AfD leader, notoriously demanded that Germany "perform a 180-degree turn-around" when recalling its past and stop atoning for Nazi crimes.[81] Calls for an end to Germany's "culture of guilt" or Shoah remembrance are regularly associated with the AfD.[82] The party's 2017 election platform called on Germany not to focus so much on its Nazi heritage but to open up the German culture of remembrance "in favour of a broader understanding of history, which also encompasses the positive, identity-establishing aspects of German history."[83] In a striking progression of the cultural normalization of Nazism, a Konstanz theater created a public scandal in 2018 when it offered free seats to audience members prepared to wear a swastika armband to performances of an anti-Hitler farce by George Tabori. Paying audience members were asked to wear a Star of David armband.[84] Alexander Gauland, the AfD leader, said in 2018 that Hitler and the Nazis are "just a speck of bird poop in more than one thousand years of successful German history," drawing strong criticism for the trivialization of the Nazi past.[85] In the UK, a school known for its right-wing proclivities included discussion of *Mein Kampf* in a 2017 forum for senior students examining "the most beautifully disturbed and disturbing ideas, all of them presented without trigger warnings."[86]

Clearly, the growing far-right ascendancy in Germany and beyond cannot be attributed to a scholarly edition of a single text. It is impossible to know whether the IfZ's *Mein Kampf* edition has played any role in *dampening* the far right's growth, as the editors presumably aspired to do, but there is no evidence to suggest it. Yet by presenting Hitler's ideas as requiring extensive public discussion, and by providing the media with an opportunity for often sensational reporting, the spectacular lifting of the *Mein Kampf* boycott undeniably raised the salience of Nazism among a middle-class readership and, in doing so, contributed to the AfD's efforts to distance itself from the extremes of German politics. Just as ongoing academic exchange with Israeli universities, even in a critical mode, serves to normalize the oppression of Palestinians, even a critical engagement with the text of *Mein Kampf* served to raise the visibility of Nazi ideas in the public sphere.

The idea that intellectual exchange is an absolute good in itself, and that calls for boycott should therefore be automatically rejected, was always preposterous. The cultural boycott of Israel is parallel: it is clear – or it should be – that there is no correlation whatsoever between musical or other performances in Israel and progress in peace talks, reductions in IDF and settler violence or moderation of the siege of Gaza. Quite the contrary, when a prominent musician publicly violates the boycott to perform in Israel, the legitimizing and normalizing effects of doing so are considerable. The same holds in the case of academics' presentations at Israeli conferences or of Israeli academic officials' presentations at overseas ones: the best chance for justice for Palestine is not the academic show going on, but the political pressure exerted on Israel when the boycott is enforced. That is, indeed, confirmed by the fact that Israel seeks out international academic connections as evidence of its good standing in the global "community" and by the lengths to which it will go in combatting academic BDS.

Both revolutionary political radicalism and fascist terror have been attributed to an excess of reason or education, an excessive quota of thought, in the population.[87] Here, by contrast, we have been considering ways in which, in academia, intellectual activity does not necessarily facilitate progress but can dampen it. That conclusion does not depend on fully accepting the present arguments for the regressive effect of either of the examples examined here. Even if someone believes that, despite the case made in this chapter, the anti-torture conference or the *Mein Kampf* republication was, on balance, politically desirable, the discussion here shows that this conclusion is not self-evident but must be argued for. It simply cannot be *automatically* assumed that research activities are necessarily progressive and must never therefore be disrupted. For academic BDS, the consequence is clear: the suspension of academic work that the boycott constitutes cannot be used as an argument against it. There should be no presupposition that intellectual life must be held immune from boycott. Keeping thinking no matter what is not always the most politically productive option. Academics – like other intellectual workers – must consider the political consequences of their activity since, as Rima Najjar Kapitan put is, "if academics may not be political actors, they will become political pawns."[88]

Chapter 6

The Opium of the Educated

In urging academics to reject certain forms of (Israeli-sponsored) intellectual activity, the boycott invites progressives to the latest installment of one of their favorite dramas: the old struggle between "ideas" and "actions," "theory" and "practice," "consciousness" and "spontaneity" in social change.[1] The interdependence of thought and action has been an article of faith – and, often, no small source of personal dilemma – for radicals since at least Marx. Academic Boycott, Divestment and Sanctions (BDS) brings a novel variation to the theme: rather than seeing thinking and acting as necessarily intertwined, it divorces one from the other, making political action out of the *refusal* to participate in theoretical reflection on one patch of its native turf, the university. Where any number of thinkers have insisted that thinking and theorizing are politically effective in themselves, the boycott is a case where action is constituted not by theories and their institutions but by their suspension.

In one sense, then, the academic boycott offers an example of the progressive potential of a certain kind of *anti*-intellectualism and suggests a model for a different politics of intellectual work. This suggestion is likely to raise eyebrows. For many people, any questioning of intellectualism should be immediately refused. Progressives of all kinds often appeal to a widely held conviction about the essential role of critical intellectualism and theoretical debate in advancing social progress – in its academic mode, the ideal of the university as the theoretical vanguard of social progress. This ideal is particularly common in arguments against the academic boycott. "The ability to keep thinking and keep talking," according to two recent critics of BDS, "might be the best weapon that the true friends of peace possess": a gratifying sentiment for professional thinkers and talkers, whichever side they are on.[2]

The immemorial question of the various connections between doing politics and theorizing about it is, for academic supporters of the Palestine solidarity movement, particularly acute. But accurately assessing the relations between thought and action, theory and politics is especially critical – and difficult – in the current era, in which analysis and reflection have been thoroughly alienated from engagement with living political forces. Despite the relentless crises of contemporary politics, the horizon of possible "political" engagement for many academic intellectuals today is still publishing articles in specialist journals, or, at best, "balanced" commentary in the mainstream media – in contrast to "unbalanced" and "unscholarly" polemic, and even more in contrast to non-discursive action: boycotting, going on strike, picketing, demonstrating, participating in a campaign group or public meeting or simply distributing material to promote a concrete political cause. At the same time that direct political engagement has become less and less typical of academics, the conviction that academic work is *inherently* of political value, even in the absence of any direct articulation with living social forces, is a frequent unspoken assumption. So convinced are many academics of the intrinsic political value of ideas – the *inherently political* nature of theorizing – that they have largely forgotten what ideas look like when they are actually at work in the world.

Contemporary progressivism has been profoundly marked by the legacy of Marxist debates about the critical role that theory can play in political struggle. "Without revolutionary theory," Lenin famously stated in *What Is To Be Done?* "there can be no revolutionary movement"; long after Bolshevism's many deaths, the conviction that intellectual work is indispensable to transformative change is still deeply rooted on the left.[3] And not just on the left. Hossam Haik, a professor at Israel's Technion, an institution deeply involved in the theft of Palestinian land and the perpetuation of the occupation, reflects just such a conception of academic intellectualism when he says that "if the Middle East was like the Technion, we would already have peace."[4] Outside the campus, too, intellectualism has standardly been seen as the sine qua non of radical politics.[5]

It is, however, worth exploring the opposite hypothesis and considering the ways in which, far from providing the conceptual lift emancipatory projects need to become airborne, theoretical activity risks creating drag that prevents them leaving the ground. As I will demonstrate, the demand for intellectual depth, reflection or even critique in political debate does not *always* advance the struggle for a better world: not infrequently, it serves as the "opium of the educated," anesthetizing or impeding progressive political energies and "smartwashing" inaction.[6] Zionist opposition to the academic boycott on the grounds of the necessity of intellectually rich "dialogue" and respect for the "complexity" of politics in Palestine and Israel is a striking case in point.

THE DRAG OF THEORY

"We've been talking for years and nothing changes," a Palestinian student anonymously interviewed by Noemi Casati says, "there aren't many things that are effective, real in politics: everything is words without implementation."[7] The sentiment is ubiquitous: thinking, talking or writing about things isn't the same as actually doing them. "These days, everyone is talking about peace in the Middle East, and about the peace process," says Jamal Khader. "So far, however, these are simply words."[8] "I often . . . think that instead of writing we should do something," observes an Israeli occupation scholar.[9] Politicians and other political actors are expected not just to act but to think as well. But for political thinkers, as these remarks suggest, action is an optional extra – a reflection, as Omar Barghouti puts it, of "the static hierarchy that treats intellectuals as the patriarchs and activists as the helpless masses who are in desperate need of direction."[10]

Assessments of the political valence of intellectual work often neglect an important consideration: the fact that the very *form* of intellectual reflection itself, quite independently of its political *substance*, has significant conservatizing potential. The Marxist category of "praxis," which refers to the dialectical connection of systematic thinking and political intervention, provides a clear counterpoint to the traditional conception of the relation of intellectualism to politics. On the traditional conception, in Sinéad Murphy's words, "politically, the mature thinker should do his thinking in *private*, that is, only when he is removed from the nuts-and-bolts workings of the world, only when he is thinking for the sake of thinking itself."[11] In praxis, by contrast, theorizing is ideally oriented, even if at multiple removes, to developing proposals for action. This kind of theoretical activity is not interested in analyses purely for their own sake but in generating ideas about what can be done.[12]

Emphasizing the importance of orienting thought to action contravenes one widespread understanding of intellectuals, especially academic intellectuals: the expectation that they should speak in the name of *disinterested, abstract* or *pure* values and hold themselves aloof from the actual exercise of political power.[13] Fascism often criticizes intellectuals, and intellectualism, for just this characteristic: valuing action as "beautiful in itself," fascists often believe that it therefore "must be taken before, or without, any previous reflection" – a belief that can prompt a virulent contempt for intellectuals' typical disengagement from concrete politics.[14] Since Judaism has often been associated with intellectualism, this disdain can also have a racist dimension.[15] There is obviously no question of any such perspective in the argument I will be making here. With the European and American far right being regularly courted by the Israeli political establishment, it is Zionism, not anti-Zionism or BDS, whose fascist affiliations are clear.[16]

By drawing attention to the regressive possibilities of intellectualism *in general*, I will also not be suggesting that intellectual preparation and analysis – thinking – could somehow be dispensed with in political ventures. There is no place for febrile voluntarism in serious political projects, especially those with the gumption to aim at genuine social transformation. Anyone who has participated in Palestine activism knows only too well that what is needed in the elaboration of political interventions is not a hot-headed "propaganda of the deed" but painstaking analysis, deliberation and planning. For this reason, as long as there is a public domain in which ideas are debated, the Palestine solidarity movement will need its intellectuals and activist scholars. So the point is certainly not to elevate the purity of the unreflective deed into the greatest political good. Instead, it is to suggest that *for many intellectuals, and in particular those who oppose the academic boycott, thinking about the world is not a precursor to changing it but an alternative to doing so*. For many intellectuals, cognitive effort is an evasion of, or proxy for, political activity, not part of a praxis from which politics cannot be erased. The claim applies especially to professional intellectuals – journalists, artists, academics like me – who rely for patronage on states or private capital. The figure of the academic is emblematic. The characteristic description of the intellectual as someone for whom ideas matter purely "for their own sake, rather than for that of their causal relationships to whatever other ends" highlights the quietism and disengagement running deeply through the culture of theoretical reflection, especially in its current center of gravity in the university.[17] Most academics, even those whose work deals directly with political questions, do not consider themselves as activist scholars; most do not explicitly articulate their intellectual activity with concrete social projects, falling back on confidence in the vague educational or cultural influence exerted by their academic work as the main source of the political effect they often claim for it. Relatedly, Tiya Miles has written of academic antiracists that "ceaseless statement-writing as an act of protest is sucking us dry – of time, rest, energy, creativity and our place in the public square." "Beyond judiciously choosing the words to put on the page," she continued, "we would be wise to follow in the great social-movement tradition of matching our words with bodies in action."[18]

In the case of debate about Palestine, belief that academic analysis is, on the contrary, intrinsically a political act is encouraged by the fact that Zionists often try to make it so. The political effect of even verbal criticism of Israel in universities is massively amplified by Zionist opposition: as any number of academic Palestine supporters have learned, merely expressing pro-Palestinian views in an academic context can call down the full fury of Zionist reaction, massively boosting the wider public significance of work that would otherwise be "purely academic."[19] This means that the divorce of intellectual analysis from political action outside the academy is, in some ways, *less* marked for academic Palestine supporters than it is for other activists: the highly charged character of Palestine advocacy in universities means that even the most abstruse scholarship can be treated by Zionists as a political intervention first and a scholarly one second and risks being escalated into a political controversy that extends well beyond the campus. Simply telling the truth about the situation in Gaza and the West Bank, and articulating the necessity of justice, can lead to an academic being targeted – a fact which makes it heavily ironic that Zionists themselves emphasize the indispensability for "peace" efforts in the Middle East of the very intellectual activity they doggedly repress on campus.

Even in a university department dominated by theorists committed to praxis, the act of theorizing society and politics "directly" or analyzing or criticizing issues of the day insightfully ultimately means no more than *expressing a rational view about* them. In itself, that is no more a political act than expressing a view that skiing is a winter sport. Debates in the academy about Palestine, as about any other topic, usually take place at multiple removes from real-world effect, and without any mechanism for ideas' implementation. "For all their critical analysis," Jeff Halper says in relation to the politics of Palestinian liberation, academics "have not been active participants in 'translating' their powerful theories into political forms of use to activists and decision makers. In particular, they have not partnered with critical activists 'on the ground' to formulate a political end-game."[20] Researchers and lecturers, whatever their field, mostly advise and teach others, rather than acting themselves. This simple point is regularly ignored in discussions of academic and other intellectualism, where it is assumed that the mere fact that thought is made public qualifies it as a political "intervention" that contributes to wider political "pressure." That assumption is mistaken. As the realm of opinion and persuasion, politics always involves language and discourse. But if all politics is discursive, not all language or discourse is "political": not all discourse that is *about* politics has any substantive effect *on* it, even when it purports or is intended to do so. In the hands of a political actor, an *opinion* becomes a *position* – a location or obstacle to actors going in different directions, which has to be removed or navigated around and so contributes to the shaping of political space. But when it is divorced from explicit political campaigning, when ideas are advanced for the purposes of debate rather than of political change, analyzing or voicing ideas about politics cannot be the same as doing it.

This is not to say that intellectual analysis *never* has any "real-world" effects. When they talk about politics, intellectual spectators and commentators, like everyone else in the world, may exert various kinds of weak and multiply refracted influences on it – one example would be when they directly address public appeals or demands to politicians. In the right circumstances, *any* action may assume political significance: drawing a cartoon, dressing in a particular way, shaking hands with someone or turning one's back on them. Talk is no different. In the right circumstances, any piece of talk – and especially talk about Palestine and Israel – can take on a political function. But the fact that *some* talk is political doesn't mean that, intrinsically, all and any talk is. Most talk, including most talk engaged in by academics and other intellectuals, is politically insignificant, whatever its intellectual importance, just like most cartoons, handshakes or styles of dress. Academic talk does not become "political" simply through being declared to be so. Political importance mostly comes, as Edward Said noted, "from the closeness of a field to ascertainable sources of power in political society."[21] But academics' separation from concrete political power is inherent to their very status; this is what makes them spectators and commentators rather than actors.

It is true that, to politicians, academics' activities or ideas can sometimes offer the prospect of legitimation – a sign that a policy has more substantial thought behind it than can be expressed in a Twitter thread or a media sound bite. Political actors do therefore sometimes care about the ideas that have currency in universities. But it's easy to overstate the extent to which this is the case. So accustomed are we to focusing on the exceptional cases where intellectual activity in universities becomes politically relevant that we can forget the important fact that, nine times out of ten, the world of "official" politics, at least, is oblivious to it.

Contrary to the typical definition of the category, then, academic intellectuals' specificity lies precisely in their activity's *lack* of effect on politics outside the intellectual sphere, its "theoretical" character. In the eyes of many people, thinking is supposed either to abstain from immediate political questions or, more often, only to confront them in the name of their general or abstract aspects, not their concrete and therefore supposedly "anecdotal" ones. It is not to theoreticians that one usually turns for suggestions about political tactics. Given the contrast between theory and application, it is no surprise that the more useful "theoretical" work is to specific political questions, the less distinctively theoretical and academic it becomes. The code of conduct for the Israeli Defense Force (IDF), written by philosopher Asa Kasher – like his code of ethics for political speech in Israeli universities – contains none of the abstract theorizing of his philosophical and linguistic investigations.[22]

Whether in universities or outside them, intellectuals in the ordinary sense are, then, largely redundant in politics. In moments of acute political crisis, their irrelevance often stands out: the uprising of May 1968 in Paris provoked "an astonishing – and short-lived – crisis of modesty in intellectuals," as well as "the fear of being historically ridiculous or out of place";[23] Hilla Dayan reports Israeli academics lamenting "the marginality, irrelevance, and futility of critical knowledge in the absence of any meaningful hope for change" in Israel's stance toward Palestine.[24] The coincidence of intellectualism and direct political engagement in a single figure does not make the two activities' divorce any less absolute. Most intellectuals are not activists; when they are, their engagement is likely to be viewed with suspicion by their peers: intellectuals committed to political causes or movements do not generally command the same respect as their supposedly "independent" peers, as many academics committed to the cause of concrete Palestine solidarity have discovered. Activist scholarship is often seen less as scholarship and more as activism. At best, if their political activity does not discredit them, an intellectual who engages with political issues politically – one who is involved in political organizing, campaigning or lobbying – is just that: an intellectual who *also* does politics.

THOUGHT AND INACTION

Received wisdom, then, is clear: analysis, thought and reflection are most themselves when they are furthest from effective political action. Attempts to politicize academic research by calling for boycotts are therefore seen as quintessentially anti-intellectual. On this understanding, reason is essentially disinterested, independent of the contingencies of any world in which it might have to be applied. Thought is inert: it does nothing to reality "except just know it," as John Dewey put it.[25] Dewey's formula expresses thought's consternation when called to account by the need to effect actual change in the world.

When the opposition of thinking and acting has been contested, it has usually been by claiming that thought *is* action. "Thinking," according to BDS opponent Nancy Koppelman, "is a kind of doing, and all other kinds of doing, especially in college, ought to be based on it."[26] It is rare to maintain the opposite and see in action the truest accomplishment of thought. Gramsci is an exception to the standard divorce of action and thought. For him, even the purest form of thought, philosophy, must be bound to concrete action: "the real philosopher," he wrote, "cannot be other than the politician, the active man [*sic*] who modifies the environment."[27] From the perspective of ordinary understandings of how abstract thought and politics relate, the claim is outlandish. Yet, while denying that politics could ever be a form of philosophy, academics and other intellectuals often argue that philosophy and other forms of theoretical activity are well and truly a form of politics.[28] But if philosophy, like other varieties of theoretical reflection, is in fact political, it is not because it is a kind of praxis or action but precisely because it is a kind of *in*action. Regardless of whatever standard definition of politics we adopt, theorizing, whether in philosophy or elsewhere, fails to qualify. If we define politics as the "organization of means in view of calculable ends," then theorizing cannot count, since the ends to which it is directed – greater understanding, clarity or accuracy – are contested and perspective-dependent and so not calculable: whether or how far theoretical activity has directly contributed to a concrete political initiative cannot usually be settled.[29] Nor does theorizing qualify if politics is understood as efforts "to share power or . . . influence the distribution of power, either among states or among groups within a state."[30] nor does it form, other than in exceptional cases, part of "the practices by which people contribute, cooperatively or in struggle, to shape the way power and authority are exercised in their lives."[31] Theorizing is the choice to contain thought in the lee of politics, to shelter it from what Adorno labeled the "pre-censorship" of praxis.[32]

If thought could, in fact, be genuine political action, then intellectual exchange could take on all the qualities of political struggle. If thought were action, the phrase "the battle of ideas" would be more than merely metaphorical. But there can be no literal "battle" of ideas, unless something can count as a battle where winners and losers are self-declared and where it can often be unclear whether the enemy has even been engaged. Ideas, which have no existence outside the kaleidoscope of their interpretations, cannot come to blows. In theory, contradictory or opposing positions can coexist: intellectual life unfolds in a permanent antebellum. Even its precise content is indeterminate: "with every thinker," Gramsci observed, "it is possible . . . to cast doubt on whether he really said such and such a thing."[33] Quarantined in disputation, ideas never escape the realm of intellectualism, no matter how radically they might claim to contest the existing order. Without actualization, that claim remains a dead letter. When they are activated politically, ideas are no longer just ideas: they are programs, translatable into action, accountable for their failure or success and understood instrumentally as prescriptions for change.

It is, as a consequence, strikingly idealistic to hold that political *ideas* are the front line of struggle, that "the most subversive act would be to make research, reveal facts, and produce knowledge that governments can neither hide nor resist," as Ariel Handel and Ruthie Ginsberg put it – a belief that would necessarily rule out academic boycotts of any kind.[34] The contention that the balance of forces can be shifted by intellectuals' contributions in their standard textual formats (books, lectures, opinion columns, expert reports, essays, etc.) is open to critique for embodying what has been called a "magical" conception of ideology. In this conception, intellectuals' written words inherently convey a political value that "somehow insinuates itself into consciousness" – how, exactly, no one knows. Having been deposited in people's minds through textual transmission, the political values espoused by intellectuals then go on to function as the "*contents of thought*" that mysteriously "come into play in real situations" in unexplained ways.[35] This is exactly the mythological conception of ideas' political efficacy that animates intellectualism and its conviction of the intrinsically progressive character of theoretical work.

In ignoring the vital questions of the transmission and implementation of ideas in practice, this "magical" conception of the value of scholarship is alive and well among opponents of the academic boycott. The outrage which meets BDS attempts to disrupt intellectual activity trades on a widespread belief that such activity possesses an intrinsic political efficacy that does not require articulation with any other kind of political work – the idea that justice in the Middle East can somehow be forged in the parallel sessions of international conferences. If denying this is anti-intellectual, then a dose of "anti-intellectualism" is sorely needed in the struggle for justice for Palestine.

STOPPING TO THINK

I've been suggesting that there are many reasons for skepticism about the indispensability of traditional forms of intellectual activity to radical political projects. In discussing some of them, we've discovered grounds to be less upset when these interventions are undermined by the academic boycott. As I have stressed, however, the boycott is aimed at increasing Palestinians' access to education and so is wholly oriented toward *boosting*, not suppressing, the possibilities of systematic thought: it targets a narrow range of academic activities in order to *further* opportunities for higher education, as well as the possibility of other basic rights, for Palestinians. From this point of view, there is nothing anti-intellectual whatsoever about the academic boycott. Indeed, boycott supporters are typically at the forefront of the struggle for a greater place for decolonial and marginalized knowledges in university curricula, in opposition to the academy's traditional intellectual norms.

But there is another way in which the academic boycott promotes thinking and therefore should not be considered as undesirably anti-intellectual. This consists in the concrete intellectual activity required to plan and execute BDS activities. Planning and executing political campaigns involves a form of collective organizing or "groupthink" – a term that should be reclaimed from its current uniquely pejorative sense. The groupthink of political organizing involves, in itself, a sophisticated exercise of intellectual capacities. In fact, a stronger claim is justified: in reconciling thought, discourse and politics, political organizing of the kind involved in boycott activism provides a *model* for ways in which intellectual and practical work on the left can relate. Boycott organizing, like other forms of political organizing, is a perfect example of praxis. Advertising and holding a meeting to plan a campaign over a political issue is in itself a political act on all three definitions of politics we entertained earlier: it is the "organization of means in view of calculable ends," an effort to "influence the distribution of power" and a contribution to shaping how "power and authority are exercised."[36] Campaign-organizing meetings are, by definition, aimed at bringing further actions into being – the boycotts, public meetings, demonstrations or whatever other events activists happen to be working on. This organizing is thoroughly "intellectual" in nature, but it contrasts in many points with the traditional model of theoretical intellectualism that is still so entrenched in academia, and which the academic boycott disrupts.

Traditional intellectual expression is geared to articulating a structured discursive whole. Its characteristic mode is therefore the monologue: the theoretical text, whether written or orally delivered, is steeped in the single author's voice. For the same reason, an intellectual speaks at length: haunted by the specter of stupidity, theoretical reflection obeys a restless logic of self-suspicion. The long form – the lecture, the essay, the monograph, the extended presentation – is therefore the genre of choice. Authorial paranoia, the constant fear of contradiction by a more astute responder, leads to prolixity, overcomplication and the escalation of subtlety, especially in written formats. At the same time, intellectual expression often serves as a comforting haven or safe space where the thinker is, for once, in control, far from the tensions and uncertainties of political action. All this cannot but emphasize a strong individualism. Differentiation of the author's position, rather than its convergence with that of others, is what is emphasized. "The hope of the intellectual," according to Said's paraphrase of Adorno, "is not that he will have an effect on the world, but that someday, somewhere, someone will read what he wrote exactly as he wrote it."[37] Accordingly, the texts intellectuals generate are often not modulated for their audience to any significant extent – or, if they are, this is understood as a concession which distorts the original integrity of the thought they express. Intellectuals' heightened sense of the inherent significance of their work is, perhaps, one of the drivers of their frequent aloofness from the social dynamics that might translate their ideas into motive political forces.

The abstracting and generalizing regimes of intellectual work often risk distancing the thinker from the grain of the real. Eyal Weizman comments that the IDF's "seductive use of theoretical and technological discourse seeks to portray war as remote, quick and intellectual, exciting." This allows violence to "be projected as tolerable and the public encouraged to support it."[38] The emotional attitudes that often accompany abstract theoretical work can accomplish a similar effect. Rather than amplifying political energies, theoretical work can often mute them, suggesting that before they can do anything, activists must *study* and *understand* – and that the mode of understanding is one that consists, precisely, in not acting.[39] Whether for writers or readers, intellectualism's temporality is that of retreat: the withdrawal from the contingencies of events in order to reflect. Slavoj Žižek is explicit on the point:

> A clear analysis of the present global constellation – one which offers no clear solution, no "practical" advice on what to do, and provides no light at the end of the tunnel, since one is well aware that this light might belong to a train crashing towards us – usually meets with reproach: "Do you mean we should do *nothing*? Just sit and wait?" One should gather the courage to answer: "YES, precisely that!" There are situations when the only truly "practical" thing to do is to resist the temptation to engage immediately and to "wait and see" by means of a patient, critical analysis.[40]

In a situation where "engagement seems to exert its pressure on us from all directions," the appropriate response, Žižek says, is to go, like Lenin, "to a solitary place to learn, learn and learn!"[41]

No one could deny the political necessity of "learning." But learning and thinking, thought and theory are insatiable: once they start, they are never enough – no question is ever adequately explored or thought through, no position ever justified as fully as it could be. While progressives have stopped to think, the right is busy ransacking the environment, winding back democratic prerogatives and consolidating attacks on Palestinians. Intellectualism should inspire new political agents to act. But even radical intellectualism risks creating drag on the impetus for action by alienating struggle's main protagonists – non-intellectuals – from the logic of political engagement and suggesting that political energy needs not just planning but also theoretical warrant. This "smartwashing" can be highly counterproductive. For the drag it creates to be justified, the compensations – in sharpened analysis, better appreciation of the possibilities of and constraints on change – must be overwhelming. In cases where a highly contested position is being argued, as is almost always the case when pro-Palestine intellectuals intervene publicly in favor of the boycott, stopping and thinking are essential to building a political case. Elsewhere, the payoff of intellectual interventions is often less clear. Academics and intellectuals often have little to offer experienced political actors by way of advice about *politics*.

The individualism and monologic nature of intellectual contributions allows politics' nature as the clash of *social forces* to be easily lost from view. Politics' social character means that political momentum is propagated collectively: time-honored catalysts of change like demonstrations, strikes, boycotts, occupations and so on are intrinsically collective. With respect to such activities, however, intellectualism is often a freely spinning wheel. As

Shlomo Sand has recently observed, "close or similar philosophical ideas can give rise to opposed and contradictory political positions": ideas, in other words, are not a political *force* in their own right.[42] Offered without any concern for their uptake, theoretical interventions are letters in a bottle, intrinsically disengaged from either the dissemination or the actuation of the ideas they propound, animated by the vague hope of "influencing opinion" or simply "contributing to the debate." This is true regardless of how penetrating or accurate they are, or of whatever other reasons there might be for writing or reading them. Publishing a book or a newspaper article leaves to chance the ideas' activation: ideas are imagined to exert an effect of contagion, insinuating themselves into the body politic in viral or subterranean ways.

Consistent with its lack of concern with the implementation of its own ideas, traditional intellectualism fosters illusions in a logic of dialogue and reason rather than the one of force and interests which governs political life.[43] It fuels the fantasy of a civil public sphere in which reason triumphs and suggests that political change is a debate or a conversation rather than a battle. Whether written or spoken, the extended textual form encourages a faith that if people only understood, then they could not but agree. This contrasts strongly with a politics of activism and disruption, which is predicated not on an ideal of mutual understanding but on the reality of discord. Political progress is often achieved through mass mobilizations and disruptions to the established order, which offer proof of the feasibility of effective popular agency and draw new actors into political activity. Necessarily, this involves repertoires of action available to everyone. But there is nothing either disruptive or universally accessible in conference presentations, theoretical articles or disquisitions packaged within the conventionality of dust-jackets and author photos, no matter how radical their content. Theoretical interventions are rarely the most potent way of forwarding a political position.

Even more popular and widely read theoretical trickle-downs, like the opinion columns published by the mainstream media, are a double-edged sword. Of course, progressives need to disseminate their ideas. A respected or resolute voice speaking out can certainly encourage others to do so too and thereby contribute to shifting "public opinion," as the relentless public advocacy of Palestinian intellectuals like Noura Erakat or Steven Salaita shows. But ideas are only worth spreading, and public "opinion" only worth shifting, if doing so contributes to change. Public analysis can most directly engage with the levers of social change if it is construed as a prelude to concrete political action. Such an orientation rings out loud and clear in Palestinian intellectuals' public analysis, but it is largely alien to the modes of political writing disseminated by progressive mainstream commentators, even the most insistent. Even strong condemnation of politicians' decisions is typically couched in a confessional mode, as the isolated reasoning or *cri de cœur* of an individual conscience. As such, analysis or opinion takes on a purely expressive role which risks substituting for concrete opposition, rather than functioning as an instance of or prelude for it.

Whether the target is the complicity of the Israeli academy with that country's crimes or some other case of serious injustice, those committed to political change need to beware of the idea that more analysis, debate or dialogue is the highest priority. The central critical task in bringing about social change is usually not mainly an analytical or an epistemological but a *political* one. Obviously, awareness needs to be raised about what is actually happening in occupied Palestine. But the "strategy" that proposes to remedy Palestinians' exclusion from basic rights simply by "raising awareness" about it in international conferences, or, even more implausibly, simply by participating in conferences on unrelated subjects with Israeli academic officials, is as feeble as the one that believes that the overthrow of academic neoliberalism can be achieved simply through the textual interventions of its critics.[44] "Dialogue during ongoing conflict," as Noura Erakat reminds us, "is paralyzing and serves to reify the current status quo."[45] We mostly do not need to *understand* more about what is wrong with the status quo in the Middle East: we need to act together to change it.

AGAINST SMARTWASHING

As well as increasing the "stock" of knowledge, thinkers are often seen as having a role of deepening and "problematizing" issues, questioning assumptions, demonstrating that things aren't as simple as people thought. There's an obvious sense in which doing that is often necessary for progressive purposes – this book, for instance, is an attempt to persuade readers of the well-foundedness of the academic boycott and to debunk the simplifications and distortions on which its critics usually rely. But it's not enough to show that important political questions are inevitably more complicated than they are presented as being. If thought and analysis are to serve political action, not inhibit and smartwash it, then their role should also be to *simplify* issues – not in the sense of inaccurate *over*simplification but in that of *clarification*, showing the ways in which they often are, in fact, actually simple enough to allow people to take a stand on a particular side. Political reflection is most authentic when it is not idle but connected to political action. Yet, if we're to act politically, the world needs to be sufficiently clear to permit a political choice. Hence, clarificatory simplification, not complexification, should be the aim of progressive political analysis.[46]

Zionists continually stress how "complex" the political realities of Zionism are, and how little interest BDS supporters have in exploring them.

According to Nancy Koppelman, whose view that thinking is a form of doing we encountered earlier, academic boycott supporters "profess the conclusion that there is a quite simple solution to the conflict – just end the occupation, preferably today – which is naïve at best and ethically irresponsible at worst when proffered by intellectuals who ought to know better how international politics actually works – 'not like the nursery,' as Hannah Arendt once wrote."⁴⁷ Possessing a supposedly deeper insight into the occupation, Zionists "smartwash" their support for oppression with an elaborate structure of intellectual mystification: "academic boycotters are forcing a retreat away from serious engagement of the issues and into anti-intellectual demonology"; "the BDS movement is not interested in reflection"; "the settlement enterprise ... is far more diverse and complicated than the standard settler colonialist rubric can admit"; "activists and academics who demand that we see the Zionist movement as a colonizing movement not only ignore the complexity of Zionism but rapidly transform the Jewish population of Israel from an oppressed people fleeing persecution and genocide into an aggressive colonial settler."⁴⁸ As these quotations suggest, claims of complexity have the function of discrediting political action by implying that it rests on a simplistic misapprehension of the true nature of the situation on the ground. The corollary of this is that only experts have the right to take a political position – exactly the view denounced by Chomsky and Said, as we saw in the previous chapter. Susie Linfield, a Zionist opponent of BDS, criticizes Chomsky for failing to "grapple with multiplicity" in his analyses of Palestine: "The array of forces in the Arab-Israeli conflict is multifaceted, indeed Byzantine," Linfield writes. "The historian, political analyst, or activist of this conflict must, therefore, be able to recognize, juggle, and synthesize many contradictory factors." But Chomsky, she claims, "is peculiarly unsuited to this task. In lieu of grappling with multiplicity, he takes one partial, small seed and engorges it so that it stands in for the knotty whole."⁴⁹

This is a textbook case of smartwashing. In using claims of complexity to discount support for Palestinians, Zionists weaponize a move that is part of the stock-in-trade of academic disputation in general. In an article called "Fuck Nuance," Kieran Healy delivers a sharp critique of calls for greater nuance in academic sociology as typically constituting "a holding maneuver": displaying "sensitivity to nuance," Healy writes, "is a manifestation of one's distinctive ... ability to grasp and express the richness, texture, and flow of social reality itself. This is the nuance of the *connoisseur*. It is mostly a species of self-congratulatory symbolic violence," since "connoisseurship gets its aesthetic bite from the easy insinuation that the person trying to simplify things is a bit less sophisticated a thinker than the person pointing out that things are more complicated."⁵⁰

An emphasis on the extraordinary complexity of a situation is a powerful incentive to believe that change is impossible. Thus, while they stress the complexity of the politics of Palestine liberation, many Zionists, especially liberals, also often declare how pessimistic they are about a resolution. Pessimism about an end to the occupation is, of course, a natural reaction in the face of Israel's overwhelming military superiority, and of the disastrous politics of the Palestinian Authority, "a proxy arm of Israel's occupation," in Noura Erakat's description.[51] Despair can even be the driving force that motivates action. The Israeli anti-occupation activist David Shulman has written of the "good despair" that drives him from bed in the morning to the South Hebron hills to join with local Palestinians in resisting settlers:

> I recommend despair as a place to start. It is in the nature of acting, of doing the right thing, that despair recedes at least for a moment, and its place is taken by something else: hopeless hope, for example. Those who work these furrows know that hope is not contingent. Sometimes the worse things get, the more hope there is, for hope is an act of the deeper self, or the freer part of the person, what some would call a spiritual act, though "spiritual" is not a word I use. In this sense, hope bears no relation to the superficial, mentalistic mode called optimism.[52]

But the despair that one encounters most often is not this kind of catalyst to activism; it is, instead, a brake on it. In their 2015 anti-BDS tract, *Boycotting Israel Is Wrong*, Australian BDS opponents Philip Mendes and Nick Dyrenfurth say they are "highly pessimistic about the chances of a peace deal being struck in the near future," devoting almost the whole of their book to a critique of BDS, without any serious positive program for an end to the occupation.[53] In cases like this, the main effect of articulating pessimism is to discourage in the audience any commitment to acting for change. As Ramzig Keucheyan has pointed out, political pessimism can sometimes approach a form of decadence or "dandyism" – "the 'aristocratic' renunciation of politics, based on a 'catastrophist' diagnosis of the irremediably corrupted nature of society."[54] Pessimism and depression are infectious and lead inexorably back to the status quo. On the surface, liberal Zionists may lament the fact that progress in Israel seems unlikely, but the effect is to deliver exactly the same message as Zionist hard-liners: nothing is going to change, so Palestinian resistance is futile.

IN PRAISE OF GROUPTHINK

The political organizing undertaken by BDS and other activists is a clear example of how radical thought can contribute to political progress. Political organizing contrasts with intellectuals' textual (oral or written) interventions in every point. When members of an activist collective or a political organization come together to plan a political campaign, the work of reflection is harnessed to particular concrete goals (determining these goals, indeed, is often one of the main purposes of meeting). Analysis and reflection are therefore closely disciplined not by the solipsistic logics of textual closure but by the possibilities of a real-world uptake of ideas. Reflection is anything but monological, as it generally is in lectures, conference talks or academic articles: it is, instead, "groupthink," developing collectively as the emergent product of different participants' contributions, none of whom can monopolize the floor. Speaking turns are limited; addressing the meeting is understood not mainly as an expressive or confessional act in which the speakers evacuate themselves of an idea but as a constructive one which contributes to the joint elaboration of a common project.[55]

In this kind of groupthink, the virtues of thinking – its ability to synthesize details, infer consequences, reconcile contradictions, imagine different worlds, penetrate through ideological distortions – are amplified through being the products of more than a single mind. A similar amplification results from ideas' directedness in organizing contexts, the fact that they are addressed to a specific audience. Forced to confront the reality of differing sensibilities, experiences and casts of mind, an idea's originator in a political organizing meeting has to exercise a significantly higher degree of rigor and responsiveness in promoting it in the meeting than within the discursive safety of a text. Promotion of an idea must be immediately responsive to its actual reception: from the start, intellectual elaboration is shaped by the dialectical necessities of communication with the other participants. Contributions in an organizing meeting are therefore experiments in feasibility: an idea is tested by being articulated, and its potential for generating results is a function of its ability actually to do so – by, in the first instance, winning acceptance as a guide to action, free of the prevarications and abstraction of pure reflection.

It is in the DNA of standard theoretical discourse to be oriented toward a utopian order of rationality in which understanding, even understanding of complexity or ambiguity, can be achieved once and for all: the audience of a book or lecture is offered the inducement of theoretical enlightenment as the end of the textual game. In organizing contexts, this is replaced by the necessity of "pragmatic" clarification, in which conceptual resolution is sought insofar as it is useful from the perspective of collective action and the furthering of political objectives. This difference has immediate consequences for the distribution of power within organizing collectives. The ambition of conceptual sophistication or complexity so characteristic of academic intellectual formats intrinsically divides the audience into those who do and don't understand. An organizing meeting, by contrast, submits the dissemination of ideas to the opposite logic. Rather than an aloof, unaccountable author, the originator of an idea is thrust into direct reciprocity with their audience. The onus is on them to make themselves understood through appeal not to intellectual authority but to shared standards of evaluation and legitimacy – standards which also require the "audience" to receive the idea constructively. The collective character of political organizing prohibits participants from fashioning bespoke intellectual criteria to justify their claims. Argument, not appeals to theoretical authority or scholarly genealogies, must be the default mode of justification.

A written text is fundamentally addressed to no one and makes no claim on its silent and anonymous audience. An activist meeting, by contrast, illustrates that the meaning of an idea is the sum of the practical consequences that flow from it: ideas are not expressed simply to be read or heard but to be responded to, refined and acted on. The fusion of thought and action in political organizing means that the speaker, just as much as the listener, is responsible when communication breaks down.

Those aspects of academic discourse that engender the suspicion that the author is engaging in intellectual display or indulging the fetishism of difficulty or the narcissism of small differences simply cannot survive the constraints of an organizing meeting. Once floated, a proposal's fate is to be hybridized and collectively refined. As successive speakers develop different aspects, drawing out what was only previously implicit, discovering weaknesses or unintended implications, developing rationales, it becomes genuine *groupthink* – the joint creation of multiple minds, not the exclusive product of a single one. Lines of intellectual responsibility are blurred: it becomes harder to say where an idea came from; the question of who it might "belong" to is meaningless. In contrast to the pretense of the determinate authorship and ownership of texts, political decisions display their collective character, illustrating the principle that the essence of an idea is realized, and discovered, in the interpretations it engenders.

The temporality of political organizing, too, contrasts strongly with intellectuals' theoretical textual interventions. Meeting times of political organizing meetings are fixed; participants are uniformly subject to a timetable set externally by the political calendar and internally by the business of the meeting itself. Whereas the author of a text determines its subject matter, pace and, often, its length, these parameters are not under the control of a speaker in an organizing meeting, limited as they are by speaking times and protocols, as well as by the meeting's own agenda. Speaking turns rotate: the person speaking now will soon be in the role of listener. This goes some way to leveling differences (of experience, authority, supposed insightfulness) among the participants and installing a certain parity among them. A text's author is its creator: the very status of author lies under the shadow of the figure of the prophet or the lone genius, consigning their declarations to the hazards of their subsequent interpretations. A contributor to a political discussion is not the distant genius of authorship but a collaborator, submitted not only to the requirement of relevance and comprehensibility but also to that of personal accountability: someone who does not follow through on the proposals or undertakings they originate in an organizing space risks being discredited. Textual interventions, by contrast, engender no such expectation of sincerity or personal commitment.

Unlike textual production, organizing contributions are embodied, engaging capacities and faculties other than merely intellectual ones. Speaker and listeners are face to face, sitting around the same table or sharing the same teleconference in a relation of mutuality, a world away from the didacticism of theory, the lecturer at the podium addressing a silent audience. Their interactions are not limited to the channel of words: intonation, body language, posture and other nonverbal cues all embed thought in a world of actual subjects. Ideas are thereby grounded in a particular set of interpreters: no longer letters in a bottle, they are tailored to their reception by a specific community with a specific physical instantiation and defined political goals. The remoteness of theory from concrete struggles, by contrast, distances readers from the opportunities, risks and compromises of real political action, absorbing them into the hesitation and overdetermination of reflection. Hence, intellectuals are often uncomfortable about the element of risk and uncertainty in political action. Ilan Pappé, for example, has criticized BDS for being "an impulse, not a strategy" – a criticism that ignores the fact that *all* political initiatives are uncertain, that none can be fully sketched out in advance or guaranteed to succeed and that, as a result, all are, in that sense, "impulses."[56] BDS certainly has no lack of strategic thinking behind it; if it counts as no more than an impulse, any number of other political campaigns do as well. In one sense, progress in the natural sciences – the traditional paradigm of rationality – is just as much a matter of "impulse" as is political campaigning: there is, in science, no methodology that unfailingly guides the empirical scientist to the best explanation of the phenomenon under investigation.[57] Like political action, theory-building in science is a matter of imagination and creativity and carries no guarantee of success. In just the same way, political campaigns advance conjectures about what will work in the real world and adapt their strategy in light of results. This is an eminently rational procedure, but it intrinsically involves risk, uncertainty and improvisation, qualities far removed from those typically prized by the logic of scholarly debate.

In the same way, the absence of traditional intellectual content in much political organizing – assigning practical tasks, arranging the many banal details of concrete political action – continually recalls thinkers to the necessities of the real world, impressing on them their particular material responsibilities in the world of action, where, after all, the most urgent necessity is often not refining a theoretical analysis but organizing venues or making more photocopies. The sheer tedium of much of what goes on in organizing meetings is, certainly, one of the most commonly cited disincentives to participating in them. This aversion reflects a basically unserious attitude to politics in which political action is envisaged as entertainment or even relaxation – an escape from activity, rather than an integral part of it. Chomsky has been particularly clear – and modest – on the point:

> Last night I gave a talk in Berkeley to a big mob of people about U.S. and the Middle East, and Israel and Palestine, and Turkey, and these things. Who is responsible for that talk? Not me. I flew in from Boston, came over and gave a talk. The people responsible for that are the people working on it, the people working day after day to create the organizational structures, the support systems, to go up and back to work with oppressed people over there. Maybe their names won't enter some record, but they're the ones who are leading everything. I come in and it's a privilege for me to be able to join them for an hour, but that's easy. You know, get up and give a talk, it's no big deal. Working on it day after day, all the time, that's hard, and that's important, and that's what changes the world, not somebody coming in and giving a talk.[58]

THE ANTI-INTELLECTUALISM WE NEED

Transcending the distinction between manual and intellectual work is an old ambition of the left, imagined as a consequence of the abolition of exploitation and class conflict. A similar goal was also prominent in early Zionism, and it still weakly survives in different pockets of today's world: one example would be Palestinian universities' requirement that students complete unpaid community work as a condition of their graduation.[59] In political organizing, the ambition is already partly realized. For all its ubiquity, political organizing embarrasses the usual terms in which we understand collective action in society. These terms come up strikingly short when faced with the need to account both for groupthink – the collective emergence of ideas in organizing contexts – and the way those ideas blend thought and action. So contradictory are thought and action as usually imagined that a special category exists to name situations where both must happen simultaneously. This category is *improvisation*, a distinctive form of practice-thought in which planning and execution are collapsed into the same moment, in which we "make it up as we go along." Outside of contexts of improvisation, in which it is contemporaneous with thought, action is considered to be lifeless and dumb – the armor-plating that thought puts on to step out into the world.

Action, on the usual construal, should simply *realize* what's already been created intellectually and shouldn't involve any creative aspect. The fact that improvisation is typically thought of as disconcerting and anxiety-inducing indicates the distance maintained by our usual categorizations between acting and thinking.

Political organizing, however, illustrates a kind of collective, distributed thinking that, since it involves assembling and deploying political forces, is also simultaneously action. To apply the full resources of human intelligence to politics does not require thinkers to withdraw into the abstraction of individual theorizing, thereby distancing themselves from the realities of political activity with all its risks and opportunities. If, accordingly, political movements have their organic intellectuals, their role is not to direct the movement from the splendid isolation of their minds but to help the movement fashion a discursive expression in which it can recognize and propagate itself, in exactly the way that so many of the Palestine solidarity movement's current intellectuals do. They are in a relationship of collective reciprocity, not of leadership, with respect to the movement's other activists.

Equipped with the view of political organizing as groupthink that I have been defending, we would lose patience with the intellectualist preconception that writing articles and essays necessarily trumps organizing collective action. We would grow tired of attempts to elevate battles of ideas into the foremost political arena, disconnected from political parties, social movements or campaign groups. Often it is not the sobrieties of published analysis but its opposite – live invective, ridicule, jokes – which will do the most to advance a political agenda.[60] The advice of an academic to antiracist student protesters in South Africa – "Don't raise your voice. Improve your argument" – betrays a real naivety about the mechanisms of political change: the protest movement in question, Rhodes Must Fall, which aimed to remove a statue of Cecil Rhodes from the University of Cape Town, started when an activist flung excrement over the statue and was successful after students staged a sit-in of the university's administration building.[61]

If Judaism has, as we have seen, often been associated in stereotypical western representations with intellectualism, Palestinians are typically placed on the other end of the spectrum and presented not just as non- or anti-intellectual but as uncultivated and barbaric – as, indeed, "Philistines," a term whose original meaning is, precisely, "Palestinian."[62] This etymology speaks volumes about the anti-Palestinianism lodged deep in western intellectual attitudes and the Islamophobic prejudices at the heart of the Eurocentric "geography of reason."[63] The fact that Palestinians are stigmatized in this way should lead us to question the nature of the intellectual aptitudes they have so often been claimed to lack. In the case of the academic boycott specifically, if it is "anti-intellectual" to oppose the ideological infrastructure of Palestinian oppression and its thinkers, then the tactic of the academic boycott is indeed anti-intellectual – proudly so – and this book should be understood as advocating a certain form of anti-intellectualism. Academics do not, however, have to resign themselves to the conclusion that their professional intellectual activities intrinsically commit them to political or moral quietism, or, worse, to open opposition to political progress. Simply "leading the life of an academic in the face of daily denials of rights is not the way to peace and happiness," as Gabi Baramki has written, either for academics or for society.[64] Both thought and education can and should be harnessed to the elimination of exploitation and injustice – the very condition, indeed, in which they are arguably most vigorous.

On the left, denunciations of anti-intellectualism are common: anti-humanism; bourgeois philistinism; narcissistic, paradoxically *intellectual* perversity; pre-fascistic decadence; book-burning. But thought and intellectualism are not equivalent: the first becomes the second only once it is seen as the preserve of a privileged caste of thinkers, defined by their characteristic abstention from concrete political interventions and aloofness from popular political initiatives. Dissolving the privilege of intellectualism and recognizing, with Gramsci, that everyone is an intellectual, is a long-standing ambition of radical politics; Palestine solidarity is just one of the many political domains which would benefit from the rehabilitation of "anti-intellectualism" of this very particular, democratizing kind.

Omar Barghouti, one of the original proponents of the academic boycott, has asserted that

> in contexts of colonial oppression, intellectuals, especially those who advocate and work for justice, cannot be just – or mere – intellectuals in the abstract sense; they cannot but be immersed in some form or another of activism, to learn from fellow activists through real-life experiences, to widen the horizons of their sources of inspiration, and to organically engage in effective, collective emancipatory processes aimed at reaching justice without the self-indulgence, complacency, or ivory-towerness that might otherwise blur their moral vision.[65]

This applies just as much to academics as it does to any other category of intellectual. Perhaps what is most striking in Barghouti's comment is his observation that it is in abandoning the position of the intellectual that academics can *actually learn* and attain *clarity of moral vision*. Clearly, then, his critique of intellectualism is in no way motivated by anti-intellectual considerations but is driven by the desire for intellectuals to *learn* and attain a particular kind of *clarity*. Commenting on this passage, Steven Salaita highlights the affinity of "ivory-towerness" with "the main elements of colonial decorum," "disinterest, civility, and moderation": the very demand for academic disengagement, in other words, reflects a structural bias against colonized people like Palestinians. Salaita goes on to assert the importance of eroding, in both thought and practice, the distinction between "the interests of the university and the imperatives of the activist."[66]

Salaita's ideal of thinkers and thought at work in the world, beyond a closed coterie of intellectuals, has, as we have seen, often been keenly felt.[67] In the face of the "infrahumanity" imposed on Palestinians and their de facto exemption from the universality of justice, it should be clear how weak is the conviction that intellectual activity – political debate, truth-telling, analysis – is a powerful motor of political change in its own right, independent of any coupling with more "concrete" political work.[68] We mostly do not need to understand more about what is wrong with the status quo in the Middle East – we need to act together to change it. I have suggested that we can best do this by participating in a collective "groupthink" that sets aside the smartwashing, mystification and individualism that is such a feature of traditional intellectualism. Truly radicalizing progressive thought should mean socializing the forms in which thinking is conducted and expressed. In the first instance, this entails recognizing the intellectual depth and complexities of political organizing – in this case, the intellectual complexities involved in organizing the boycott. In this light, the dilemmas faced by so many progressives – to think or to act? how much thought is needed before acting? – reflect, ultimately, a false dichotomy. In advocating the theorized, organized, collective refusal of official intellectual collaboration with Israel, the academic boycott exemplifies a way to connect thinking about politics with actually doing it that applies not only to the project of Palestinian liberation but also to many others besides.

Notes

INTRODUCTION

1. International Middle East Media Center (IMEMC), "Open Letter from Academics at Birzeit University in Palestine," January 9, 2018, accessed April 28, 2022, imemc.org/article/open-letter-from-academics-at-birzeit-university-in-palestine/.

2. For a compilation of the statements, see the "Palestinian Campaign for the Academic & Cultural Boycott of Israel (@PACBI)," Twitter, May 21, 2021, 1:33 a.m., accessed April 28, 2022, twitter.com/PACBI/status/1395402203699978241. Two statements released within a matter of weeks of each other in Denmark are indicative: a May 25, 2021, BDS statement in support of Palestine gathered 51 signatures, while a statement in support of Danish academic freedom against government interference garnered over 1,000 local signatories, among the total of 2,700 international names: "Forskere og undervisere med speciale i Mellemøsten: Danmark bør påtage sig en ledende rolle i kampen mod israelsk apartheid," *Politiken*, May 25, 2021, accessed April 28, 2022, politiken.dk/debat/debatindlaeg/art8219285/Danmark-b%C3%B8r-p%C3%A5tage-sig-en-ledende-rolle-i-kampen-mod-israelsk-apartheid; "3241 forskere i opråb til regeringen: Tag klart afstand fra angrebet på forskningsfriheden. Det kan føre til selvcensur," *Politiken*, June 8, 2021, accessed April 28, 2022, politiken.dk/debat/debatindlaeg/art8237629/Tag-klart-afstand-fra-angrebet-p%C3%A5-forskningsfriheden.-Det-kan-f%C3%B8re-til-selvcensur.

3. Muhammad Ali Khalidi, "BDS and the Morality of Boycott," *Institute for Palestine Studies* (blog), December 2, 2020, accessed April 28, 2022, www.palestine-studies.org/en/node/1650796.

4. See Abdel Razzaq Takriti, "Before BDS: Lineages of Boycott in Palestine," *Radical History Review* 134 (2019): 60.

5. "Palestinian Civil Society Call for BDS," BDS Movement (website), July 9, 2005, accessed April 28, 2022, bdsmovement.net/call. The differences between the boycott of South Africa and of Israel will be discussed in chapter one.

6. "Palestinian Civil Society Call for BDS."

7. See "L'Université Paris VI (Jussieu) vote pour l'arrêt de la coopération avec Israël," *EuroPalestine*, December 19, 2002, accessed April 28, 2022, europalestine.com/2002/12/19/luniversite-paris-vi-jussieu-vote-pour-larret-de-la-cooperation-avec-israel/. See also Hilary Rose and Steven Rose, "Israel, Europe and the Academic Boycott," *Race and Class* 50 (2008): 1–20.

8. In Omar Barghouti, *BDS: Boycott, Divestment, Sanctions: The Global Struggle for Palestinian Rights* (Chicago: Haymarket, 2011), 236.

9. Adam Horowitz, "University of Johannesburg to Officially Sever Ties with Israel's Ben-Gurion University," *Mondoweiss*, March 23, 2011, accessed April 28, 2022: mondoweiss.net/2011/03/university-of-johannesburg-to-officially-severed-ties-with-israel%E2%80%99s-ben-gurion-university/.

10. See Nora Barrows-Friedman, *In Our Power: U.S. Students Organize for Justice in Palestine* (Charlottesville, VA: Just World Books, 2014).

11. For two recent announcements of the "failure" of BDS, see Steven A. Cook, "The Anti-Israel BDS Movement Has Already Lost," *Foreign Policy*, May 19, 2022, accessed June 12, 2022, foreignpolicy.com/2022/05/19/bds-movement-boycott-israel-palestine-harvard-crimson/; Eric Alterman, "Altercation: Israel and Palestine and the Absence of a Solution," *The American Prospect*, June 3, 2022, accessed June 12, 2022, prospect.org/world/altercation-israel-palestine-absence-of-a-solution/. On Israeli state expenditure against BDS, see Adnan Abu Amer, "Israel Is Frustrated at the Failure to Tackle the BDS Movement," *Middle East Monitor*, August 27, 2020, accessed April 28, 2022, www.middleeastmonitor.com/20200827-israel-is-frustrated-at-the-failure-to-tackle-the-bds-movement/.

12. Jewish Telegraphic Agency (JTA), "Israel Okays $72 Million Anti-BDS Project," *Times of Israel*, December 29, 2017, accessed April 28, 2022, www.timesofisrael.com/israel-okays-72-million-anti-bds-project/.

13. Already in 2010 the "Jerusalem Declaration" signed by four European far-right leaders expressed support for Israel's anti-Palestinianism: see Tom Heneghan, "Europe Far Right Courts Israel in Anti-Islam Drive," *Reuters*, December 21, 2010, accessed April 28, 2022, www.reuters.com/article/us-europe-islam-far-right-idUSTRE6BJ37120101220.

14. Steven Salaita, *Inter/Nationalism: Decolonizing Native America and Palestine* (Minneapolis: University of Minnesota Press, 2016), 49.

15. See Jamie Stern-Weiner, ed., *Antisemitism and the Labour Party* (London: Verso, 2019).

16. Sam Biddle, "Facebook's Secret Rules about the Word 'Zionist' Impede Criticism of Israel," *The Intercept*, May 15, 2021, accessed June 25, 2022, theintercept.com/2021/05/14/facebook-israel-zionist-moderation/.

17. On this question, see, for instance, Marc Lamont Hill and Mitchell Plitnick, *Except for Palestine: The Limits of Progressive Politics* (New York: The New Press, 2021), 36–48.

18. See, for instance, Ilan Pappé, *A History of Modern Palestine*, 2nd ed. (Cambridge: Cambridge University Press, 2006), 53.

19. Salaita, *Inter/Nationalism*, 39.

20. Salaita, *Inter/Nationalism*, 38.

1. INSTITUTIONS OF OCCUPATION AND RESISTANCE

1. Fayez A. Sayegh, *Zionist Colonialism in Palestine* (Beirut: Research Centre Palestine Liberation Organization, 1965), 31, 52.

2. John Dugard and John Reynolds, for example, state that Israeli apartheid is "not only reminiscent of – and, in some cases, worse than – apartheid as it existed in South Africa" but "in breach of the legal prohibition of apartheid" itself: see "Apartheid, International Law, and the Occupied Palestinian Territory," *European Journal of International Law* 24, no. 3 (2013): 912. See also Raef Zreik and Azar Dakwar, "What's in the Apartheid Analogy? Palestine/Israel Refracted," *Theory & Event* 23, no. 3 (2020): 664–705; Robert Wintemute, "Israel-Palestine through the Lens of Racial Discrimination Law: Is the South African Apartheid Analogy Accurate, and What If the European Convention Applied?" *King's Law Journal* 28, no. 1(2017): 89–129; Richard Falk and Virginia Tilley, *Israeli Practices towards the Palestinian People and the Question of Apartheid* (*Palestine and the Israeli Occupation, Issue No. 1*, United Nations Economic and Social Commission for Western Asia, 2017), accessed April 28, 2022, opensiuc.lib.siu.edu/ps_pubs/9/. In 2021, the Israeli NGOs B'Tselem and Human Rights Watch both published reports confirming the apartheid character of the Israeli regime. Amnesty International, Harvard Law School's International Human Rights Clinic and Al Haq, Addameer and Habitat International Coalition all followed in 2022.

3. Samer Abdelnour, "Beyond South Africa: Understanding Israeli Apartheid," *Al Shabaka: The Palestinian Policy Network*, April 4, 2013, accessed April 28, 2022, al-shabaka.org/briefs/beyond-south-africa-understanding-israeli-aparthei/.

4. Adam Raz, "When the Shin Bet Chief Warned That Educated Arabs Are a 'Problem' for Israel," *Haaretz*, September 16, 2021, accessed April 28, 2022, www.haaretz.com/israel-news/.premium-when-the-shin-bet-chief-warned-that-educated-arabs-are-a-problem-for-israel-1.10214323. On Palestine as a historic center of learning, see Nur Masalha, *Palestine: A Four Thousand Year History* (London: Zed Books, 2018). On the immediate pre-Nakba period, see Ami Ayalon, *Reading Palestine: Printing and Literacy, 1900–1948* (Austin: University of Texas Press, 2004).

5. Gabi Baramki, *Peaceful Resistance: Building a Palestinian University under Occupation* (London: Pluto Press, 2010), 35. On Palestinians' commitment to, and involvement in, higher education, see Nabeel Shaath, "High Level Palestinian Manpower," *Journal of Palestine Studies* 1, no. 2 (1972): 80–95; Ibrahim Abu Lughod, "Educating a Community in Exile: The Palestinian Experience," *Journal of Palestine Studies* 2, no. 3 (1973): 94–111.

6. Ido Zelkowitz, *Students and Resistance in Palestine: Books, Guns and Politics* (Abingdon: Routledge, 2015), 99. See also Sam Bahour, "Exporting Palestinian Education to Palestinians: Documenting Yet Another Step Forward," *Jadaliyya*, July 9, 2018, accessed April 28, 2022, www.jadaliyya.com/Details/37749/Exporting-Palestinian-Education-to-Palestinians-Documenting-Yet-Another-Step-Forward.

7. Ibrahim Abu Lughod, "Palestinian Higher Education: National Identity, Liberation, and Globalization," *boundary 2* 27, no. 1 (2000): 88–89.

8. Christa Bruhn, "Higher Education as Empowerment: The Case of Palestinian Universities," *American Behavioral Scientist* 49, no. 8 (2006): 1127.

9. Omri Shafer Raviv discusses recommendations to increase the educational level of Palestinians in the occupied territories after 1967, "focusing on professions that were in high demand in neighboring Arab countries" since "[e]ach emigration wave of young men . . . had the potential to spur a larger wave of families in its aftermath." This proposal, on one estimate, promised to reduce the Palestinian population by one per cent annually: see "Studying an Occupied Society: Social Research, Modernization Theory and the Early Israeli Occupation, 1967–8," *Journal of Contemporary History* 55, no. 1 (2020): 175. See Gil Feiler on the "Israeli effort to push the Palestinian population out of the West Bank and Gaza Strip": "Palestinian Employment Prospects," *Middle East Journal* 47, no. 4 (1993): 639. See also Muhsin D. Yusuf, "The Potential Impact of Palestinian Education on a Palestinian State," *Journal of Palestine Studies* 8, no. 4 (1979): 70–93.

10. Abu Lughod, "Palestinian Higher Education," 82–83. According to Baramki, universities did not exacerbate the brain drain but reversed it: see Baramki, *Peaceful Resistance*, 166. Bethlehem University also presents its establishment as intended to stem the exodus of young people from Palestine: "About Bethlehem University," accessed June 11, 2022, www.bethlehem.edu/aboutbu/#more-info.

11. As stated, for example, on the "History and Traditions" webpage of An-Najah National University, accessed April 28, 2022, www.najah.edu/en/about/history-and-traditions/.

12. Abaher El Sakka, "Les universités palestiniennes: entre hiérarchisations académiques et attente sociale," *Hérodote* 168 (2018): 146.

13. Ibrahim Abu-Lughod, *Palestine Open University: Feasibility Study. General Report* (Paris: UNESCO, 1980), 10.

14. Muhammad Hallaj, "Mission of Palestinian Higher Education," *Journal of Palestine Studies* 9, no. 4 (1980): 86.

15. See *Birzeit University Annual Report, 2014–2015*, 44, accessed April 28, 2022, www.birzeit.edu/en/content/annual-report-2014-2015.

16. *Al Fajr* editorial, February 20, 1987, quoted by Anthony Thrall Sullivan, *Palestinian Universities under Occupation* (Cairo: American University in Cairo Press, 1988), 18.

17. El Sakka, "Les universités palestiniennes,"144; my translation.

18. See, for instance, Moath al-Amoudi, "Dahlan Bloc Upends Election at Fatah University in Gaza," *Al-Monitor*, March 12, 2019, accessed April 28, 2022, www.al-monitor.com/pulse/originals/2019/03/gaza-al-azhar-university-abbas-fatah-dahlan-dispute.html. Cary Nelson, in *Not in Kansas Anymore: Academic Freedom in Palestinian Universities* (Washington, DC: Academic Engagement Network, 2021), claims that the politicization of West Bank and Gazan campuses by Palestinians themselves, not the Israeli occupation, is the most serious obstacle to academic freedom in Palestinian higher education. Quite aside from the fact that Palestinians do not regularly bomb, shell or invade their own campuses or impose large-scale restrictions on the freedom of staff and students, Nelson ignores the fact that Palestinian politics is aimed at self-determination through freedom from the Israeli occupation and siege

and that it is therefore the latter, and not any notional Palestinian "cultural values" incompatible with free enquiry (44), that must bear ultimate responsibility for Palestinian universities' many problems. See chapter two for further discussion of Nelson's critique of Palestinian universities.

19. Noemi Casati, "Political Participation in a Palestinian University: Nablus Undergraduates' Political Subjectivities through Boredom, Fear and Consumption," *Ethnography* 17, no. 4 (2016): 524. On Palestinian universities and activism, see Mazin B. Qumsiyeh, *Popular Resistance in Palestine: A History of Hope and Empowerment* (London: Pluto, 2010).

20. "Right to Education Campaign Condemns Israeli Arrest of Birzeit University's Head of Student Council," *Palestine News & Info Agency (WAFA)*, November 19, 2018, accessed April 29, 2022, english.wafa.ps/page.aspx?id=CQT8Yca1065040159 59aCQT8Yc; see also Anat Matar, "In Its War on Palestinian Students, Israel Deems Book Fairs and Falafel Sales a Crime," *+972 Magazine*, February 3, 2021, accessed April 29, 2022, www.972mag.com/palestinian-university-students-israel-arrests/.

21. Daphna Golan, *Teaching Palestine on an Israeli University Campus: Unsettling Denial* (London: Anthem Press, 2020), 36–37.

22. Saree Makdisi, *Palestine Inside Out: An Everyday Occupation* (New York: W.W. Norton, 2010), 204.

23. For a detailed description of West Bank checkpoints, see Makdisi, *Palestine Inside Out*.

24. According to a university staff member I interviewed in Bethlehem in 2019, some students say they wear the hijab and/or long dresses because it makes them feel safer or better covered when crossing checkpoints, or in case they are manhandled by police or IDF.

25. See Association of Academics for the Respect of International Law in Palestine (AURDIP), "Palestinian Universities under Occupation," AURDIP (website), July 1, 2015, accessed April 29, 2022, www.aurdip.org/palestinian-universities-under.html.

26. See El Sakka, "Les universités palestiniennes," 141–50.

27. In 2019, for instance, Bethlehem University had, according to one of its staff members whom I interviewed that year, no or almost no academics from Ramallah.

28. See *Overview of the Higher Education System – Palestine* (Luxembourg: Publications Office of the European Union, 2017), 13.

29. Stuart Laing, "Letter from BRISMES Protesting against Israeli Violations of Palestinian Academic Freedom," BRISMES (website), 2019, accessed June 11, 2022, www.brismes.ac.uk/files/download/documents/BRISMES_Israeli_Gvt.pdf.

30. "Birzeit University Says Israel's Denial of Permit for Foreign Lecturers Hampers Education," *WAFA*, July 12, 2018, accessed April 29, 2022, english.wafa.ps/page.aspx?id=CQT8Yca98401742670aCQT8Yc.

31. See the Academia for Equality petition available at docs.google.com/forms/d/e/1FAIpQLSfxbyzS9gPuiuNqD1vDpvbm2Cc9VgAm0OD5lRR8wf8IVdZRig/viewform. See also "Israel Forcing International Lecturers Out of West Bank Palestinian Universities," Adalah – The Legal Center for Arab Minority Rights in Israel (website), April 20, 2021, accessed April 29, 2022, www.adalah.org/en/content/view/9767; Scientists for Palestine, "Impact of the Israeli Occupation on Palestinian

Science, Education, and Research," conversation streamed live on September 26, 2020, YouTube video, 1:24:27, accessed April 29, 2022, youtu.be/KRa_-n6D2FA.

32. "Israel to Decide Which Foreign Lecturers Allowed to Teach in Palestinian Universities," *Middle East Eye*, March 8, 2022, accessed April 29, 2022, www.middleeasteye.net/news/israel-palestine-lecturers-allowed-teach-universities.

33. Ruhan Nagra, *Academia Undermined: Israeli Restrictions on Foreign National Academics in Palestinian Higher Education Institutions* (Ramallah: Right to Enter, 2013), 20.

34. *Country Programming Document for Palestine 2014–2017* (Ramallah: UNESCO Office Ramallah, 2014), 9, accessed April 29, 2022, unesdoc.unesco.org/ark:/48223/pf0000230212.

35. See Addameer Prisoner Support and Human Rights Association, *Opened – Books on Cuffed – Hands: The Cultural and Educational Life of Palestinian Political Prisoners in Israeli Prisons and Detention Centers* (Ramallah: Addameer, 2020), 45.

36. See Addameer, *Opened – Books on Cuffed – Hands*, 48–49 and 57ff; Addameer Prisoner Support and Human Rights Association, "Access to Education," December 2015, accessed July 7, 2022, mail.addameer.org/key_issues/access_to_education.

37. In the words of a student quoted by Baramki, "All we have now is education, so I study." Baramki, *Peaceful Resistance*, 147.

38. Quoted by Robert Boyce, "Denial of Academic Freedom in the West Bank," *British Committee for the Universities of Palestine (BRICUP) Newsletter* 99 (May 2016): 5–6.

39. See Ida Audeh, ed., *Birzeit University: The Story of a National Institution* (Birzeit: Birzeit University Publications, 2010), xiv.

40. Jaclynn Ashly, "Israel Is Turning Palestinian Students into Criminals," *+973 Magazine*, October 31, 2019, accessed April 29, 2022, www.972mag.com/birzeit-student-arrests-israel/. The Palestinian Authority and Hamas also arrest academics and students on political grounds: see Budour Youssef Hassan, "Palestinian Authority Arrests Dissident Professor," *The Electronic Intifada*, February 5, 2016, accessed April 29, 2022, electronicintifada.net/content/palestinian-authority-arrests-dissident-professor/15526; Human Rights Watch, *Two Authorities, One Way, Zero Dissent: Arbitrary Arrest and Torture under the Palestinian Authority and Hamas* (Human Rights Watch, 2018), 38–41, 70–71.

41. "Statement about the Israeli Occupation's Arrest of Birzeit University Students, Faculty Members," Birzeit University (website), January 23, 2020, accessed April 29, 2022, www.birzeit.edu/en/news/statement-about-israeli-occupations-arrest-birzeit-university-students-faculty-members.

42. Baramki, *Peaceful Resistance*, 57.

43. Gabi Baramki, "Running a University under Israeli Military Occupation," in *Birzeit University: The Story of a National Institution*, ed. Ida Audeh (Birzeit: Birzeit University Publications, 2010), 54.

44. "Imad Ahmad Barghouthi Released," *BRICUP Newsletter* 104 (November 2016): 8; "Barghouthi Ordered to Two Months in Administrative Detention by Ofer Military Court," Samidoun – Palestinian Prisoner Solidarity Network (website), May 11, 2016, accessed April 29, 2022, samidoun.net/2016/05/

barghouthi-ordered-to-two-months-in-administrative-detention-by-ofer-military-court/. See also the Scientists for Palestine, "Academic Freedom in Palestine: A Conversation with Imad Barghouthi," seminar streamed live on August 28, 2021, Facebook video, 1:31:28, accessed April 29, 2022, www.facebook.com/watch/live/?ref=watch_permalink&v=280813893414963.

45. "Palestinian Professor Essam al-Ashqar Ordered to Two More Months in Administrative Detention," Samidoun – Palestinian Prisoner Solidarity Network (website), July 7, 2017, accessed April 29, 2022, samidoun.net/2017/07/palestinian-professor-essam-al-ashqar-ordered-to-two-more-months-in-administrative-detention/; "Statement about the Israeli Occupation's Arrest of Birzeit University Students, Faculty Members."

46. See Joseph Nasr, "Book Ban Ends Rare Arab-Israeli Cultural Exchange," *Reuters*, October 1, 2008, accessed April 29, 2022, www.reuters.com/article/us-israel-books-ban/book-ban-ends-rare-arab-israeli-cultural-exchange-idUSTRE49004R20081001; David M. Halbfinger, "Arabic Readers in Israel Have to Hope the Border Guards Are Sloppy," *New York Times*, September 23, 2019, accessed April 29, 2022, www.nytimes.com/2019/09/20/world/middleeast/arab-books-israel-lebanon.html; AURDIP, "Palestinian Universities under Occupation." For details on censorship in an earlier period, see Sullivan, *Palestinian Universities under Occupation*, 15.

47. *Overview of the Higher Education System – Palestine*, 11.

48. Except where otherwise indicated, press releases from the Ma'an and the Palestinian Authority's WAFA news agency are the source of all the details conveyed here: english.wafa.ps/, www.maannews.com. Not all of the original media releases are still available.

49. These details are from "Israeli Occupation Forces Assault on the Abu Jihad Centre for Captive Movements at Al Quds University," *BRICUP Newsletter* 118 (February 2018): 4.

50. "Israeli Forces Kill Palestinian Student, Former Prisoner during Clashes in Qalqiliya," *Ma'an*, January 16, 2018, accessed December 27, 2018, www.maannews.com/Content.aspx?id=779753, original webpage discontinued.

51. "Israeli Forces Attack Students of Hebron Technical University," *WAFA News Agency*, March 4, 2018, accessed April 29, 2022, english.wafa.ps/page.aspx?id=ru3OGoa96754258227aru3OGo.

52. "Israeli Army Abducts a University Student, and a Former Political Prisoner, near Jenin," *International Middle East Media Center (IMEMC) News*, March 6, 2018, accessed April 29, 2022, imemc.org/article/israeli-army-abducts-a-university-student-and-a-former-political-prisoner-near-jenin/.

53. "Our Students Imprisoned Away from Sunlight," Right2Edu: Right to Education Campaign – Birzeit University (website), April 18, 2018, accessed April 29, 2022, right2edu.birzeit.edu/our-students-imprisoned-away-from-sunlight/.

54. "Army Abducts a University Student in Hebron, Injures Several Others," *IMEMC News*, April 25, 2018, accessed April 29, 2022, imemc.org/article/army-abducts-a-university-student-in-hebron-injures-several-others/.

55. "Israeli Soldiers Close Kadoorie University's Entrances, Injure Four Students," *IMEMC News*, April 26, 2018, accessed April 29, 2022, imemc.org/article/israeli-soldiers-close-kadoorie-universitys-entrances-injure-four-students/.

56. News article, Ma'an News Agency, 2018, accessed December 27, 2018, www.maannews.com/Content.aspx?id=780946, original webpage discontinued.

57. News article, Ma'an News Agency, 2018, accessed December 27, 2018, www.maannews.com/Content.aspx?id=781150, original webpage discontinued.

58. News article, Ma'an News Agency, 2018, accessed December 27, 2018, www.maannews.com/Content.aspx?id=781843, original webpage discontinued.

59. "Israel Will No Longer Recognize Degrees from Al-Quds University," *IMEMC News*, December 5, 2018, accessed May 2, 2022, imemc.org/article/israel-will-no-longer-recognize-degrees-from-al-quds-university/.

60. See "Israel Attacks Palestinian University in Jerusalem," *Middle East Monitor*, December 13, 2018, accessed May 2, 2022, www.middleeastmonitor.com/20181213-israel-attacks-palestinian-university-in-jerusalem/.

61. "Army Injures Many Palestinians near Hebron," *IMEMC News*, December 23, 2018, accessed May 2, 2022, imemc.org/article/army-injures-many-palestinians-near-hebron-2/.

62. Makdisi, *Palestine Inside Out*, 204.

63. All details in UNESCO, *Rapid Assessment of Higher Education Institutions in Gaza: Data Analysis Report* (United Nations Education, Scientific and Cultural Organization in collaboration with Enabling Education Network CIC, 2015).

64. Amr EL-Tohamy, "Palestine's Education Institutions Are Victims of Conflict Again," *Al-Fanar Media*, May 18, 2021, accessed May 2, 2022, www.al-fanarmedia.org/2021/05/palestines-education-institutions-are-victims-of-conflict-again/.

65. Sunaina Maira, *Boycott! The Academy and Justice for Palestine* (Oakland: University of California Press, 2018), 8.

66. Judith Butler, "Exercising Rights: Academic Freedom and Boycott Politics," in *Who's Afraid of Academic Freedom?* eds. Alex Bilgrami and Jonathan R. Cole (New York: Columbia University Press, 2015), 293.

67. David Newman, "The Failure of Academic Boycotts," *Geographical Review* 106, no. 2 (2016): 267.

68. For lack of protest as a criterion of complicity, see Anton Leist, "Israel and the Boycott, Divestment, Sanctions Campaign: Academic Freedom and the Palestinian Academic Boycott," *Journal of Holy Land and Palestine Studies* 16, no. 2 (2017): 230.

69. For two recent overviews, see Lisa Taraki, "The Complicity of the Israeli Academy in the Structures of Domination and State Violence," in *Against Apartheid: The Case for Boycotting Israeli Universities*, eds. Ashley Dawson and Bill V. Mullen (Chicago: Haymarket, 2015), 21–29; Ronit Lentin, "Colonial Academic Control in Palestine and Israel: Blueprint for Repression?" in *Enforcing Silence: Academic Freedom, Palestine and the Criticism of Israel,* eds. David Landy, Ronit Lentin and Conor McCarthy (London: Zed Books, 2020), 207–30.

70. "Technion History," Technion: Israel Institute of Technology (website), accessed May 2, 2022, www.technion.ac.il/en/history-of-the-technion/.

71. In Carl Alpert, *Technion: The Story of Israel's Institute of Technology* (New York: American Technion Society, 1982).

72. "Higher Education in Israel: The Hebrew University of Jerusalem," Jewish Virtual Library (website), accessed May 2, 2022, www.jewishvirtuallibrary.org/the-hebrew-university-of-jerusalem.

73. Yfaat Weiss, "'Nicht durch Macht und nicht durch Kraft, sondern durch meinen Geist': Die Hebräische Universität in der Skopusberg-Enklave," *Simon Dubnow Yearbook* 14 (2015): 12. See also Diana Dolev, *The Planning and Building of the Hebrew University, 1919–1948: Facing the Temple Mount* (Lanham, MD: Lexington Books, 2016).

74. On Beersheba, see Ilan Pappé, *The Ethnic Cleansing of Palestine* (London: Oneworld, 2006), 195; on al-Shaykh Muwannis, see Pappé, *The Ethnic Cleansing of Palestine*, 103, and "Welcome To al-Shaykh Muwannis," PalestineRemembered.com (website), accessed May 2, 2022, www.palestineremembered.com/Jaffa/al-Shaykh-Muwannis/index.html. On HUJ's Mount Scopus campus, see Omar Barghouti and Lisa Taraki, "Freedom versus 'Academic Freedom': Debating the British Academic Boycott," in *BDS: Boycott, Divestment, Sanctions: The Global Struggle for Palestinian Rights*, by Omar Barghouti (Chicago: Haymarket, 2011), 114–15; Yfaat Weiss, "Resting in Peace in No Man's Land: Human Dignity and Political Sovereignty at the British Commonwealth's Jerusalem War Cemetery, Mount Scopus," *Jerusalem Quarterly* 72 (2017): 71–76; "Explanatory Note" to "Statement by Legal Scholars and International Lawyers against Holding ESIL Forum at the Hebrew University in East Jerusalem," Critical Legal Thinking (website), November 23, 2017, accessed May 2, 2022, criticallegalthinking.com/2017/11/23/statement-against-holding-esil-at-the-hebrew-university/; The Land Research Center (LRC), "Hebrew University Expansionist Plans," Poica: Eye on Palestine (website), December 7, 2004, accessed May 2, 2022, poica.org/2004/12/hebrew-university-expansionist-plans/; Ilan Pappé, *The Biggest Prison on Earth* (London: Oneworld, 2017), 84–85.

75. "Higher Education in Israel: The Hebrew University of Jerusalem," Jewish Virtual Library (website), accessed June 12, 2022, www.jewishvirtuallibrary.org/the-hebrew-university-of-jerusalem.

76. "Higher Education in Israel"; Nir Hasson, "Hebrew University to Become First Israeli School to Recognize Palestinian Authority Test Scores," *Haaretz*, March 3, 2017, accessed May 2, 2022, www.haaretz.com/israel-news/.premium-hebrew-university-to-recognize-palestinian-authority-test-scores-1.5443610; Nir Hasson, "Hebrew U. to Offer Preparatory Course for East Jerusalem Palestinians," *Haaretz*, May 20, 2015, accessed May 2, 2022, www.haaretz.com/.premium-hebrew-u-to-offer-course-for-e-jlem-palestinians-1.5364130.

77. See A. L. Tibawi, "The Project for a British University in Palestine," *Journal of the Royal Central Asian Society* 40, no. 3–4 (1953): 225.

78. Pinhas Ofer, "A Scheme for the Establishment of a British University in Jerusalem in the Late 1920s," *Middle Eastern Studies* 22, no. 2 (1986): 274–85.

79. Tibawi, "The Project for a British University in Palestine," 230.

80. Lior Dattel, "Number of Arabs in Israeli Higher Education Grew 79% in Seven Years," *Haaretz*, January 24, 2018, accessed May 2, 2022, www.haaretz.com/israel-news/number-of-arabs-in-israeli-higher-education-grew-79-in-seven-years-1.5763067.

81. See Yarden Skop, "Tel Aviv University Tells Call Center Workers Not to Speak Arabic," *Haaretz*, February 17, 2016, accessed May 2, 2022, www.haaretz.com/israel-news/.premium-tel-aviv-u-tells-call-center-workers-not-to-speak-arabic-1.5405493.

82. Gish Amit, "Salvage or Plunder? Israel's 'Collection' of Private Palestinian Libraries in West Jerusalem," *Journal of Palestine Studies* 40, no. 4 (2011): 6–23.

83. Ilan Pappé, *The Idea of Israel: A History of Power and Knowledge* (London: Verso, 2014); Nadia Abu El-Haj, *Facts on the Ground: Archeological Practice and Territorial Self-Fashioning in Israeli Society* (Chicago: University of Chicago Press, 2001); *The Genealogical Science: The Search for Jewish Origins and the Politics of Epistemology* (Chicago: University of Chicago Press, 2012); Gil Eyal, "Dangerous Liaisons between Military Intelligence and Middle Eastern Studies in Israel," *Theory and Society* 31, no. 5 (2002): 653–93; Gad Yair and Noa Apeloig, "Israel and the Exile of Intellectual Caliber: Local Position and the Absence of Sociological Theory," *Sociology* 40, no. 1 (2006): 51–69; Sylvain Cypel, *Walled: Israeli Society at an Impasse* (New York: Other Press, 2006); Tikva Honig-Parnass, *False Prophets of Peace: Liberal Zionism and the Struggle for Palestine* (Chicago: Haymarket, 2011).

84. Yonatan Mendel, *The Creation of Israeli Arabic: Political and Security Considerations in the Making of Arabic Language Studies in Israel* (Basingstoke: Palgrave, 2014), 224. See Amit Levy, "German Philology, Zionist Ideology: The Contested Linguistic Legacy of Arabic Studies in Palestine/Israel," paper presented at the Labex TransferS-SHESL-SLP Conference, "La circulation des savoirs linguistiques et philologiques entre l'Allemagne et le monde, XVI-XXe siècles," Paris, January 2018. For wider exploration, see Edward Said, *The Question of Palestine* (London: Vintage, 1992), 26.

85. Amit Levy, "A Man of Contention: Martin Plessner (1900–1973) and his Encounters with the Orient," *Naharaim* 10, no. 1 (2016): 97.

86. Nir Hasson, "Right-Wing NGO Funding Tel Aviv University Dig in East Jerusalem," *Haaretz*, June 13, 2013, accessed May 2, 2022, www.haaretz.com/right-wing-ngo-funding-e-j-lem-dig-1.5279147; "Teens Find Ancient Coins in Samaria," *Israel National News*, October 26, 2021, accessed May 2, 2022, www.israelnationalnews.com/news/315757.

87. El-Haj, *Facts on the Ground*, 280–81.

88. "About Us," Emek Shaveh (website), accessed May 2, 2022, emekshaveh.org/en/about-us/; Haggai Matar, "Because BDS, Israeli Archaeologists Want West Bank Work Kept Secret," BDS Movement (website), November 22, 2016, accessed May 2, 2022, bdsmovement.net/news/because-bds-israeli-archeologists-want-west-bank-work-kept-secret. See Ziv Stahl's December 2017 report for the Israeli NGOs Emek Shaveh and Yesh Din: *Appropriating the Past: Israel's Archaeological Practices in the West Bank,* accessed December 11, 2020, emekshaveh.org/en/wp-content/uploads/2017/12/Menachsim-Eng-Web.pdf.

89. See Nur Masalha, "New History, Post-Zionism and Neo-Colonialism: A Critique of the Israeli 'New Historians,'" *Holy Land Studies* 10, no. 1 (2011): 1–53.

90. See Ilan Pappé, *Out of the Frame* (London: Pluto Press, 2010).

91. B. N. [anonymous author], "How the Israeli Right Conspired to Shut Down 'Lefty' Department at BGU," *+972 Magazine*, October 24, 2012, accessed November 21, 2020, www.972mag.com/who-and-what-are-behind-the-attacks-on-ben-gurion-universitys-politics-and-government-department/.

92. Chen Misgav, "The Silence of Israeli Academics," *Haaretz*, March 21, 2017, accessed May 2, 2022, www.haaretz.com/opinion/.premium-the-silence-of-israeli-academics-1.5451128. See also Moshe Shoked, "In Our Very Own Weimar Republic,

Israeli Academics Stay Resoundingly Silent," *Haaretz*, February 19, 2016, accessed May 2, 2022, www.haaretz.com/opinion/.premium-passive-in-our-israeli-weimar-republic-1.5406433; Lisa Taraki, "The Silence of the Israeli Intelligentsia," *Counterpunch*, September 10, 2010, accessed May 2, 2022, www.counterpunch.org/2010/09/10/the-silence-of-the-israeli-intelligentsia/. In 2013, the *Haaretz* Education correspondent wrote that "faced with the campaign being waged by the right to reshape reality, academia – as an institution based on values like skepticism, tolerance and pluralism – has barely raised its voice": Or Kashti, "Toppling Israel's Ivory Tower," *Haaretz*, January 20, 2013, accessed June 11, 2022, www.haaretz.com/opinion/2013-01-20/ty-article/.premium/or-kashti-silence-of-the-academics/0000017f-f7fc-d318-afff-f7ffb1c10000.

93. Baramki, *Peaceful Resistance*, 79.

94. Yarden Skop, "Israeli University Faculty Protest Expansion of Gender-Segregated Programs," *Haaretz*, May 30, 2017, accessed May 2, 2022, www.haaretz.com/israel-news/.premium-university-faculty-protest-expansion-of-gender-segregated-programs-1.5478470.

95. Amira Haas, "Israeli University Heads Say Won't Intervene in Discrimination against Palestinian Schools," *Haaretz*, August 28, 2019, accessed May 2, 2022, www.haaretz.com/israel-news/.premium-israeli-university-heads-say-won-t-intervene-in-discrimination-against-palestinians-1.7764492.

96. Haim Bresheeth-Žabner, *An Army Like No Other: How the Israel Defense Forces Made a Nation* (London: Verso, 2020), 154.

97. Omri Shafer Raviv, "Studying an Occupied Society: Social Research, Modernization Theory and the Early Israeli Occupation, 1967–1968," *Journal of Contemporary History* 55, no. 1 (2020): 169.

98. Bresheeth-Žabner, *An Army Like No Other*, 82.

99. Ahmed Abbes and Ivar Ekeland, "The Technion: An Elite University for Israeli Student-Soldiers," *The New Arab*, November 9, 2014, accessed May 2, 2022, www.alaraby.co.uk/english/features/2014/11/9/the-technion-an-elite-university-for-israeli-student-soldiers; Allison Deger, "Israeli University Gaining a Toehold in Manhattan Specializes in Weapons Development," *Mondoweiss*, December 23, 2011, original webpage discontinued, screenshot accessed May 2, 2022, web.archive.org/web/20210211115827/https://mondoweiss.net/2011/12/israeli-university-gaining-a-toehold-in-manhattan-specializes-in-weapons-development/.

100. Technion Research and Development Foundation, *Industry Guide to Technion: Research Projects, Research Services, Technology Transfer* (Haifa: Technion – Israel Institute of Technology, 2014), 79, accessed May 2, 2022, www.technion.ac.il/wp-content/uploads/2014/07/INDUSTRY-GUIDE-TO-TECHNION_L.pdf.

101. Abbes and Ekeland, "The Technion: An Elite University for Israeli Student-Soldiers."

102. "Ben-Gurion University to Receive NIS 55 Million Upgrade Ahead of IDF Move to Negev," Ben-Gurion University of the Negev (website), October 16, 2018, accessed May 2, 2022, in.bgu.ac.il/en/pages/news/upgrade_idf.aspx; "It's Official: IDF Tech Corps Moving to Ben-Gurion University," Ben-Gurion University of the Negev (website), November 6, 2018, accessed May 2, 2022, in.bgu.ac.il/en/pages/news/idf_tech.aspx.

103. Maya Mirsky, "How This Israeli University Is Creating Robotic Life in the Desert," *The Jewish News of Northern California*, July 26, 2018, accessed May 2, 2022, www.jweekly.com/2018/07/26/beyond-sci-fi-israels-ben-gurion-university-of-the-negev-moves-forward-with-robot-technology/.

104. Yara Sa'di, "Warmongering Hebrew University Tries to Muzzle Palestinian Students," *The Electronic Intifada*, October 10, 2014, accessed May 2, 2022, electronicintifada.net/content/warmongering-hebrew-university-tries-muzzle-palestinian-students/13941.

105. Yaniv Cogan, "Academia, Weapons and Occupation: How Tel Aviv University Serves the Interests of the Israeli Military and Arms Industry," BDS Movement (website), May 4, 2022, accessed June 25, 2022, bdsmovement.net/news/academia-weapons-and-occupation-how-tel-aviv-university-serves-interests-israeli-military-and; "TAU and IDF Launch Air and Space Power Center," Tel Aviv University (website), January 5, 2022, accessed June 25, 2022, english.tau.ac.il/news/air-and-space-power. See also "Tel Aviv University – A Leading Israeli Military Research Centre," Urgent Briefing Paper 4493, SOAS Palestine Society, February 2009, accessed July 15, 2022, bdsmovement.net/sites/default/files/SOAS-Palestine-Society-Paper-TAU-Military-Complicity-Feb-2009_0.pdf.

106. "Students Connect to Combat Anti-Israel Incitement Online," *Heights: University of Haifa Magazine*, Spring 2017, accessed June 26, 2022, magazine.haifa.ac.il/index.php/inside-5/31-students-connect-to-combat-anti-israel-incitement-online.

107. See "The Public Diplomacy Program," Reichman University (website), accessed May 2, 2022, www.runi.ac.il/en/special-programs/pd/; Daniel Lark, "Call of Duty," *Jewish Currents*, August 10, 2020, accessed May 2, 2022, jewishcurrents.org/call-of-duty/.

108. See Shira Kadari-Ovadia, "Jerusalem's Hebrew U to Give Students Credit for Volunteering with Right-Wing Group That Blacklists Academics," *Haaretz*, February 13, 2020, accessed May 2, 2022, www.haaretz.com/israel-news/.premium-hebrew-university-to-give-students-credit-for-volunteering-with-right-wing-group-1.8528417.

109. "The National Security Studies Center – Home Page," University of Haifa (website), accessed May 2, 2022, nssc.haifa.ac.il/index.php/en/./.

110. Eyal Pascovich, "Security and Intelligence Studies in Israel," *The International Journal of Intelligence, Security, and Public Affairs* 19, no. 2 (2017): 137.

111. Udi Dekel and Kim Lavi, "Questions and Answers on the INSS Plan: A Strategic Framework for the Israeli-Palestinian Arena," INSS: The Institute for National Security Studies (website), November 6, 2018, accessed May 2, 2022, www.inss.org.il/publication/questions-answers-inss-plan-strategic-framework-israeli-palestinian-arena/.

112. "The INSS Plan: A Political-Security Framework for the Israeli-Palestinian Arena," INSS: The Institute for National Security Studies (website), accessed May 2, 2022, www.inss.org.il/inss-plan-political-security-framework-israeli-palestinian-arena/.

113. Udi Dekel, "Operation Guardian of the Walls: Envisioning the End," *INSS Insight*, no. 1468, May 19, 2021, accessed May 2, 2022, www.inss.org.il/publication/operation-ending.

114. Udi Dekel, "Operation Guardian of the Walls: The Need for an Integrated Multi-Front Strategy," *INSS Insight*, no. 1467, May 16, 2021, accessed May 2, 2022, www.inss.org.il/publication/guardian-of-the-walls/.

115. See Gabi Siboni, "Disproportionate Force: Israel's Concept of Response in Light of the Second Lebanon War," *INSS Insight*, no. 74, October 2, 2008, accessed May 2, 2022, www.inss.org.il/publication/disproportionate-force-israels-concept-of-response-in-light-of-the-second-lebanon-war/.

116. See "About the Moshe Dayan Center (MDC)," The Moshe Dayan Center for Middle Eastern and African Studies (website), accessed March 22, 2020, dayan.org/content/about-moshe-dayan-center-mdc. For a discussion of the Dayan Center and its earlier incarnation, the Shiloah Institute, see Gil Eyal, *The Disenchantment of the Orient: Expertise in Arab Affairs and the Israeli State* (Stanford: Stanford University Press, 2006), 197–206.

117. See "Mission," BESA: The Begin-Sadat Center for Strategic Studies, Bar-Ilan University (website), accessed May 2, 2022, besacenter.org/about/mission/.

118. See Pascovich, "Security and Intelligence Studies in Israel," 138.

119. Hillel Frisch, "Another Round, Not More Extortion, Is Needed in Gaza," BESA: The Begin-Sadat Center for Strategic Studies, Bar-Ilan University (website), BESA Center Perspectives Paper no. 1017, November 27, 2018, accessed May 2, 2022, besacenter.org/perspectives-papers/gaza-fighting-extortion/.

120. Larry D. Weiss, "Boycott Palestine," BESA: The Begin-Sadat Center for Strategic Studies, Bar-Ilan University (website), BESA Center Perspectives Paper no. 2,052, May 27, 2021, accessed May 2, 2022, besacenter.org/boycott-palestine/; Gershon Hacohen, "Lessons of the Gaza War," BESA: The Begin-Sadat Center for Strategic Studies, Bar-Ilan University (website), BESA Center Perspectives Paper no. 2,059, May 31, 2021, accessed May 2, 2022, besacenter.org/lessons-of-the-gaza-war/.

121. Bresheeth-Žabner, *An Army Like No Other*, 81. For details of the historically "dynamic partnership among colonial administrators, army officers, intelligence operatives and academics" (22), see Taraki, "The Complicity of the Israeli Academy in the Structures of Domination and State Violence."

122. Judy Maltz, "Why Adelson Is Pouring Millions into an Israeli University in the West Bank," *Haaretz*, July 20, 2017, accessed May 2, 2022, www.haaretz.com/israel-news/.premium-why-adelson-pours-millions-into-a-west-bank-university-1.5431239.

123. Tsivya Fox, "For First Time, IDF Will Fully Fund Soldier University Scholarships," *Israel365 News*, November 23, 2016, accessed May 2, 2022, www.breakingisraelnews.com/79016/first-time-idf-will-fully-fund-soldier-university-scholarships/.

124. "Full Scholarships to Veteran IDF Combat Soldiers," Bar-Ilan University (website), June 23, 2022, accessed June 26, 2022, www.biu.ac.il/en/article/11369.

125. This decision was taken voluntarily by universities. See Adir Yanko, "Who Is Responsible for Providing 2 Credit Points for Students in the Army Reserves?" *Ynet* [Hebrew], April 30, 2018, accessed May 2, 2022, www.ynet.co.il/articles/0,7340, L-5246374,00.html; Oren Oppenheim, "Knesset Advances Bill Granting Academic Credit to Reserve Soldiers," *Jerusalem Post*, June 26, 2018, accessed May 2, 2022, www.jpost.com/Israel-News/Knesset-advances-bill-granting-academic-credit-to-reserve-soldiers-560880.

126. Ali Abunimah, "Israeli Universities Lend Support to Gaza Massacre," *The Electronic Intifada*, July 25, 2014, accessed May 2, 2022, electronicintifada.net/blogs/ali-abunimah/israeli-universities-lend-support-gaza-massacre.

127. "University of Haifa Wins Tender for Military Colleges," *Arutz Sheva News*, June 25, 2018, accessed May 2, 2022, www.israelnationalnews.com/News/News.aspx/247962; Yaakov Lappin, "Israel's 'West Point' Increasingly Shapes the IDF Ground Forces," BESA: The Begin-Sadat Center for Strategic Studies, Bar-Ilan University (website), BESA Center Perspectives Paper no. 1,859, December 29, 2020, accessed May 2, 2022, besacenter.org/idf-tactical-command-college/.

128. See Pascovich, "Security and Intelligence Studies in Israel," 141.

129. Christopher Rhoads, "Secret Weapon: How an Elite Military School Feeds Israel's Tech Industry," *The Wall Street Journal*, July 6, 2007, accessed May 2, 2022, www.wsj.com/articles/SB118368825920758806; Jason Gewirtz, "Inside the IDF's Super-Secret Elite Brains Trust," *The Tower Magazine* 37 (April 2016), www.thetower.org/article/inside-the-idfs-super-secret-elite-brain-trust-talpiot/; "School of Military Medicine in Israel," Hadassah University Medical Center (website), accessed June 11, 2022, www.hadassah.org.il/en/militarymedschool/.

130. Ali Abunimah, "'Warrior Students': How Israeli Universities Are Supporting War Crimes in Gaza," *The Electronic Intifada*, August 18, 2014, accessed May 2, 2022, electronicintifada.net/blogs/ali-abunimah/warrior-students-how-israeli-universities-are-supporting-war-crimes-gaza.

131. "Following Outcry, Hebrew University Issues Pro-IDF Ad," *Jewish News Syndicate*, January 7, 2019, accessed June 11, 2022, www.jns.org/following-outcry-hebrew-university-issues-rare-pro-idf-ad/. See the translation of the advertisement in Yoni Molad, "As a Faculty Member, I No Longer Have Faith in the Administration of the Hebrew University [English translation of David Enoch's article]," Facebook, no date, www.facebook.com/notes/yoni-molad/as-a-faculty-member-i-no-longer-have-faith-in-the-administration-of-the-hebrew-u/10155718056647121/.

132. Chaim Levinson, "Israeli Universities Providing Data on Graduates to Shin Bet," *Haaretz*, June 11, 2015, accessed May 2, 2022, www.haaretz.com/.premium-universities-give-shin-bet-data-on-graduates-1.5371033.

133. Ilana Hammerman, "What I Saw at a Shin Bet Lecture at Jerusalem's Hebrew University," *Haaretz*, April 3, 2018, accessed May 2, 2022, www.haaretz.com/opinion/.premium-what-i-saw-at-a-shin-bet-lecture-at-hebrew-university-1.5974392.

134. James Eastwood, *Ethics as a Weapon of War: Militarism and Morality in Israel* (Cambridge: Cambridge University Press, 2017), 23, 232.

135. See Boycott, Divestment and Sanctions (BDS) Movement, "Hebrew University, Which Is Partially Built on Stolen Palestinian Land in Occupied East Jerusalem, Lends Its Rooftop to Israeli Police Surveilling the Palestinian Neighborhood of Issawiya," Facebook, January 17, 2020, www.facebook.com/BDSNationalCommittee/photos/a.129952410382961/2965413960170111/?type=3&theater.

136. For details, see the publicly available letter from Adalah to the OECD: Sawsan Zaher, Muna Haddad and Katie Hesketh, "Re: Adalah's Response to OECD Reports on Education in Israel, 2015 & 2016," Adalah: The Legal Center for Arab Minority Rights in Israel (website), September 1, 2016, accessed May 2, 2022, www.adalah.org/uploads/

uploads/Adalah_Response_to_OECD_1.9.2016.pdf; see also the report *Second Class: Discrimination against Palestinian Arab Children in Israel's Schools*, Human Rights Watch, September 30, 2001, accessed May 2, 2022, www.hrw.org/report/2001/09/30/second-class/discrimination-against-palestinian-arab-children-israels-schools.

137. See Omar Mizel, "'I Lost My Identity in the Halls of Academia': Arab Students on the Use of Arabic in Israeli Higher Education," *Issues in Educational Research* 31, no. 3 (2021); Yarden Zur, "Survey: Half of Arabs in Israeli Universities Suffer Racism – Israel News," *Haaretz*, July 5, 2017, accessed June 26, 2022, www.haaretz.com/israel-news/2017-07-05/ty-article/.premium/survey-half-of-arabs-in-israeli-universities-suffer-racism/0000017f-e605-df2c-a1ff-fe55d34e0000?lts=1656231694734; Jonathan Shamir, "A Revolution in Arabic Studies Is Shaking Up Israeli Universities," *Haaretz*, June 1, 2022, accessed June 26, 2022, www.haaretz.com/israel-news/2022-06-01/ty-article-magazine/.premium/a-revolution-in-arabic-studies-is-shaking-up-israeli-universities/00000181-1e66-db47-a5dd-9f6f7fb40000; Khalid Arar and Yonis Abu El-Hija, "Also a University for the Arab Minority in Israel: Stake Holders' Perceptions and Proposed Models," *Higher Education Policy* 31 (2018): 75–96; "Adalah's Initial Position on the Absorption of Discharged Soldiers Law – 1994 (Amendment No. 24, 2022), Which Was Approved by the Israeli Knesset on 23 May 2022," Adalah: The Legal Center for Arab Minority Rights in Israel (website), May 26, 2022, accessed June 26, 2022, www.adalah.org/en/content/view/10632.

138. Greer Fay Ashman, "Making History: First Arab Woman Appointed Dean at Hebrew University," *Jerusalem Post*, July 28, 2018, accessed May 2, 2022, www.jpost.com/Opinion/Making-history-first-Arab-woman-appointed-dean-at-Hebrew-University-563645. For details see Uri Ram, *Israeli Sociology: Text in Context*, (Cham: Palgrave Macmillan), 154; Tamar Hager and Yousef Jabareen, "From Marginalisation to Integration: Arab-Palestinians in Israeli Academia," *International Journal of Inclusive Education* 20, no. 5 (2016): 455–73; Golan, *Teaching Palestine on an Israeli University Campus*, 41.

139. Among many possible examples, see Shira Kadari-Ovadia, "Israeli University Cancels Event Marking Nakba Day, Citing Violation of Law," *Haaretz*, May 16, 2019, accessed June 26, 2022, www.haaretz.com/israel-news/2019-05-16/ty-article/.premium/in-first-israeli-university-bans-political-event-citing-violation-of-nakba-law/0000017f-e8be-df2c-a1ff-feff380b0000; "Adalah Appeals to Supreme Court against Haifa University's Decision to Prohibit Activities of Arab Student Clubs on Campus," Adalah: The Legal Center for Arab Minority Rights in Israel (website), June 5, 2014, accessed May 2, 2022, www.adalah.org/en/content/view/8287; Tamar Pileggi, "Haifa U. Arab Students Cleared for Nakba Day Event," *The Times of Israel*, September 16, 2014, accessed May 2, 2022, www.timesofisrael.com/haifa-u-arab-students-cleared-for-nakba-day-event/. In 2017, HUJ gave in to right-wing pressure and canceled a conference on the Palestinian prisoners' movement: see Yarden Skop, "After Right-Wing Pressure, Hebrew U. Cancels Confab on Palestinian Prisoners," *Haaretz*, May 15, 2017, accessed May 2, 2022, www.haaretz.com/israel-news/.premium-hebrew-u-cancels-confab-on-palestinian-prisoners-1.5471659. In 2018, a conference in East Jerusalem on Muslim endowment and property was

prevented from taking place, and fifteen participants were detained: see "Anger after Israel Shuts Down Palestinian Universities in East Jerusalem," *The New Arab*, July 15, 2018, accessed May 2, 2022, www.alaraby.co.uk/english/news/2018/7/15/anger-after-israel-shuts-down-palestinian-universities-in-jerusalem.

140. "Demonstrators Shut Roads, Airport as Women Strike to Protest Violence," *The Times of Israel*, December 4, 2018, accessed May 2, 2022, www.timesofisrael.com/demonstrators-shut-roads-airport-as-women-strike-to-protest-violence/.

141. Or Kashti, "Ben-Gurion University Slammed for Nixing Breaking the Silence's Prize," *Haaretz*, July 5, 2016, accessed May 2, 2022, www.haaretz.com/israel-news/.premium-bgu-slammed-for-nixing-breaking-the-silence-s-prize-1.5405871; Rami Younis, "Hebrew U. Threatens Palestinian Students with Expulsion over Political Activities," *+972 Magazine*, October 24, 2014, accessed May 2, 2022, 972mag.com/hebrew-u-threatens-palestinian-students-with-expulsion-for-political-activities/97987/; Yarden Zur, "Tel Aviv University Prevents Student from Holding Pro-Peace Events Because of Red Tape," *Haaretz*, May 28, 2018, accessed May 2, 2022, www.haaretz.com/israel-news/tau-prevents-student-pro-peace-events-based-on-permit-issue-1.6130870.

142. See, for instance, Chaim Hames, "South Africa's Shameful Capitulation to Anti-Israel Thuggery," *Haaretz*, November 28, 2018, accessed May 2, 2022, www.haaretz.com/world-news/south-africa-s-shameful-capitulation-to-anti-israel-thuggery-1.6698178; Or Kashti, "Israeli University Rebukes Professor Who Expressed Sympathy for Both Israeli, Gazan Victims," *Haaretz*, July 29, 2014, accessed May 2, 2022, www.haaretz.com/.premium-israeli-prof-rebuked-over-anti-war-message-1.5257329; Amira Hass, "Israeli University Heads Say Won't Intervene in Discrimination against Palestinian Schools," *Haaretz*, August 28, 2019, accessed May 2, 2022, www.haaretz.com/israel-news/.premium-israeli-university-heads-say-won-t-intervene-in-discrimination-against-palestinians-1.7764492; Judith E. Tucker and Laurie Brand, on behalf of the Middle East Studies Association Committee on Academic Freedom, "Public Smear Campaign against Nadera Shalhoub-Kevorkian and Hebrew University's Failure to Protect Her," Middle East Studies Association (website), March 15, 2019, accessed May 2, 2022, mesana.org/advocacy/committee-on-academic-freedom/2019/03/15/public-smear-campaign-against-nadera-shalhoub-kevorkian-and-hebrew-universitys-failure-to-protect-her; Somdeep Sen, "Israeli Apartheid on Campus," *Al Jazeera*, June 29, 2021, accessed May 2, 2022, www.aljazeera.com/opinions/2021/6/29/israeli-apartheid-on-campus.

143. Yarden Skop, "Israeli University Faculty Protest Expansion of Gender-Segregated Programs," *Haaretz*, May 30, 2017, accessed May 2, 2022, www.haaretz.com/israel-news/.premium-university-faculty-protest-expansion-of-gender-segregated-programs-1.5478470.

144. Yarden Zur, "Israeli Universities Urged to Bar Professors from Calling to Boycott Israel," *Haaretz*, March 25, 2018, accessed May 2, 2022, www.haaretz.com/israel-news/universities-urged-to-bar-professors-from-calling-to-boycott-israel-1.5938431; Alison Abbott, "In the Palestinian Territories, Science Struggles against All Odds," *Nature* 563, no. 7731 (2018): 308–11.

145. See Or Kashti, "Tel Aviv University Shutting Down Center for Peace Research," *Haaretz*, December 27, 2019, accessed May 2, 2022, www.haaretz.com/israel-news/.premium-tel-aviv-university-shutting-down-center-for-peace-research-1.8321470.

146. Batya Jerenberg, "'No Longer a Stepchild': University in Samaria Finally Recognized as an Equal," *World Israel News*, June 20, 2022, accessed June 21, 2022, worldisraelnews.com/no-longer-a-stepchild-university-in-samaria-finally-recognized-as-an-equal/.

147. Ilan Pappé, "The Tantura Case in Israel: The Katz Research and Trial," *Journal of Palestine Studies* 30, no. 3 (2001): 19–39; Jonathan Ofir, "The Tantura Massacre of 1948 and the Academic Character Assassination of Teddy Katz," *Mondoweiss*, March 3, 2016, accessed May 2, 2022, mondoweiss.net/2016/03/the-tantura-massacre-of-1948-and-the-academic-character-assassination-of-teddy-katz/.

148. David Rodin and Michael Yudkin, "Academic Boycotts," *The Journal of Political Philosophy* 19, no. 4 (2011): 477.

149. See F. W. Lancaster and Lorraine J. Haricombe, "The Academic Boycott of South Africa: Symbolic Gesture or Effective Agent of Change?" *Perspectives on the Professions* 15, no. 1 (1995): 2–4; Lorraine J. Haricombe and F. W. Lancaster, *Out in the Cold: Academic Boycotts and the Isolation of South Africa* (Arlington: Information Resources Press, 1995).

150. The fact that Israeli institutional funding is not a boycott trigger is regularly misunderstood by BDS opponents, including Cary Nelson, most recently in his book *Israel Denial: Anti-Zionism, Anti-Semitism, & the Faculty Campaign against the Jewish State* (Washington, DC: Academic Engagement Network and Bloomington: Indiana University Press, 2019). Nelson concentrates on statements by Judith Butler, which are contrary to the official boycott guidelines at bdsmovement.net/pacbi/academic-boycott-guidelines. These guidelines state that "an Israeli academic is entitled, as a taxpayer, to receive funding from his/her government or institution in support of academic activities, such as attendance of international conferences and other academic events, so long as this is not conditioned upon serving Israel's policy interests in any way, such as public acknowledgement of this support by the organizers of the conference or activity/event. Mere affiliation of the academic to an Israeli institution does not subject the conference or activity to boycott."

151. For example, David Newman incorrectly claims that the boycott asks scholars to "cease *all forms of collaboration with Israeli scientists and scholars*, regardless of their political positions on the Israel-Palestine conflict and the status of the Occupation." See Newman, "The Failure of Academic Boycotts," 264, emphasis added. Dan Avnon's entire case against his own boycotting in Australia in 2012 rests on the false premise that he was "singled out for boycott merely because of . . . being a Jewish-Israeli scholar": Dan Avnon, "BDS and the Dynamics of Self-Righteous Moralism," *Plus61JMedia: Australia, Israel and the Jewish World*, October 17, 2015, accessed May 2, 2022, plus61j.net.au/70th-anniversary-special/bds-and-the-dynamics-of-self-righteous-moralism/. Avnon was, in fact, subject to boycott because his visit to the University of Sydney was made possible through an institutional exchange agreement between Sydney and HUJ.

152. Rodin and Yudkin, "Academic Boycotts," 474.

153. 2014 figures: see UNESCO, "Six Ways to Ensure Higher Education Leaves No One Behind," Global Education Monitoring Report: Policy Paper 30, April 2017, accessed May 2, 2022, unesdoc.unesco.org/ark:/48223/pf0000247862.

154. Palestinian Campaign for the Academic and Cultural Boycott of Israel (PACBI), "Israel's Universities: A Pillar of Occupation and Apartheid," BDS Movement (website), November 8, 2014, accessed May 2, 2022, bdsmovement.net/news/israel%E2%80%99s-universities-pillar-occupation-and-apartheid. For some recent critique of the Palestinian BDS National Committee, see Naji Handallah, "A Tactic Not a Trademark: How the BDS National Committee Supports the Liberal Zionist Agenda," JISR Collective (website), July 5, 2022, accessed July 8, 2022, jisrcollective.com/pages/a-tactic-not-a-trademark.html.

155. Rifat Odeh Kassis, "Levelling the Scales by Force: Thoughts on Normalisation," in *Generation Palestine*, ed. Rich Wiles (London: Pluto Press, 2013), 83–84.

156. "Why Boycott Israeli Universities?" BDS Movement (website), accessed May 2, 2022, bdsmovement.net/academic-boycott#guidelines.

157. Baramki, *Peaceful Resistance*, 126.

158. On normalization, see Kassis, "Levelling the Scales by Force," 79–84.

2. THE ACADEMY AND ITS FREEDOMS

1. Russell A. Berman, "The Boycott as an Infringement on Academic Culture," in *The Case against Academic Boycotts of Israel*, eds. Cary Nelson and Gabriel Noah Brahm (Chicago: MLA Members for Scholars' Rights, 2014), 49.

2. Hilary Rose and Steven Rose, "Israel, Europe and the Academic Boycott," *Race and Class* 50, no. 1 (2008): 16.

3. David Rodin and Michael Yudkin, "Academic Boycotts," *The Journal of Political Philosophy* 19, no. 4 (2011): 479.

4. Steven Salaita, *Inter/Nationalism: Decolonizing Native America and Palestine* (Minneapolis: University of Minnesota Press, 2016), 42. David Feldman, ed., *Boycotts Past and Present: From the American Revolution to the Campaign to Boycott Israel* (Cham: Palgrave Macmillan, 2019) gives useful context.

5. Pierre Bourdieu, *Homo Academicus*, trans. Peter Collier (Stanford: Stanford University Press, 1988), 11. See also Brian Martin, *Tied Knowledge: Power in Higher Education* (published on the web, 1998), 7, accessed May 3, 2022, www.bmartin.cc/pubs/98tk/.

6. As Matthew Abraham, *Intellectual Resistance and the Struggle for Palestine* (New York: Palgrave Macmillan, 2014), 33, puts it, "one group's use of academic freedom may restrict another group's ability to realize its academic freedom."

7. Rima Najjar Kapitan, "Academic Freedom as a Fundamental Human Right in American Jurisprudence and the Imposition of 'Balance' on Academic Discourse about the Palestinian-Israeli Conflict," *Arab Studies Quarterly* 33, no. 3–4 (2011): 276.

8. See Rodin and Yudkin, "Academic Boycotts," 476.

9. See, for instance, Noura Erakat, "Toward an Ethic of Legitimate Dissent: Academic Boycott at the American Studies Association," *Journal of Palestine Studies* 43, no. 3 (2014): 60.

10. Nick Riemer, "Academics Should Boycott International Conferences in the US until Trump's 'Muslim Ban' Is Lifted," *Wildcat Dispatches*, February 2, 2017, accessed May 3, 2022, wildcatdispatches.org/2017/02/02/nick-riemer-academics-should-boycott-conferences-in-the-us-until-trumps-muslim-ban-is-lifted/; Mark Levine, "Boycott UAE & UAE-Based Universities until Matthew Hedges Released and Academic Freedom Guaranteed," Care2Petitions (website), accessed May 3, 2022, www.thepetitionsite.com/fr/takeaction/827/377/366/.

11. Palestinian Campaign for the Academic and Cultural Boycott of Israel (PACBI), "Western Academy's Hypocrisy: Sanctions against Russia but not Israel," BDS Movement (website), April 5, 2022, accessed May 3, 2022, bdsmovement.net/news/western-academys-hypocrisy-sanctions-against-russia-not-israel.

12. "What Is the Role of Academia in Political Change? The Case of BDS and Israeli Violations of International Law [Public Policy Forum at the December 2014 American Anthropological Association conference – Panel discussion transcript by Samantha Brotman]," *Jadaliyya*, accessed May 3, 2022, www.jadaliyya.com/Details/31909.

13. "What Is the Role of Academia in Political Change?"

14. "What Is the Role of Academia in Political Change?"

15. Eyal Sivan and Armelle Laborie, *Un boycott légitime. Pour le BDS universitaire et culturel de l'État d'Israël* (Paris: La Fabrique, 2016), 132.

16. Ben White, *Cracks in the Wall: Beyond Apartheid in Palestine/Israel* (London: Pluto Press, 2018), 113.

17. Cary Nelson, *Not in Kansas Anymore: Academic Freedom in Palestinian Universities* (Washington, DC: Academic Engagement Network, 2021), 5, 143.

18. Nelson, *Not in Kansas Anymore*, 19.

19. Nelson, *Not in Kansas Anymore*, 44.

20. Nelson, *Not in Kansas Anymore*, 38, 100.

21. Nelson, *Not in Kansas Anymore*, 98.

22. See Human Rights Watch, *Two Authorities, One Way, Zero Dissent: Arbitrary Arrest and Torture under the Palestinian Authority and Hamas* (Human Rights Watch, 2018), 38–41, 70–71; Addameer Prisoner Support and Human Rights Association (website), "Suspended Graduation: The Targeting and Political Detention of Palestinian University Students," March 3, 2020, accessed July 7, 2022, www.addameer.org/publications/suspended-graduation-targeting-and-political-detention-palestinian-university-students.

23. Nelson, *Not in Kansas Anymore*, 80, 86.

24. See, for example, "Statement of Position: Palestinian Federation of Unions of University Professors and Employees – Concerning the University of Johannesburg's Relations with Ben Gurion University," Right2Edu: Right to Education Campaign, Birzeit University (website), January 19, 2011, accessed May 3, 2022, right2edu.birzeit.edu/statement-positionpalestinian-federation-unions-university-professors-employees/; Palestinian Union of Social Workers and Psychologists (PUSWP),

"Palestinian Union of Social Workers and Psychologists Urges Colleagues Not to Participate in International Meeting in Tel Aviv," BDS Movement (website), October 2, 2018, accessed May 3, 2022, bdsmovement.net/news/palestinian-union-social-workers-and-psychologists-urges-colleagues-not-participate; University Teachers' Association in Palestine (UTA) and Palestinian Students' Campaign for the Academic Boycott of Israel (PSCABI), "Letter from Gaza Academics and Students: Eight American Universities Normalize Occupation, Colonization and Apartheid!" BDS Movement (website), September 24, 2010, accessed May 3, 2022, bdsmovement.net/news/letter-gaza-academics-and-students-eight-american-universities-normalize-occupation; Workers in Palestine (@WorkersinPales1), "Palestinian Trade Unions Call for Immediate and Urgent Action from International Trade Unions," Twitter, May 22, 2021, 7:27 p.m., accessed May 3, 2022, twitter.com/WorkersinPales1/status/1396034862432260099.

25. David Newman, "The Failure of Academic Boycotts," *Geographical Review* 106, no. 2 (2016): 269.

26. Salaita, *Inter/Nationalism*, 43.

27. Berman, "The Boycott as an Infringement on Academic Culture," 57. Ilan Pappé notes that "academics quite often lag behind social activists when it comes to challenging realities that are taken for granted." See Ilan Pappé, *The Idea of Israel: A History of Power and Knowledge* (London: Verso, 2014), 234. Activism, not academia and its "dialogue," emerges in this account as the locus of intellectual progress. The influence of theorizing done by activists on academics is discussed by Colin Barker and Laurence Cox, "'What Have the Romans Ever Done for Us?': Academic and Activist Forms of Movement Theorizing," in *Proceedings of the Eighth International Conference on Alternative Futures and Popular Protest*, eds. Colin Barker and Mike Tyldesley (Manchester: Manchester Metropolitan University, 2002), 7, mural.maynoothuniversity.ie/428/.

28. Palestinian Campaign for the Academic and Cultural Boycott of Israel, "PACBI Guidelines for the International Academic Boycott of Israel," July 9, 2014, accessed June 26, 2022, bdsmovement.net/pacbi/academic-boycott-guidelines.

29. William I. Robinson, "My Ordeal with the Israel Lobby and the University of California," in *We Will Not Be Silenced*, eds. William I. Robinson and Maryam S. Griffin (London: Pluto Press, 2017), 68.

30. Judith Butler, "Israel/Palestine and the Paradoxes of Academic Freedom," *Radical Philosophy* 135 (January/February 2006), www.radicalphilosophy.com/article/israelpalestine-and-the-paradoxes-of-academic-freedom, emphasis added. Like most other discussions of academic freedom, Butler also ignores the different arenas in which that "free exchange of ideas" might be exercised – the classroom, appointment and tenure decisions, conferences, publication – in a way which allows the freedom of academic exchange to be exaggerated. For some relevant discussion, see Steven Salaita, *Uncivil Rights*: *Palestine and the Limits of Academic Freedom* (Chicago: Haymarket, 2015). Salaita is right to say that "the preservation of academic freedom as a rights-based structure . . . shouldn't be the focus of our [anti-Zionists'] work. We should focus on the development and maintenance of just labor conditions and the disengagement of our institutions from the exercise of state violence" (91).

31. Conrad Russell, *Academic Freedom* (London: Routledge, 1993), 15.

32. Piya Chatterjee and Sunaina Maira, "The Imperial University: Race, War and the Nation-State," in *The Imperial University: Academic Repression and Scholarly Dissent*, eds. Piya Chatterjee and Sunaina Maira (Minneapolis: University of Minnesota Press, 2014), 37.

33. The American Association of University Professors' (AAUP) 1940 Statement of Principles on Academic Freedom and Tenure, for instance, states that "teachers are entitled to freedom in the classroom in discussing their subject, but they should be careful not to introduce into their teaching controversial matter which has no relation to their subject." See "1940 Statement of Principles on Academic Freedom and Tenure," AAUP: American Association of University Professors (website), accessed May 3, 2022, www.aaup.org/report/1940-statement-principles-academic-freedom-and-tenure#B4.

34. Chatterjee and Maira, "The Imperial University," 23.

35. Chatterjee and Maira, "The Imperial University," 21. See also C. Heike Schotten, "Against Academic Freedom: 'Terrorism,' Settler Colonialism and Palestinian Liberation," in *Enforcing Silence: Academic Freedom, Palestine and the Criticism of Israel*, eds. David Landy, Ronit Lentin and Conor McCarthy (London: Zed Books, 2020), 282–309.

36. See "Retraction Watch," accessed May 3, 2022, retractionwatch.com.

37. Rodin and Yudkin, "Academic Boycotts," 479.

38. See Carl Alpert, *Technion: The Story of Israel's Institute of Technology* (New York: American Technion Society, 1982), 44ff. for a detailed account; Dennis Kurzon, "The Language War: Hebrew and Other Languages in Pre-First World War Palestine," in *The Studies on the Hebrew Language / İbrani Dili Üzerine Araştırmalar*, eds. Ali Küçükler and Hüseyin İçen (Newcastle upon Tyne: Cambridge Scholars Publishing, 2014), 39–49.

39. For a critical discussion, see the chapters by Yehonatan Alsheh and Lee Jones in Feldman, *Boycotts Past and Present*.

40. See F. W. Lancaster and Lorraine J. Haricombe, "The Academic Boycott of South Africa: Symbolic Gesture or Effective Agent of Change?" *Perspectives on the Professions* 15, no. 1 (1995): 2–4.

41. See Association of University Teachers in England, "Boycott of South African Universities [March 1988]," British Committee for the Universities of Palestine (BRICUP) (website), accessed February 14, 2021, www.bricup.org.uk/downloads/academic%20boycott%20of%20south%20africa.doc (URL discontinued). This policy was not, however, as absolute as this might suggest, since it did not exclude "visits from academics (black or white) known for their opposition to apartheid."

42. See the ANC's 1989 "Position Paper on the Cultural and Academic Boycott: Adopted by the National Executive Committee of the African National Congress, May 1989 – Lusaka," SAHO: South African History Online (website), accessed May 3, 2022, www.sahistory.org.za/archive/position-paper-cultural-and-academic-boycott.

43. Rodin and Yudkin, "Academic Boycotts," 468.

44. See Simon Baker, "Invasion of Ukraine Raises Issue: Do Academic Boycotts Work?" *Inside Higher Ed*, March 10, 2022, accessed May 3, 2022, www.insidehighered.com/news/2022/03/10/invasion-ukraine-raises-issue-do-academic-boycotts-work.

45. Jonathan Cook, "Over 500 Scholars Launch Fightback against Israel Lobby's Antisemitism Smear of UK Academics," *Scheerpost*, October 28, 2021, accessed May 3, 2022, scheerpost.com/2021/10/28/over-500-scholars-launch-fightback-against-israel-lobbys-antisemitism-smear-of-uk-academics/.

46. Goda Naujokaitytė, "Russian Rectors' Support for Putin Prompts UK Universities to Cut Links," *Science|Business*, March 10, 2022, accessed May 3, 2022, sciencebusiness.net/news/russian-rectors-support-putin-prompts-uk-universities-cut-links.

47. See "The Cost of Knowledge," accessed May 3, 2022, thecostofknowledge.com/.

48. See Scott Jaschik, "Language of Protest," *Inside Higher Ed*, November 2, 2015, accessed May3, 2022, www.insidehighered.com/news/2015/11/02/editors-and-editorial-board-quit-top-linguistics-journal-protest-subscription-fees; Eric Baković and Kai von Fintel, "*Lingua* Is Dead: Long Live *Glossa*!" *Language Log* (blog), November 8, 2015, accessed May 3, 2022, languagelog.ldc.upenn.edu/nll/?p=22162.

49. See Peter Suber's list at "Journal Declarations of Independence," Open Access Directory (website), accessed May 3, 2022, oad.simmons.edu/oadwiki/Journal_declarations_of_independence.

50. Lindsay Ellis, "In Talks with Elsevier, UCLA Reaches for a Novel Bargaining Chip: Its Faculty," *Chronicle of Higher Education*, December 12, 2018, accessed May 3, 2022, www.chronicle.com/article/In-Talks-With-Elsevier-UCLA/245311.

51. John Villasenor, "The Trouble with Institution-Led Boycotts," *Chronicle of Higher Education*, December 19, 2018, accessed May 3, 2022, www.chronicle.com/article/The-Trouble-With/245367.

52. Colleen Flaherty, "How Good Is Your Gaydar? How Good Is Your Science?" *Inside Higher Ed*, September 12, 2017, accessed May 3, 2022, www.insidehighered.com/news/2017/09/12/new-paper-artificial-intelligence-can-mostly-correctly-pick-self-identified-gays-and; Colleen Flaherty, "AI Gaydar Study Gets Another Look," *Inside Higher Ed*, September 13, 2017, accessed May 3, 2022, www.insidehighered.com/news/2017/09/13/prominent-journal-accepted-controversial-study-ai-gaydar-reviewing-ethics-work.

53. See "The History of World Archaeological Congress," World Archaeological Congress (website), accessed May 3, 2022, worldarch.org/history-wac/.

54. Elisabeth Pain, "In Plagiarism Protest, Expat Researchers to Boycott Romanian Conference," *Science*, September 21, 2012, accessed May 3, 2022, www.sciencemag.org/news/2012/09/plagiarism-protest-expat-researchers-boycott-romanian-conference.

55. Ian Sample, "US Scientists Boycott Nasa Conference over China Ban," *Guardian*, October 5, 2013, accessed May 3, 2022, www.theguardian.com/science/2013/oct/05/us-scientists-boycott-nasa-china-ban.

56. See "The Men Who Are Taking a Stand against 'Dude Fests,'" *BBC News*, May 23, 2016, accessed May 3, 2022, www.bbc.com/news/blogs-trending-36333700.

57. "In Solidarity with People Affected by the 'Muslim Ban': Call for an Academic Boycott of International Conferences Held in the US," petition and list of signatures last updated March 6, 2017, accessed May 3, 2022, docs.google.com/a/insidehighered.com/forms/d/e/1FAIpQLSeNN_2HHREt1h-dm_CgWpFHw8NDPGLCkOwB4lLRFtKFJqI25w/viewform.

58. "Academic Boycott I," *Political Prisoners in Thailand* (blog), May 29, 2016, accessed May 3, 2022, thaipoliticalprisoners.wordpress.com/2016/05/29/academic-boycott-i/.

59. Benjamin Haas, "'Killer Robots': AI Experts Call for Boycott over Lab at South Korea University," *Guardian*, April 5, 2018, accessed May 3, 2022, www.theguardian.com/technology/2018/apr/05/killer-robots-south-korea-university-boycott-artifical-intelligence-hanwha; Megana Sekar, "California and UCLA Restrict Travel to Oklahoma in Response to Anti-LGBTQ Law," *Daily Bruin*, June 4, 2018, accessed May 3, 2022, dailybruin.com/2018/06/04/california-and-ucla-restrict-travel-to-oklahoma-in-response-to-anti-lgbtq-law/.

60. Zack Beauchamp, "These Scholars Are Trying to Stop Kirstjen Nielsen from Getting a Soft Landing," *Vox*, April 9, 2019, accessed May 3, 2022, www.vox.com/2019/4/9/18300584/kirstjen-nielsen-secretary-homeland-security-boycott.

61. "Pledge Your Support for the UCU Boycott of London Metropolitan University," UCU London Region (website), July 25, 2016, accessed June 11, 2022, uculondonregion.wordpress.com/tag/lmu/; "Global Boycott of University of Leicester Begins Today," UCU: University and College Union (website), May 4, 2021, last updated July 7, 2021, accessed May 3, 2022, www.ucu.org.uk/article/11533/Global-boycott-of-University-of-Leicester-begins-today.

62. Audrey McNamara and Harini Shyamsundar, "UC Berkeley Faculty Members Call for Boycott of Classes during 'Free Speech Week,'" *The Daily Californian*, September 13, 2017, last updated September 14, 2017, accessed May 3, 2022, www.dailycal.org/2017/09/13/uc-berkeley-faculty-members-call-boycott-classes-free-speech-week/.

63. Paul Daley, "WHO Worries That Melbourne University's Links to Arms Industry Will Threaten Joint Medical Research," *Guardian*, January 22, 2021, accessed May 3, 2022, www.theguardian.com/australia-news/2021/jan/22/who-worries-that-melbourne-universitys-links-to-arms-industry-will-threaten-joint-medical-research.

64. Klaus Dörre, Stephan Lessenich and Ingo Singe, "German Sociologists Boycott Academic Ranking," *Global Dialogue: Magazine of the International Sociological Association*, April 28, 2013, accessed May 3, 2022, globaldialogue.isa-sociology.org/german-sociologists-boycott-academic-ranking/; Sheetal Banchariya, "Why Older IITs Are Boycotting Times Higher Education Rankings 2020," *Times of India*, June 3, 2020, timesofindia.indiatimes.com/home/education/news/why-older-iits-are-boycotting-times-higher-education-rankings-2020/articleshow/75291276.cms.

65. See Baker, "Invasion of Ukraine Raises Issue."

66. Newman, "The Failure of Academic Boycotts," 267.

67. Newman, "The Failure of Academic Boycotts," 267.

68. "Israeli Lecturers Back Theater Boycott," *WAFA News Agency*, August 31, 2010, accessed May 3, 2022, english.wafa.ps/page.aspx?id=xVXWYHa1399933487 7axVXWYH.

69. Gili S. Drori and Yagil Levi, "Presidential Statement, 18 February 2018," Israeli Sociological Society (website), accessed May 3, 2022, www.israel-sociology.org.il/uploadimages/ISSdeclaration_EN.pdf.

70. Yarden Skop and Reuters, "Leading Israeli Sociologist Calls for Boycott of West Bank University," *Haaretz*, March 14, 2016, accessed May 3, 2022, www.haaretz.com/israel-news/leading-israeli-sociologist-calls-for-boycott-of-west-bank-university-1.5417305.

71. Judy Maltz, "Why Adelson Is Pouring Millions into an Israeli University in the West Bank," *Haaretz*, July 20, 2017, accessed May 3, 2022, www.haaretz.com/israel-news/.premium-why-adelson-pours-millions-into-a-west-bank-university-1.5431239.

72. Or Kashti, "Israeli Anthropological Association: We Won't Cooperate with Institutions in the West Bank," *Haaretz*, June 26, 2018, accessed May 3, 2022, www.haaretz.com/israel-news/.premium-leading-israeli-academic-body-to-ban-institutions-in-the-west-bank-1.6217574. It is entirely characteristic of these initiatives that they have the effect of combating the international academic boycott of Israel by dissociating Israeli academics from the most flagrant kind of complicity with the occupation – the theft of Palestinian land for Israeli higher education. The IAA had written to the American Anthropological Association in 2014 to dissuade it from voting to support BDS. See Lidar Gravé-Lazi, "20 Israeli Academics Encourage BDS, Im Tirtzu Says," *Jerusalem Post*, May 27, 2016, accessed May 3, 2022, www.jpost.com/Israel-News/20-Israeli-academics-encourage-BDS-Im-Tirtzu-says-455181.

73. Some boycott supporters are targeted by the anti-BDS websites Israel Academia Monitor (israel-academia-monitor.com) and Know the Anti-Israel Israeli Professor (knowbdsinisrael.com/).

74. See Shlomo Piotrkowski, "Hershkovitz Assigns 'Boycott Grants' to Boycotted Scholars" (Hebrew), *Arutz Sheva/Israel National News*, January 13, 2011, accessed May 3, 2022, www.inn.co.il/news/214090; Omar Barghouti, "Israeli Govt Forms Strategy to Fight Boycott," *The Real News Network*, February 18, 2014, accessed May 3, 2022, therealnews.com/omarbarghouti12182014; Rafael Medoff, "Could Pro-BDS Professors Benefit from Tel Aviv University's New 'Anti-BDS' Fund?" *The Algemeiner*, September 25, 2017, accessed July 7, 2022, www.algemeiner.com/2017/09/25/could-pro-bds-professors-benefit-from-tel-aviv-universitys-new-anti-bds-fund/.

75. Tanya Reinhart, "Why Academic Boycott – A Reply to an Israeli Comrade [Indymedia Israel – May 17, 2002]," Mona Baker (website), January 4, 2016, accessed May 3, 2022, www.monabaker.org/2016/01/04/why-academic-boycott-a-reply-to-an-israeli-comrade/. See also Sara Roy, "Humanism, Scholarship, and Politics: Writing on the Palestinian-Israeli Conflict," *Journal of Palestine Studies* 36, no. 2 (2007): 54–65.

76. See Alberto Baccini and Giuseppe De Nicolao, "Academics in Italy Have Boycotted Assessment: What Has It Achieved?" *Times Higher Education*, April 21, 2016, accessed May 3, 2022, www.timeshighereducation.com/comment/academics-in-taly-have-boycotted-assessment-what-has-it-achieved-alberto-baccini-university-of-siena-giuseppe-de-nicolao-university-of-pavia.

77. David Holmes, "Academic Freedom Isn't the Issue with Lomborg's Consensus Centre," *The Conversation*, October 6, 2015, accessed May 3, 2022, theconversation.com/academic-freedom-isnt-the-issue-with-lomborgs-consensus-centre-48586.

78. Michael McGowan, "Sydney University Academics Denounce Western Civilisation Degree," *Guardian*, June 8, 2018, accessed May 3, 2022, www.theguardian.

com/australia-news/2018/jun/08/sydney-university-academics-denounce-western-civilisation-degree. The present author was the principal drafter of the open letter in question in this article.

79. Seth Shulman, "Math Society Votes Down Funding by SDI, Military," *The Scientist*, May 2, 1988, accessed May 3, 2022, www.the-scientist.com/news/math-society-votes-down-funding-by-sdi-military-62998.

80. See Jan Petter Myklebust, "Boycott of Opening of New Racism Research Institute," *University World News*, August 21, 2015, accessed May 3, 2022, www.universityworldnews.com/article.php?story=20150818160250889.

81. See Martha Nussbaum, "Against Academic Boycotts," in Nelson and Brahm, *The Case against Academic Boycotts of Israel*: "It doesn't make practical sense to boycott scholars, typically among the most powerless of society's members, and it also doesn't make symbolic sense" (46); "boycotts of academic individuals deeply compromise the core values of a university" (47).

82. See Igor Primoratz, "Boycott of Serbian Intellectuals," *Public Affairs Quarterly* 10, no. 3 (1996): 267–78; Carlos Fuentes, "Academic Boycott," *New York Review*, January 7, 1971, accessed May 3, 2022, www.nybooks.com/articles/1971/01/07/academic-boycott/; Sarah Bridger, *Scientists at War. The Ethics of Cold War Weapons Research* (Cambridge, MA: Harvard University Press, 2015), 201, 261–62.

83. Taly Krupkin, "Israel's Travel Ban Backlash: Over 100 Jewish Studies Scholars Threaten to Not Visit Israel in Protest," *Haaretz*, March 10, 2017, accessed May 3, 2022, www.haaretz.com/us-news/.premium-100-jewish-studies-scholars-threaten-to-not-visit-israel-over-travel-ban-1.5447119.

84. Adam Smulevich, "Il rettore dell'università La Sapienza a favore del 'boicottaggio del BDS,'" *Osservatorio antisemitismo*, February 23, 2016, accessed May 3, 2022, www.osservatorioantisemitismo.it/articoli/il-rettore-delluniversita-la-sapienza-a-favore-del-boicottaggio-del-bds/.

85. Alan Dershowitz, "Combating BDS by Legislation: Different Approaches, Same Goal," *Jerusalem Post*, June 22, 2016, accessed May 3, 2022, www.jpost.com/opinion/combating-bds-by-legislation-different-approaches-same-goal-457507.

86. Magid Shihade, "The Academic Boycott of Israel and Its Critics," in *Against Apartheid: The Case for Boycotting Israeli Universities*, eds. Ashley Dawson and Bill V. Mullen (Chicago: Haymarket, 2015), 15.

87. See Cary Nelson, "BDS Boycotts: Personal Reflections," *TELOSscope* (blog), January 2, 2017, accessed May 3, 2022, www.telospress.com/bds-boycotts-personal-reflections/.

88. See Phan Nguyen, "Cary Nelson, the AAUP, and the Privilege of Bestowing Academic Freedom," *Mondoweiss*, January 17, 2014, accessed May 3, 2022, mondoweiss.net/2014/01/privilege-bestowing-academic/; David Palumbo-Liu, "Not So Much Anti-Boycott as Pro-Israel [Review of *The Case against Academic Boycotts of Israel*, eds. Cary Nelson and Gabriel Noah Brahm]," *symploke* 23, no. 1–2 (2015): 425–57.

89. See Herbert Marcuse, "Repressive Tolerance," in *A Critique of Pure Tolerance*, eds. Robert P. Wolff, Barrington Moore, Jr and Herbert Marcuse (London: Jonathan Cape, 1969), 95–118.

90. In the commercial arena, the French president, Emmanuel Macron, restated his opposition to BDS and his determination to repress it in the same 2017 interview in which he also *advocated* for a consumer boycott of companies that practice employment discrimination. See Ali Abunimah, "What Will France's Election Mean for Palestine?" *The Electronic Intifada*, April 19, 2017, accessed May 3, 2022, electronicintifada.net/blogs/ali-abunimah/what-will-frances-election-mean-palestine.

91. See Rodin and Yudkin, "Academic Boycotts," for a clear exposition of this idea.

92. We would obviously not think that academic exchange was worth engaging in if it made the world worse, and there are some forms of academic exchange which *do* make the world worse and which should therefore not be engaged in, such as weapons research, research into environmentally destructive resource-extraction or use processes, into technical means of social control and so on.

93. Berman, "The Boycott as an Infringement on Academic Culture," 52.

94. Omar Barghouti, *BDS: Boycott Divestment Sanctions: The Global Struggle for Palestinian Rights* (Chicago: Haymarket, 2011), 105–6.

95. Primoratz, "Boycott of Serbian Intellectuals," 272.

3. LITTLE ISRAELS

1. Chris Lorenz, "If You're So Smart, Why Are You under Surveillance? Universities, Neoliberalism, and New Public Management," *Critical Enquiry* 38, no. 3 (2012): 607; Jacob Mikanowski, "The Austro-Hungarian Officer Corps – and Us," *The Chronicle Review*, November 19, 2017, accessed May 6, 2022, www.chronicle.com/article/Academic-Life-Isnt-As-Modern/241785.

2. So says David Saranga, then senior foreign policy advisor to the president of Israel: David Saranga, "Tel Aviv Gay Murders Shocked Our Tolerant Nation: Israeli Spokesman," *The Huffington Post*, September 9, 2009, accessed May 6, 2022, www.huffingtonpost.com/david-saranga/tel-aviv-gay-murders-shoc_b_254284.html. See also Saree Makdisi, "Apartheid / Apartheid / [ ]," *Critical Inquiry* 44 (2018): 304–30.

3. See OECD, *OECD Economic Surveys: Israel 2020* (Paris: OECD Publishing, 2020), accessed June 27, 2022, doi.org/10.1787/d6a7d907-en; "Israel Has an Increasingly Strong and Resilient Economy," Invest in Israel: Ministry of Economy and Industry State of Israel (website), accessed May 6, 2022, www.investinisrael.gov.il/InvestInIsrael/Pages/WhyIsrael.aspx. In 2016, Israel had the highest poverty in the OECD: Lidar Gravé-Lazi, "More Than 1 in 5 Israelis Live in Poverty, Highest in Developed World," *Jerusalem Post*, December 15, 2016, accessed May 6, 2022, www.jpost.com/Israel-News/More-than-1-in-5-Israelis-live-in-poverty-highest-in-developed-world-475444.

4. For a representative critique of academic political correctness, see David Bromwich, "The New Campus Censors," *Chronicle of Higher Education*, November 5 2017, accessed May 6, 2022, www.chronicle.com/article/the-new-campus-censors/. Erwin Chemerinksy and Howard Gillman, *Free Speech on Campus* (New Haven: Yale University Press, 2017) give numerous examples of the kinds of action

that motivate the critique. See also Jon A. Shields and Joshua M. Dunn, *Passing on the Right: Conservative Professors in the Progressive University* (New York: Oxford University Press, 2016).

5. Cary Nelson, *No University Is an Island: Saving Academic Freedom* (New York: New York University Press, 2010), 173.

6. Max Weber, "Politics as a Vocation," in *From Max Weber: Essays in Sociology*, eds. H. H. Gerth and C. Wright Mills (Milton Park: Routledge, 1991), 78.

7. Daniel W. Drezner, *The Ideas Industry* (New York: Oxford University Press, 2017), 100.

8. Sarah Brown and Shannon Najmabadi, "Shock, Despair, and Outrage: Academics Condemn Trump's Immigration Crackdown," *Chronicle of Higher Education*, January 29, 2017, accessed May 6, 2022, www.chronicle.com/article/shock-despair-and-outrage-academics-condemn-trumps-immigration-crackdown/.

9. Ruth Steinhardt, "University Urges Dialogue, Not Partisanship, in Wake of Election," *GW Today*, November 30, 2016, accessed May 6, 2022, gwtoday.gwu.edu/university-urges-dialogue-not-partisanship-wake-election.

10. Edward Said, "Opponents, Audiences, Constituencies, and Communities," *Critical Inquiry* 9, no. 1 (1982): 20.

11. Exactly this was among the conclusions reached in the 2002 UC Berkeley "Intifada curriculum" controversy. See Robert C. Post, "Academic Freedom and the 'Intifada Curriculum,'" *Academe* 89, no. 3 (2003): 16–20.

12. Matthew Abraham, *Out of Bounds: Academic Freedom and the Question of Palestine* (New York: Bloomsbury Academic, 2014), 133.

13. Norman G. Finkelstein, "Civility and Academic Life," in *Academic Freedom in the Post-9/11 Era*, eds. Edward J. Carvalho and David B. Downing (New York: Palgrave Macmillan, 2010), 122.

14. Nelson, *No University Is an Island*, 173; Finkelstein, "Civility and Academic Life," 119.

15. Lorenz, "If You're So Smart, Why Are You under Surveillance?" 607, italics added.

16. Lee Jones, "UCU's Rush to E-Ballot Reflects the Weakness of Union Democracy," *Medium*, March 29, 2018, accessed May 6, 2022, medium.com/@drleejones/ucus-rush-to-e-ballot-reflects-the-weakness-of-union-democracy-c892e316ebf.

17. Theodor W. Adorno, "Politics and Economics in the Interview Material," in Adorno et al., *The Authoritarian Personality* (New York: Harper and Brothers, 1950), 662.

18. Cary Nelson charts the decline in the membership of the American Association of University Professors (AAUP) in *No University Is an Island*.

19. Scott Jaschik, "MLA Votes to 'Refrain' from Backing Israel Boycott," *Inside Higher Ed*, June 15, 2017, accessed May 6, 2022, www.insidehighered.com/news/2017/06/15/mla-votes-large-margin-refrain-backing-israel-boycott; David Palumbo-Liu, "Learning, and Not Caring: On the MLA's Palestine Resolution," *Los Angeles Review of Books*, February 18, 2018, accessed May 6, 2022, lareviewofbooks.org/article/learning-and-not-caring-on-the-mlas-palestine-resolution. See also Jeffrey Sacks, "The Resistance to Boycott: Palestine, BDS, and the Modern Language Association," *Radical History Review* 134 (2019): 233–44.

20. Eyal Weizman, *The Least of All Possible Evils: Humanitarian Violence from Arendt to Gaza* (London: Verso, 2011), 58.

21. Russell A. Berman is one scholar who notes that the call for BDS "politicizes" scholarship. See Russell A. Berman, "The Boycott as an Infringement on Academic Culture," in *The Case against Academic Boycotts of Israel*, eds. Cary Nelson and Gabriel Noah Brahm (Chicago: MLA Members for Scholars' Rights, 2015), 50.

22. Stefan Collini, *Speaking of Universities* (London: Verso, 2017), 85.

23. Ramzy Baroud, "Palestine's Global Battle That Must Be Won," in *Generation Palestine: Voices from the Boycott, Divestment and Sanctions Movement*, ed. Rich Wiles (London: Pluto Press, 2013), 13.

24. See, for instance, Sinéad Murphy, *Zombie University*: *Thinking under Control* (London: Repeater Books, 2017). No better illustration exists of this enclosure than the stupendous sums academics and their employers are willing to pay in subscription costs to corporate publishers who literally enclose – put out of public reach – publicly funded research. See Mark C. Wilson, "Universities Spend Millions on Accessing Results of Publicly Funded Research," *The Conversation*, December 12, 2017, accessed May 6, 2022, theconversation.com/universities-spend-millions-on-accessing-results-of-publicly-funded-research-88392.

25. Proponents of the academic boycott argue, apparently paradoxically, that the overall inclusiveness of academic life is best secured by the exclusion of the deans and presidents who have made themselves accountable for Israeli universities' support for Israeli apartheid by taking on leadership positions in them. As we explored in chapter two, this is not, in fact, such an uncommon strategy: it is no more unreasonable to expect overall inclusiveness in Palestine and Israel to be advanced by the exclusion of Israeli universities' deans and presidents from international fora than it is to expect gender equity in academia to be advanced by limiting the number of men delivering plenary sessions in academic conferences.

26. See Jonathan Coulson, Paul Roberts and Isabelle Taylor, *University Trends: Contemporary Campus Design* (London and New York: Routledge, 2015); Rana Sharif compares the structural inequities facing Palestinian and American students: see Rana Sharif, "The Right to Education: From La Frontera to Gaza: A Brief Communication," *American Quarterly* 62, no. 4 (2010): 855–60.

27. Alex Finnis, "Is This Really Necessary? Universities Introduce Fingerprinting for International Students," *Independent*, October 21, 2013, accessed May 6, 2022, www.independent.co.uk/student/news/is-this-really-necessary-universities-introduce-fingerprinting-for-international-students-8894007.html. See also Julia C. Oparah, "Challenging Complicity: The Neoliberal University and the Prison-Industrial Complex," in *The Imperial University: Academic Repression and Scholarly Dissent*, eds. Piya Chatterjee and Sunaina Maira (Minneapolis: University of Minnesota Press, 2014), 99–121, for discussion of the connection between US higher education and "the prisonization of the globe" (102).

28. Pierre Bourdieu, *The State Nobility: Elite Schools in the Field of Power*, trans. Lauretta C. Clough (Stanford: Stanford University Press, 1996), 12.

29. "Perché ho rifiutato un lavoro di ricerca in collaborazione con l'Università di Tel Aviv," Campagna BDS Italia (website), February 21, 2017, accessed May 6, 2022, bdsitalia.org/index.php/ultime-notizie-bac/2253-torino-tel-aviv, my translation.

30. On reprisals against academics who withhold recommendation letters from students wanting to study in Israel, see Isaac Stanley-Becker, "University of Michigan Promises to Discipline Faculty in Israel Boycott Controversy," *Washington Post*, October 11, 2018, accessed May 6, 2022, www.washingtonpost.com/news/morning-mix/wp/2018/10/11/university-of-michigan-promises-to-discipline-faculty-in-israel-boycott-controversy. See William I. Robinson and Maryam S. Griffin, eds., *We Will Not Be Silenced: The Academic Repression of Israel's Critics* (London: Pluto Press, 2017); *The Palestine Exception to Free Speech: A Movement under Attack in the US* (Palestine Legal and The Center for Constitutional Rights, 2015), accessed May 6, 2022, palestinelegal.org/the-palestine-exception.

31. See Karma Nabulsi, "Don't Go to the Doctor," *London Review of Books*, May 18, 2017, accessed June 28, 2022, www.lrb.co.uk/the-paper/v39/n10/karma-nabulsi/don-t-go-to-the-doctor.

32. Government of the United Kingdom, "Prevent Duty Guidance: For Higher Education Institutions in England and Wales," GOV.UK (website), updated April 1, 2021, accessed May 6, 2022, www.gov.uk/government/publications/prevent-duty-guidance/prevent-duty-guidance-for-higher-education-institutions-in-england-and-wales.

33. Simon Hooper, "Revealed: UK universities told to 'manage' Palestine activism," *Middle East Eye*, February 22, 2017, accessed May 6, 2022, www.middleeasteye.net/news/revealed-uk-universities-told-manage-palestine-activism; Osha Mahmoud, "Is Prevent Ending Palestinian Activism on University Campuses?" *Middle East Eye*, February 7, 2018, accessed May 6, 2022, www.middleeasteye.net/video/prevent-ending-palestinian-activism-university-campuses; Malia Bouattia, "Policing Muslims, Policing Dissent: Free Speech is under Attack at Westminster University," *Middle East Eye*, June 13, 2018, accessed May 6, 2022, www.middleeasteye.net/opinion/policing-muslims-policing-dissent-free-speech-under-attack-westminster-university.

34. Mark McGovern, "The University, Prevent and Cultures of Compliance," *Prometheus* 34, no. 1 (2016): 49–62.

35. Universities UK, *Freedom of Speech on Campus: Rights and Responsibilities in UK Universities* (London: Universities UK, February 2011), 3, italics added.

36. Universities UK, *Freedom of Speech on Campus*, 21.

37. Bano Murtuja and Waqas Tufail, *Rethinking Prevent: A Case for an Alternative Approach* (Rotherham: Just Yorkshire, 2017), 6, 20. See also Open Society Justice Initiative, *Eroding Trust: The UK's Prevent Counter-Extremism Strategy in Health and Education* (New York: Open Society Foundations, 2016).

38. Murtuja and Tufail, *Rethinking Prevent*, 21. See also Les Levidow, "Political Dissent as 'Extremism' under the PREVENT Programme," *BRICUP Newsletter* 92 (October 2015): 2–5; Les Levidow, "Counter-Extremism Agenda: Safeguarding What?" *BRICUP Newsletter* 106 (January 2017): 3–6. Waqas Tufail details a case where "a criminology lecturer ran her course's reading list past the police 'just in case there was anything too critical'." See Josh Halliday, "Prevent Scheme 'Fosters Fear and Censorship at Universities,'" *Guardian*, August 29, 2017, accessed May 6, 2022, www.theguardian.com/uk-news/2017/aug/29/prevent-scheme-fosters-fear-and-censorship-at-universities-just-yorkshire. In 2018, an article on "the ethics of revolution" was targeted by the University of Reading, with students being "warned not to access it on personal devices, to read it only in a secure setting,

and not to leave it lying around where it might be spotted." Eleni Courea, "University Alerts Students to Danger of Leftwing Essay," *Observer*, November 11, 2018, accessed May 6, 2022, www.theguardian.com/education/2018/nov/11/reading-university-warns-danger-left-wing-essay; Vikram Dodd and Jamie Grierson, "Greenpeace Included with Neo-Nazis on UK Counter-Terror List," *Guardian*, January 17, 2020, accessed May 6, 2022, www.theguardian.com/uk-news/2020/jan/17/greenpeace-included-with-neo-nazis-on-uk-counter-terror-list.

39. Lisa Visentin, "Sydney University Protest: 13 People Investigated after Public Lecture Disrupted," *Sydney Morning Herald,* April 17, 2015, accessed May 6, 2022, www.smh.com.au/nsw/sydney-university-protest-13-people-investigated-after-public-lecture-disrupted-20150416-1mmazh.html.

40. See Susan G. Drummond, *Unthinkable Thoughts*: *Academic Freedom and the One-State Model for Israel and Palestine* (Vancouver: UBC Press, 2013).

41. See Jack Grove, "What Are the Potential Perils of Ex-Politicians in University Posts?" *Times Higher Education*, June 8, 2017, accessed May 6, 2022, www.timeshighereducation.com/features/what-are-the-potential-perils-for-ex-politicians-in-university-posts.

42. See "A Note of Thanks to Ami Ayalon," *Heights: University of Haifa Magazine*, Spring 2017, accessed May 6, 2022, magazine.haifa.ac.il/index.php/inside-5/30-a-note-of-thanks-to-ami-ayalon; "Hebrew U. Board of Governors Approves Carmi Gillon as Vice-President of External Relations," The Hebrew University of Jerusalem (website), June 6, 2007, accessed May 6, 2022, www.huji.ac.il/cgi-bin/dovrut/dovrut_search_eng.pl?mesge118111567232688760. See Eyal Sivan and Armelle Laborie, *Un boycott légitime: Pour le BDS universitaire et culturel de l'État d'Israel* (Paris : La Fabrique), 78–79.

43. See Robinson and Griffin, *We Will Not Be Silenced*, for extensive documentation.

44. The phrase "totalitarianism of the private sector" is Chris Lorenz's. See Lorenz, "If You're So Smart, Why Are You under Surveillance?," 614. On Israeli universities, see Gili S. Drori, "Professional Consultancy and Global Higher Education: The Case of Branding of Academia," in *World Yearbook of Education 2016: The Global Education Industry*, eds. Antoni Verger, Christopher Lubienski and Gita Steiner-Khamsi (London: Routledge, 2016), 182. Drori notes that "seeing that most academic institutions in Israel were founded after the 1995 regulatory reform . . . they were born into the era of mediatization, marketization and managerialism in academia and were imprinted by this atmosphere."

45. Nelson, *No University Is an Island*; Cary Nelson, "The Corporate University," in Cary Nelson and Stephen Watt, *Academic Keywords: A Devil's Dictionary for Higher Education* (New York: Routledge, 1999), 84–98.

46. In the face of mounting faculty BDS efforts, all ten University of California chancellors signed an anti-BDS statement in 2018. See John Patrick, "University of California Chancellors Break with Faculty, Condemn Boycotts of Israel," *Washington Examiner*, December 18, 2018, accessed May 6, 2022, www.washingtonexaminer.com/opinion/university-of-california-chancellors-break-with-faculty-condemn-boycotts-of-israel; "University of California First to Issue New Academic Boycott Condemnation," AMCHA Initiative (website), December 13, 2018, accessed

May 6, 2022, amchainitiative.org/UC-Anti-Academic-BDS-12.13.18pr. Cornell president Martha Pollack declared her "strong opposition" to BDS in a letter to Cornell's Students for Justice in Palestine (SJP) chapter in 2019: see William A. Jacobson, "Cornell President to Students for Justice in Palestine: 'I Must Reject Your Call for BDS-Related Divestment,'" Legal Insurrection (website), February 28, 2019, accessed May 6, 2022, legalinsurrection.com/2019/02/cornell-president-to-students-for-justice-in-palestine-i-must-reject-your-call-for-bds-related-divestment/.

47. "Former Harvard President Larry Summers Calls BDS Efforts 'Deplorable,'" *Algemeiner,* January 20, 2016, accessed May 6, 2022, www.algemeiner.com/2016/01/20/former-harvard-president-calls-bds-efforts-deplorable/; Charles Ferguson, "Larry Summers and the Subversion of Economics," *Chronicle of Higher Education,* October 3, 2010, accessed May 6, 2022, www.chronicle.com/article/Larry-Summersthe/124790/.

48. Ulrich Beck, "Die Wiederkehr des Sozialdarwinismus," *Frankfurter Rundschau,* February 5, 2010, accessed May 6, 2022, www.fr.de/kultur/weltinnenpolitik-januar-2010-die-wiederkehr-des-sozialdarwinismus-a-1053045; Ferguson, "Larry Summers and the Subversion of Economics." The coincidence between university leaders' hostility to BDS and their investment in the current settings of the world economy is not, however, purely ideological. The chancellor of the University of Illinois at Urbana–Champaign (UIUC), Phyllis Wise, both opposed the American Studies Association's call to endorse BDS and sacked Israeli critic and BDS supporter Steven Salaita. Wise was, at the time of both incidents, on the board of the multinational Nike, whose Israeli business is supplied by a firm in the Barkan Industrial Zone, a West Bank settlement. For Wise, opposition to BDS aligns with her commercial commitments. Tithi Bhattacharya and Bill V. Mullen, "Salaita Firing Shows Where Zionism Meets Neoliberalism at US universities," *Electronic Intifada,* September 2, 2014, accessed May 6, 2022, electronicintifada.net/content/salaita-firing-shows-where-zionism-meets-neoliberalism-us-universities/13826.

49. For some useful remarks on the importance of interdisciplinary fields like critical ethnic, race, queer and Indigenous studies in stimulating activism, see Sunaina Maira, *Boycott! The Academy and Justice for Palestine* (Berkeley: University of California Press, 2017), 57–58. For some interesting discussion of BDS's lack of traction among scientists, see Michael Harris, "Scientists and BDS, in France and in the US," AURDIP: Association of Academics for the Respect of International Law in Palestine (website), April 13, 2016, accessed May 6, 2022, www.aurdip.org/scientists-and-bds-in-france-and.html.

50. I have explored the question of discretion in "Disciplinarity and the Boycott," in *Enforcing Silence: Academic Freedom, Palestine and the Criticism of Israel,* eds. David Landy, Ronit Lentin and Conor McCarthy (London: Zed Books, 2020), 67–90.

51. Cary Nelson, *Israel Denial: Anti-Zionism, Anti-Semitism, & the Faculty Campaign against the Jewish State* (Washington, DC, and Bloomington: Academic Engagement Network and Indiana University Press, 2019), 266.

52. Hamid Dabashi, *Can Non-Europeans Think?* (London: Zed Books, 2015), 36.

53. See Pierre Bourdieu, "Le discours d'importance: Quelques remarques critiques sur 'Quelques remarques critiques à propos de "Lire Le Capital,"'" in *Langage et pouvoir symbolique* (Paris: Seuil, 2001).

54. Michèle Lamont, *How Professors Think: Inside the Curious World of Academic Judgment* (Cambridge, MA: Harvard University Press, 2009), 162.

55. Nick Riemer, "Linguistic Form: A Political Epistemology," in *Form and Formalism in Linguistics,* ed. James McElvenny (Berlin: Language Science Press, 2019), 225–64; Nick Riemer, *L'emprise de la grammaire: Propositions épistémologiques pour une linguistique mineure* (Lyon: ENS Éditions, 2021).

56. Lamont, *How Professors Think*, 130.

57. Lamont, *How Professors Think*, 130.

58. Lamont, *How Professors Think*, 128. See also Christine Wennerås and Agnes Wold, "Nepotism and Sexism in Peer-Review," *Nature* 387 (1997): 341–43.

59. As Lamont notes, "Belief in the legitimacy of the system is essential to preserving the vitality of research and of higher education in the United States and beyond": fundamental change, that is, is inconceivable. See Lamont, *How Professors Think*, 249.

60. Saree Makdisi, *Palestine Inside Out: An Everyday Occupation* (New York: W. W. Norton, 2010). See, for instance, Robert A. H. Cohen, "Dear Simon Schama, You Need a History Lesson on Zionism," *Mondoweiss*, November 10, 2017, accessed May 6, 2022, mondoweiss.net/2017/11/schama-history-zionism/. See also the controversial special issue of *Israel Studies* 24, no. 2 (2019): "Word Crimes: Reclaiming the Language of the Israeli-Palestinian Conflict." Shlomo Sand, *The Words and the Land: Israeli Intellectuals and the Nationalist Myth*, trans. Ames Hodges (Los Angeles: Semiotext(e), 2011) discusses intellectuals' often questionable use of analogies to illuminate Israeli politics.

61. Cary Nelson, "The Problem with Judith Butler: The Political Philosophy of the Movement to Boycott Israel," *Los Angeles Review of Books*, March 16, 2014, accessed May 6, 2022, lareviewofbooks.org/article/problem-judith-butler-political-philosophy-movement-boycott-israel/. It is noteworthy that in *Israel Denial*, Nelson adds a sentence that makes this implication less stark: "Like other BDS advocates, Butler takes political self-determination as an unqualified good for Palestinians, an end result that then becomes a sine qua non for any acceptable resolution of the conflict. *They should be able to decide their own future without regard to the political wishes of Israeli citizens*. Anything less than that, she believes, will not constitute justice." See Nelson, *Israel Denial*, 97, italics added.

62. A contingent, tradition-embedded and "discretionary" character is intrinsic to any discipline in which knowledge is produced creatively, and in which interpretation, especially when uninformed by strongly empirical techniques, holds pride of place. As such, it would be neither possible nor desirable to transcend the discretionary character of humanities research entirely. The critical task is therefore to recognize the connections between the forms of symbolic authority contracted and disseminated in the seminar room, and the wider forms of social and political authority in which they are embedded, and which they can simultaneously reinforce and challenge.

63. Muriel Darmon, *Classes préparatoires: La fabrique d'une jeunesse dominante* (Paris: La Découverte, 2015), 308.

64. Paulo Freire, *Pedagogy of the Oppressed*, trans. Myra Bergman Ramos (Harmondsworth: Penguin, 2017), 46.

65. "Germaine Greer Speaks to University of Sydney Graduates," The University of Sydney (website), November 5, 2005, web.archive.org/web/20210307220455/https://www.sydney.edu.au/news/84.html?newsstoryid=761 (original webpage discontinued).

4. DISRUPTION, PROTEST, DEMOCRACY

1. It is useful to consider the discussion in this chapter in light of the numerous disruptions that can be seen online. Some examples: "Human Rights 'Champion' Irwin Cotler Disrupted at Concordia University (Part 1)," Lobby Watch Canada, recorded on June 3, 2019, posted on June 5, 2019, YouTube video, www.youtube.com/watch?v=62AsRksrPPM; "Arye Shalicar – Apartheid Representative – Disruption in Germany [Aurich Adult Education Institute]," Boycott Apartheid, recorded on May 17, 2019, posted on May 30, 2019, YouTube video, www.youtube.com/watch?v=IV-5bm2B56o&t=146s; "Aliza Lavie, Chair of Anti BDS Lobby, Interrupted at Humboldt Uni Berlin. #Humboldt3," Boycott Apartheid, recorded on June 20, 2017, posted on July 1, 2017, YouTube video, www.youtube.com/watch?time_continue=92&v=87OWhVLsRuI; "Israel's UN Ambassador Danny Danon at Columbia University," JBS [Jewish Broadcasting Service], posted on March 3, 2017, YouTube video, www.youtube.com/watch?v=gJySRamy6EU#t=24m45s; "BDS Protest at University of Sydney 11/3/15," Human Being, recorded on March 11, 2015, posted on March 12, 2015, YouTube video, 3:17, www.youtube.com/watch?v=Auwjiq6gt64.

2. Gholam Khiabany and Milly Williamson, "Free Speech and the Market State: Race, Media and Democracy in New Liberal Times," *European Journal of Communication* 30, no. 5 (2015): 572.

3. See, for example, Stavit Sinai, Majed Abusalama and Ronnie Barkan, "An Open Letter Regarding June 20th [2017] Protest Held at Humboldt University, Berlin," Speaking Up in Times of Apartheid: Civil Responsibility and Protest in Berlin (website), accessed September 13, 2019, sites.google.com/view/speakingupintimesofapartheid/home?authuser=0.

4. David Estlund, "When Protest and Speech Collide," in *Academic Freedom*, ed. Jennifer Lackey (Oxford: Oxford University Press, 2018), 152. See also the essays in Andrew Pessin and Doron S. Ben-Atar, eds., *Anti-Zionism on Campus: The University, Free Speech, and BDS* (Bloomington: Indiana University Press, 2018).

5. See Mazin B. Qumsiyeh, *Popular Resistance in Palestine: A History of Hope and Empowerment* (London: Pluto Press, 2011), for ample documentation.

6. See *The Palestine Exception to Free Speech* (Palestine Legal and The Center for Constitutional Rights, 2015), 89–90, accessed May 9, 2022, palestinelegal.org/the-palestine-exception; Riri Hylton, "Three Activists Go on Trial for Challenging Israeli Apartheid in Berlin," *Electronic Intifada*, March 4, 2019, accessed May 9, 2022, electronicintifada.net/blogs/riri-hylton/three-activists-go-trial-challenging-israeli-apartheid-berlin.

7. Saree Makdisi, *Palestine Inside Out: An Everyday Occupation* (New York: W. W. Norton, 2010), xxiv.

8. The question of censorship also has particular historical relevance to the academic boycott, given that the US Campaign for the Academic and Cultural Boycott of Israel (USACBI) was formed after discussion of the boycott was banned on the California Scholars for Academic Freedom email list. See Sunaina Maira, *Boycott! The Academy and Justice for Palestine* (Oakland: University of California Press, 2018), 53.

9. See Tavia Nyong'o and Kyla Wazana Tompkins, "Eleven Theses on Civility," *Social Text* (online), July 11, 2018, accessed May 9, 2022, socialtextjournal.org/eleven-theses-on-civility/. In 2014, the president of the University of California accused a student campaign against free trips from Israel advocacy groups as violating principles of "civility, respect, and inclusion." See "President Napolitano's Statement on Civil Discourse at UCLA," University of California (website), accessed September 10, 2019, www.universityofcalifornia.edu/press-room/napolitano-statement-civil-discourse-ucla. See also Steven Salaita, *Uncivil Rites: Palestine and the Limits of Academic Freedom* (Chicago: Haymarket, 2015). See also Nadia Abu El-Haj, "Academic Freedom at Risk: The Occasional Worldliness of Scholarly Texts," in *If Truth Be Told: The Politics of Public Ethnography*, ed. Didier Fassin (Durham, NC: Duke University Press, 2017), 205–27; C. Heike Schotten, "Against Academic Freedom: 'Terrorism,' Settler Colonialism, and Palestinian Liberation," in *Enforcing Silence: Academic Freedom, Palestine and the Criticism of Israel*, eds. David Landy, Ronit Lentin and Conor MacCarthy (London: Zed Books, 2020), 282–309; Arianne Shahvisi, "Privilege, Platforms and Power: Uses and Abuses of Academic Freedom," in *Enforcing Silence*, 310–30.

10. See Stanley Fish, "There's No Such Thing as Free Speech, and It's a Good Thing, Too," in *There's No Such Thing as Free Speech* (New York: Oxford University Press, 1994), 102–19.

11. Obstacles to pro-Palestine speakers and events can be serious: in 2017 in the UK alone, several talks by Richard Falk were canceled in UK universities, no less than two events hosted by the Centre for Palestine studies at SOAS were disrupted and the University of Central Lancashire canceled a panel event on "Debunking Misconceptions on Palestine and the Importance of BDS": see Chloe Farand, "UK Universities Cancel Talks by Co-Author of UN Report Accusing Israeli of Apartheid Regime, over Security Concerns," *Independent*, March 24, 2017, accessed May 9, 2022, www.independent.co.uk/news/uk/home-news/israel-apartheid-regime-universities-cancel-talks-un-report-co-author-name-security-concerns-palestinians-a7647986.html; House of Commons and House of Lords Joint Committee on Human Rights, *Freedom of Speech in Universities: Fourth Report of Session 2017–19* [HC 589 – HL Paper 111: Published on March 27, 2018 by authority of the House of Commons and House of Lords], 23, accessed May 9, 2022, publications.parliament.uk/pa/jt201719/jtselect/jtrights/589/589.pdf; Ben White, "Israeli Apartheid Week: How Campus Activism Is Being Shut Down by False Charges of 'Anti-Semitism,'" Ben White (website), February 23, 2017, accessed May 9, 2022, benwhite.org.uk/2017/02/23/israeli-apartheid-week-how-campus-activism-is-being-shut-down-by-false-charges-of-anti-semitism/.

12. On the history of no platforming, see Evan Smith, *No Platform: A History of Anti-Fascism, Universities and the Limits of Free Speech* (Abingdon: Routledge, 2020).

13. On censorship by digital platforms, see Michael Arria, "Zoom Cancels Panel Featuring Leila Khaled amid Protests from Pro-Israel Groups," *Mondoweiss*, September 23, 2020, accessed May 9, 2022, mondoweiss.net/2020/09/zoom-cancels-panel-featuring-leila-khaled-after-protests-from-pro-israel-groups/; Rabab Ibrahim Abdulhadi, Tomomi Kinukawa, Saliem Shehadeh and Sean Malloy, "We Will Not Be Silenced! In Solidarity with Palestinian Sumoud and Intellectual Integrity," *Mondoweiss*, May 5, 2021, accessed May 9, 2022, mondoweiss.net/2021/05/we-will-not-be-silenced-in-solidarity-with-palestinian-sumoud-and-intellectual-integrity/. The Palestinian Observatory of Digital Rights Violations tracks online suppression of Palestinians: see "We Monitor, Document and Follow Up," The Palestinian Observatory of Digital Rights Violations (7or) (website), accessed May 9, 2022, 7or.7amleh.org/.

14. See Kim Willshire, "Ban on Israel-Palestine Debate Ignites Free Speech Row at French University," *Guardian*, March 22, 2011, accessed June 30, 2022, www.theguardian.com/world/2011/mar/21/ecole-normale-superieure-debate-row; Raphaël Gibour, "Le meeting 'Palestine vaincra' interdit à Toulouse," *Le Figaro Étudiant*, December 7, 2012, accessed May 9, 2022, etudiant.lefigaro.fr/les-news/actu/detail/article/le-meeting-palestine-vaincra-interdit-a-toulouse-666/; Génération Palestine Lyon, "'Thématique potentiellement conflictuelle' nous ont-ils dit," AURDIP: Association of Academics for the Respect of International Law in Palestine (website), March 19, 2014, accessed September 10, 2019, www.aurdip.org/thematique-potentiellement.html?lang=fr; Julien Salingue, "Le Crif ordonne la censure, l'université Paris 8 obéit," *Le Club de Mediapart*, February 17, 2012, accessed June 12, 2022, blogs.mediapart.fr/edition/les-invites-de-mediapart/article/170212/le-crif-ordonne-la-censure-luniversite-paris-8-; Philippe Mercier, "Annulation d'une conférence sur la Palestine et polémique à Sciences Po Nancy," *L'Est républicain*, February 11, 2015, accessed June 30, 2022, www.estrepublicain.fr/meurthe-et-moselle/2015/02/11/polemique-a-sciences-po; L'Union Générale des Étudiants de Palestine en France (GUPS Aix-Marseille), "Aix-Marseille Université bâillonne la voix de la solidarité avec la Palestine – Halte à la censure!" Mille Bâbords (website), March 21, 2015, accessed June 30, 2022, www.millebabords.org/spip.php?article27657; Génération Palestine Paris, "Conférence censurée à Paris 1: appel à mobilisation!" Paris Luttes (website), March 26, 2015, accessed May 9, 2022, paris-luttes.info/conference-censuree-a-paris-1-2908?lang=fr; BDS France Toulouse, "Le Président de l'Université Jean Jaurès (Toulouse) veut interdire une réunion publique de la Semaine contre l'apartheid israélien," BDS France (website), March 5, 2017, accessed May 9, 2022, www.bdsfrance.org/le-president-de-luniversite-jean-jaures-toulouse-veut-interdire-une-reunion-publique-de-la-semaine-contre-lapartheid-israelien/; UET – Union des ÉtudiantEs de Toulouse, "[Urgent - Interdiction d'une conférence sur la Palestine]," Facebook, March 13, 2018, accessed May 9, 2022, www.facebook.com/UEToulouse/photos/a.691139444321376/1292184364216878/?type=3&theater; BDS France Toulouse, "La semaine internationale contre l'apartheid israélien aura bien lieu malgré les pressions des officines sionistes," BDS France (website), March 14, 2019, accessed May 9, 2022, www.bdsfrance.org/la-semaine-internationale-contre-lapartheid-israelien-aura-bien-lieu-malgre-les-pressions-des-officines-sionistes/.

15. Ali Abunimah, "Court Overturns French Ban on Palestine Solidarity Groups," *The Electronic Intifada*, May 2, 2022, accessed June 27, 2022, electronicintifada.net/blogs/ali-abunimah/court-overturns-french-ban-palestine-solidarity-groups.

16. See Michael Arria, "The Trump Administration Is Investigating UCLA over a Pro-Palestine Event and Lecture," *Mondoweiss*, January 10, 2020, accessed May 9, 2022, mondoweiss.net/2020/01/the-trump-administration-is-investigating-ucla-over-a-pro-palestine-event-and-lecture. The organization Palestine Legal tracks anti-Palestinian legislation in the US: see Palestine Legal: Legislation (website), accessed May 9, 2022, legislation.palestinelegal.org/.

17. For some detailed case studies, see Rebecca Ruth Gould, "Legal Form and Legal Legitimacy: The IHRA Definition of Antisemitism as a Case Study in Censored Speech," *Law, Culture and the Humanities* 18, no. 1 (2022): 153–86.

18. See "Palestinian Academic Suspended by UK University Using Controversial Definition of Anti-Semitism," *Middle East Monitor*, January 27, 2022, accessed May 9, 2022, www.middleeastmonitor.com/20220127-palestinian-academic-suspended-by-uk-university-using-controversial-definition-of-anti-semitism/.

19. See Alison Campsie, "Glasgow University Accused of Undermining Academic Freedom in 'Antisemitic' Ruling," *Scotsman*, October 25, 2021, accessed May 9, 2022, www.scotsman.com/education/glasgow-university-accused-of-undermining-academic-freedom-in-antisemitic-ruling-3431124; Haleh Afshar and Neve Gordon, on behalf of BRISMES, "Re: [University of Glasgow's] 'Protocol for Managing Speakers and Events,' the IHRA Working Definition of anti-Semitism, and their Implications for Middle East Studies and Academic Freedom," *BRISMES: British Society for Middle Eastern Studies*, October 19, 2021, accessed May 9, 2022, www.brismes.ac.uk/files/documents/CAF_Glasgow_19102021_signed.pdf.

20. Orge Castellano, "Spanish University Cancels 'Auschwitz/Gaza' Seminar Comparing Holocaust to Israeli-Palestinian Conflict," *JTA: Jewish Telegraphic Agency*, August 25, 2021, accessed May 9, 2022, www.jta.org/2021/08/25/global/spanish-university-cancels-auschwitz-gaza-seminar-comparing-holocaust-to-israeli-palestinian-conflict.

21. Jonathan Cook, "The Antisemitism Industry: How Antisemitism Is Being Politicized and Weaponized in Europe to Defend Israel," *Mondoweiss*, December 14, 2020, accessed May 9, 2022, mondoweiss.net/2020/12/the-antisemitism-industry-how-antisemitism-is-being-politicized-and-weaponized-in-europe-to-defend-israel/.

22. Mati Shemoelof, "In First Application of Anti-BDS Resolution, Germany Censors Israelis," *Mondoweiss*, November 3, 2020, accessed May 9, 2022, mondoweiss.net/2020/11/in-first-application-of-anti-bds-law-germany-censors-israelis/.

23. Hebh Jamal, "German Police Remove Pro-Palestinian Students from Campus Meeting," *Mondoweiss*, December 15, 2021, accessed May 9, 2022, mondoweiss.net/2021/12/german-police-remove-pro-palestinian-students-from-campus-meeting/.

24. Matthew Abraham, *Out of Bounds: Academic Freedom and the Question of Palestine* (New York: Bloomsbury Academic, 2014), 19. For the Lyon incident, see Génération Palestine Lyon, "'Thématique potentiellement conflictuelle' nous ont-ils dit."

25. Susan G. Drummond, *Unthinkable Thoughts: Academic Freedom and the One-State Model for Israel and Palestine* (Vancouver: UBC Press, 2013).

26. "Palestine Legal Publishes Report on Trends in Palestine Advocacy and Backlash in 2021," Palestine Legal (website), February 24, 2022, accessed June 27, 2022, palestinelegal.org/news/2022/2/24/palestine-legal-publishes-report-on-trends-in-palestine-advocacy-and-backlash-in-2021. See also Palestine Legal's 2015 report *The Palestine Exception to Free Speech*.

27. See Lana Tatour (@Lana_Tatour), "Just Went to a Staff Seminar Delivered by Prominent Jewish-Zionist Scholar," Twitter, August 6, 2019, 1:46 p.m., accessed May 9, 2022, twitter.com/Lana_Tatour/status/1158585158993190913.

28. International Campaign to Defend Professor Rabab Abdulhadi, "A Victory! Professor Rabab Abdulhadi Wins Second Grievance at SFSU," *Mondoweiss*, February 19, 2022, accessed May 9, 2022, mondoweiss.net/2022/02/a-victory-professor-rabab-abdulhadi-wins-second-grievance-at-sfsu.

29. European Legal Support Center (ELSC), *The Attempt to Chill Palestinian Rights Advocacy in the Netherlands* (Amsterdam: ELSC, 2021), 29, accessed May 9, 2022, elsc.support/resources/the-attempt-to-chill-palestinian-rights-advocacy-in-the-netherlands.

30. Anshuman A. Mondal, "The Shape of Free Speech: Rethinking Liberal Free Speech Theory," *Continuum* 32, no. 4 (2018): 504.

31. The linguist Roy Harris, for instance, argued that "the denial of freedom of speech, however temporarily and for whatever reason, is a violation of the humanity of those to whom it is denied." See Roy Harris, "On Freedom of Speech," in *Ideologies of Language*, eds. John E. Joseph and Talbot J. Taylor (London: Routledge, 1990), 159.

32. Slavoj Žižek, "Introduction. The Spectre of Ideology," in *Mapping Ideology*, ed. Slavoj Žižek (London: Verso, 1994), 8.

33. For Ilongot speakers in the Philippines, for example, according to Michelle Z. Rosaldo's classic analysis, language is fundamentally not communicative but social and action-oriented, based on entirely different premises from the Western communicative ones. Michelle Z. Rosaldo, "The Things We Do with Words: Ilongot Speech Acts and Speech Act Theory in Philosophy," *Language in Society* 11, no. 2 (1982): 203–37.

34. Richard Bauman and Charles L. Briggs, *Voices of Modernity: Language Ideologies and the Politics of Inequality* (Cambridge: Cambridge University Press, 2003), 59.

35. Edward Sapir, *Language: An Introduction to the Study of Speech* (New York: Harcourt Brace, 1921), 39.

36. William James, "What Is an Emotion?" in *What Is an Emotion? Classic Readings in Philosophical Psychology*, eds. Cheshire Calhoun and Robert C. Solomon (New York: Oxford University Press, 1984), 131.

37. Luiz Pessoa, "Précis on *The Cognitive-Emotional Brain*," *Behavioral and Brain Sciences* 38 (2015): 1.

38. Jesse J. Prinz, *The Emotional Construction of Morals* (Oxford: Oxford University Press, 2007).

39. Stavroula-Thaleia Kousta, Gabriella Vigliocco, David P. Vinson, Mark Andrews, Elena Del Campo, "The Representation of Abstract Words: Why Emotion Matters,"

Journal of Experimental Psychology: General 140, no. 1 (2011): 14; Marta Ponari, Courtenay Frazier Norbury and Gabriella Vigliocco, "Acquisition of Abstract Concepts Is Influenced by Emotional Valence," *Developmental Science* 21, no. 2 (2018): 1–12.

40. Rae Langton observes about discussions of freedom of expression that "as political philosophers, and philosophers of language too, we tend to be god-like in our habit of creating man in our own image: of creating human beings who match a philosophical ideal, rather than a social reality. We create paradigm political agents, whose chief interest in speech is a search for truth. We create paradigm speakers, whose chief interest in conversation is the spread of knowledge." See Rae Langton, "Beyond Belief: Pragmatics in Hate Speech and Pornography," in *Speech and Harm: Controversies over Free Speech*, eds. Ishani Maitra and Mary Kate McGowan (Oxford: Oxford University Press, 2012), 90.

41. Erwin Chemerinsky and Howard Gillman, *Free Speech on Campus* (New Haven: Yale University Press, 2017), 25.

42. V. N. Vološinov, *Marxism and the Philosophy of Language*, trans. Ladislav Matejka and I.R. Titunik (New York: Seminar Press, 1973).

43. Michael Toolan, *Total Speech: An Integrational Linguistic Approach to Language* (Durham, NC: Duke University Press, 1996), 25.

44. Richard Kemp, "Submission to the United Nations Independent Commission of Inquiry on the 2014 Gaza Conflict [Geneva, February 20, 2015]," Colonel Richard Kemp (website), February 21, 2015, accessed May 9, 2022, richard-kemp.com/submission-to-the-united-nations-independent-commission-of-inquiry-on-the-2014-gaza-conflict/.

45. Roman Jakobson, "Closing Statement: Linguistics and Poetics," in *Style in Language*, ed. Thomas Sebeok (Cambridge, MA: MIT Press, 1960), 350–77.

46. Jakobson, "Closing Statement: Linguistics and Poetics," 356.

47. Louis Althusser, "Ideology and Ideological State Apparatuses (Notes towards an Investigation)," trans. Ben Brewster, in Louis Althusser, *On the Reproduction of Capitalism: Ideology and Ideological State Apparatuses* (London: Verso, 2014), 232–72.

48. Rashid Khalidi, *Palestinian Identity: The Construction of Modern National Consciousness* (New York: Columbia University Press, 1997).

49. Lorna Finlayson, "How to Screw Things with Words," *Hypatia* 29, no. 4 (2014): 775.

50. Judith Butler, *Gender Trouble: Feminism and the Subversion of Identity* (New York: Routledge, 1999), 189.

51. Shlomo Sand, *The Invention of the Jewish People*, trans. Yael Lotan (London: Verso, 2009), 14.

52. See Mary Kate McGowan, *Just Words: On Speech and Hidden Harm* (Oxford: Oxford University Press, 2019), 5.

53. Khalidi, *Palestinian Identity*, 8.

54. David A. McDonald, "Poetics and the Performance of Violence in Israel/Palestine," *Ethnomusicology* 53, no. 1 (2009): 73, 77, 76.

55. Makdisi, *Palestine Inside Out*, contains extensive documentation of these practices.

56. See, for an example, "Video: Settlers Hurl Insults, Threaten Sexual Violence against Palestinians in Hebron," *Ma'an News Agency*, August 29, 2017, accessed September 11, 2019, www.maannews.com/Content.aspx?id=778908 (webpage discontinued, available via https://web.archive.org/web/20181209095524/https://www.maannews.com/Content.aspx?id=778908).

57. Similarly, if the speech practice *in which* the interpellation is embedded is invested with significant energy or institutional authority, its power to successfully interpellate – to form identities – is amplified. The force of an insult is increased if its recipient understands that the person insulting them is committed to the practice of insult itself, and will not stop at a single slur, but will continue insulting them indefinitely. In the same way, the interpellative power of anti-Palestinian campus speech by an Israeli diplomat or spokesperson is boosted by the seal of social and intellectual authority conferred by the fact that a university is hosting the speech, and reinforced even further by the impressive security arrangements with which such occasions are often surrounded, which flatter the speaker and their cause through a material reflection of their importance, at the same time that they foreground their supposed vulnerability to attack.

58. In the deepest sense, language does this by providing the expressions we necessarily use to speak. Words have an intrinsically social, collective aspect. Since we often know best what we think when we've managed to put it into words, interpellation functions in the very act of speech by channeling our self-expression into the public terms of language, terms which then go on to have an important influence on how others understand and behave toward us. Words always come to us secondhand: when we express ourselves in speech, we're obliged (occasional coinages aside) to use words that exist already, and which we partly make our own by articulating them. This dialectic is characteristic of language, which gives us the ability to express *ourselves* as long as we do so in *others'* terms. However much we might hesitate to phrase things in a particular way, however much we might try to suggest that what we really mean is something different from what our words initially suggest, however often we might try to coin new words or expressions to capture what we have in mind, it is clear that, mostly, we have no choice but to work with the language that is already available. "Dispossession" and "expulsion" are mere words, and they might feel inadequate to describe the particularity of the human tragedy inflicted on Palestinians in 1948, but these, and terms like them, are the ones we are stuck with, at the moment at least. Language interpellates us, then, by constituting the discursive medium for the expression of our subjectivity, including in contexts of political demands.

59. Khalidi, *Palestinian Identity*, ix.

60. Judith Butler, *Excitable Speech: A Politics of the Performative* (New York: Routledge, 1997), 31ff.

61. See, for example, Center for Constitutional Rights, "Palestinians Intervene to Sue Israeli Settlers in Airbnb Lawsuit," *Mondoweiss*, March 18, 2019, accessed May 9, 2022, mondoweiss.net/2019/03/palestinians-intervene-settlers/.

62. See Anshuman A. Mondal, *Islam and Controversy: The Politics of Free Speech after Rushdie* (Basingstoke: Palgrave Macmillan, 2014), for a pointed critique

of the "philosophical idealism within liberal discourse that separates speech from its consequences" (22).

63. Jodi Dean, *Crowds and Party* (London: Verso, 2016).

64. Note that hearer passivity is not a universal of human communicative practices. According to Michael Walsh, Australian Aboriginal "conversation" is "hearer controlled": Michael Walsh, *Cross-Cultural Communication Problems in Aboriginal Australia* (Canberra: North Australia Research Unit, Australian National University, 1997), 8–10.

65. John Ganz, "The Hannah Arendt Center's Dark Thinking: A Study in Questionable Judgment," *The Baffler*, October 25, 2017, accessed May 9, 2022, thebaffler.com/latest/hannah-arendt-center-ganz.

66. Nadia Abu El-Haj, "Disciplinary Peace Above All Else?" Somatosphere (website), April 25, 2016, accessed December 13, 2020, somatosphere.net/2016/disciplinary-peace-above-all-else.html/.

67. For some discussion of this point, see Estlund, "When Protest and Speech Collide," 157. Based on Israel on Campus Coalition figures, Cary Nelson claims that only 22 of 94 disruptions of speakers in the US between 2015 and 2018 actually prevented talks being completed. See Cary Nelson, *Israel Denial: Anti-Zionism, Anti-Semitism, & the Faculty Campaign against the Jewish State* (Washington DC and Bloomington: Academic Engagement Network and Indiana University Press, 2019), 28.

68. Palestine solidarity activists often *do* appeal to negative freedom of speech in their own defense against Zionist interference. For one example, see Tom Hickey, "UCU Fringe Meeting Attacked by Zionists," *BRICUP Newsletter* 125 (October 2018): 7–8.

69. Edward Said, *The Question of Palestine* (London: Vintage, 1992), 50.

70. For one popular exploration of performativity and hate speech, see Rae Langton, "Words That Wound: Understanding the Authority and Effect of Hate Speech," ABC (Australian Broadcasting Corporation) (website), November 8, 2018, accessed September 23, 2019, www.abc.net.au/religion/the-authority-of-hate-speech/10478626. Comparisons between "performative/performativity" and "interpellation/interpellate" between 1900 and 2008 (English corpus 2012) on the Google Ngram Viewer (books.google.com/ngrams) also reveal the dominance of the former (accessed September 23, 2019).

71. Judith Butler, *Bodies That Matter: On the Discursive Limits of "Sex"* (New York: Routledge, 1993), 2.

72. See, for example, Catharine A. MacKinnon, *Only Words* (Cambridge, MA: Harvard University Press, 1993), 21, 121. MacKinnon distances herself from the details of the account of performatives in Austin, which she nevertheless takes as "a foundational exploration of the view in language theory that some speech can be action" (121).

73. The most careful statement of this position is due to Rae Langton, "Speech Acts and Unspeakable Acts," *Philosophy and Public Affairs* 22, no. 4 (1993): 293–330.

74. Among many other discussions, see Gavan Titley, *Is Free Speech Racist?* (Cambridge: Polity, 2020); Anthony Leaker, *Against Free Speech* (Lanham: Rowman

and Littlefield, 2020); Jeff Sparrow, *Trigger Warnings: Political Correctness and the Rise of the Right* (Melbourne: Scribe, 2018).

75. Butler, *Excitable Speech*, 15.

76. Butler, *Gender Trouble*, 184.

77. The role of convention is assumed in both the "continental" and "analytical" traditions of analyses of hate speech. According to Butler (*Excitable Speech*, 34), "racist speech works through the invocation of convention." "If a performative provisionally succeeds," Butler says, "then it is not because an intention successfully governs the action of speech, but only because that action echoes prior actions, and accumulates the force of authority through the repetition or citation of a prior *and authoritative* set of practices" (51, italics added). For Butler, it is conventions' vulnerability to subversion that provides an opening for counter-hegemonic speech. St Clare, similarly, states that "hate words and their uses operate according to particular social conventions": Kameron Johnston St Clare, "Linguistic Disarmament: On How Hate Speech Functions, the Way Hate Words Can Be Reclaimed, and Why We Must Pursue Their Reclamation," *Linguistic and Philosophical Investigations* 17 (2018): 90. Rae Langton, in an important early article on performativity and pornography, also sees the force of performatives as conventional, as deriving from "informal practices of speech and communication that gradually establish *precedents and informal rules*." See Langton, "Speech Acts and Unspeakable Acts," 320, italics added.

78. Langton, "Speech Acts and Unspeakable Acts," 320. This understanding is what leads some writers, like Abigail Levin, to see a response to hate speech and pornography in an "activist state," which would regulate speech in favor of women and minorities. Well intentioned though it is, this is misguided, because it has no analysis of the vested interests and power relations that subtend the "conventions" that currently make hate speech and pornography sayable, or of the balance of forces that would turn any such regulation to the advantage of the dominant powers, as the attempt to conflate anti-Zionism and anti-Semitism, and therefore to prohibit the former, shows. See Abigail Levin, *The Cost of Free Speech: Pornography, Hate Speech, and Their Challenge to Liberalism* (Basingstoke: Palgrave Macmillan, 2010).

79. A particularly clearly expressed statement of this mystification is provided by St Clare, "Linguistic Disarmament," 79–109. Talk of resignification suggests that if the harmful interpellations of hate speech are merely a convention, they are therefore something to which the subject can choose how (and whether) to respond: cf. Jacques Bidet, "The Interpellated Subject: Beyond Althusser and Butler," *Crisis and Critique* 2, no. 2 (2015): 62–85. For a critique of the concept of "resignification," see Geoff Boucher, "The Politics of Performativity: A Critique of Judith Butler," *Parrhesia: A Journal of Critical Philosophy* 1 (2006): 127.

80. It also involves the inconvenience, noted by Abigail Levin, that if the targets of hate speech can resignify it, then so can its originators. Levin, *The Cost of Free Speech*, 147.

81. Judith Butler, *Notes toward a Performative Theory of Assembly* (Cambridge, MA: Harvard University Press, 2015), 163. "It may prove important," Butler observes, "to reconsider those forms of performativity that only operate through forms of coordinated action, whose condition and aim is the reconstitution of plural forms of agency and social practices of resistances" (9).

82. Althusser stresses how ideology is omnipresent in history, which he defines, following the *Communist Manifesto*, as the history of class struggle: Louis Althusser, *On the Reproduction of Capitalism: Ideology and Ideological State Apparatuses*, trans. G. M. Goshgarian (London: Verso, 2014), 175. An ideology, he says, "always exists in an apparatus, and its practice, or practices. This existence is material" (259). Butler sees Althusser's theory of ideology as undoing any simple contrast between the material and the cultural: Judith Butler, "Merely Cultural," *New Left Review* 227 (1998): 36.

83. Rae Langton acknowledges that the debate about pornography "is not really about ideas at all, but about people and what they do": Langton, "Speech Acts and Unspeakable Acts," 327. But even if speech is envisaged as an act, this truth is regularly lost sight of by the intense theoretical effort dedicated to exploring the *linguistic mechanisms*, which supposedly endow language itself with real-world efficacy.

84. Mondal, *Islam and Controversy*, 27.

5. THE POLITICS OF REGRESSIVE RESEARCH

1. Gabi Baramki, *Peaceful Resistance: Building a Palestinian University under Occupation* (London: Pluto Press, 2010), 33.

2. Steven Salaita, *Inter/Nationalism: Decolonizing Native America and Palestine* (Minneapolis: University of Minnesota Press, 2016), 44, italics added.

3. This point is argued for in David Rodin and Michael Yudkin, "Academic Boycotts," *The Journal of Political Philosophy* 19, no. 4 (2011): 481.

4. James Eastwood, *Ethics as a Weapon of War: Militarism and Morality in Israel* (Cambridge: Cambridge University Press, 2017).

5. On the Minerva project, see the essays and other contributions at "The Minerva Controversy," Social Science Research Council (website), accessed December 6, 2020, essays.ssrc.org/minerva/; on the Human Terrain System, see Maja Zehfuss, "Culturally Sensitive War? The Human Terrain System and the Seduction of Ethics," *Security Dialogue* 43, no. 2 (2012): 175–90.

6. Edward Said, *The Question of Palestine* (London: Vintage, 1992), xxxxii. See also Edward Said, "Opponents, Audiences, Constituencies, and Communities," *Critical Inquiry* 9, no. 1 (1982): 1–26.

7. Noam Chomsky, "The Responsibility of Intellectuals," in *The Chomsky Reader*, ed. J. Peck (New York: Pantheon, 1978). See also Nicholas Allott, Chris Knight and Neil Smith, eds., *The Responsibility of Intellectuals: Reflections by Noam Chomsky and Others after 50 Years* (London: UCL Press, 2019).

8. Noam Chomsky, "Objectivity and Liberal Scholarship," in *American Power and the New Mandarins* (New York: Pantheon Books, 1969), 72.

9. Chomsky, "The Responsibility of Intellectuals," 67. I have explored the antidemocratic consequences of the technocratization of political communication with respect to George Lakoff's theories of American politics: Nick Riemer, "Cognitive Linguistics and the Public Mind: Idealist Doctrine, Materialist Histories," *Language and Communication* 64 (2019): 38–52.

10. Said, *The Question of Palestine*, xxxiii; Edward Said, *Representations of the Intellectual: The 1993 Reith Lectures* (New York: Vintage, 1996), 82.

11. See Cary Nelson, *Israel Denial: Anti-Zionism, Anti-Semitism, & the Faculty Campaign against the Jewish State* (Washington, DC and Bloomington: Academic Engagement Network and Indiana University Press, 2019), 266–67, for an instance of this common charge, and Nick Riemer, "Disciplinarity and the Boycott," in *Enforcing Silence: Academic Freedom, Palestine and the Criticism of Israel*, eds. David Landy, Ronit Lentin and Conor McCarthy (London: Zed Books, 2020), 67–90, for further discussion.

12. Ilan Pappé, *The Idea of Israel: A History of Power and Knowledge* (London: Verso, 2014); Shlomo Sand, *The Words and the Land: Israeli Intellectuals and the Nationalist Myth*, trans. Ames Hodges (Los Angeles: Semiotext(e), 2011).

13. Frédérique Matonti, *Intellectuels communistes: Essai sur l'obéissance politique* (Paris: La Découverte, 2005), 243.

14. Miklós Haraszti, *L'artiste d'état: De la censure en pays socialiste* (Paris: Fayard, 1983), 9.

15. Ellen Schrecker, *The Lost Soul of Higher Education: Corporatization, the Assault on Academic Freedom, and the End of the American University* (New York: The New Press, 2010), 166.

16. Pierre Bourdieu, *Pascalian Meditations*, trans. Richard Nice (Stanford: Stanford University Press, 2000), 21.

17. Bourdieu, *Pascalian Meditations*, 13–15.

18. Pierre Bourdieu, "Pour un savoir engagé," *Le monde diplomatique*, no. 575 (February 2002): 3.

19. Danielle Celermajer, *The Prevention of Torture: An Ecological Approach* (Cambridge: Cambridge University Press, 2018), 25, 26.

20. Danielle Celermajer, "Ending Torture Means Engaging with Traditional Foes," *Guardian*, September 16, 2014, accessed May 10, 2022, www.theguardian.com/commentisfree/2014/sep/16/ending-torture-means-engaging-with-traditional-foes.

21. Celermajer, "Ending Torture." For details of the controversy and a discussion, see Danielle Celermajer, *Conference Report: Human Rights and the Security Sector in the Asia Pacific* (Sydney: University of Sydney, 2015), accessed May 10, 2022, ehrp.cmb.ac.lk/wp-content/uploads/2016/04/Annex-14Conference-Report-Web.pdf.

22. Celermajer, *Conference Report*, 34.

23. Celermajer, "Ending Torture."

24. Celermajer, "Ending Torture."

25. Celermajer is a critic of Israel's crimes against Palestinians and has signed a petition calling on her, and my, institution, the University of Sydney, to "suspend all forms of exchange and cooperation with Israeli institutions, including Israeli universities, which are complicit with the ongoing colonial violence exercised by the Israeli state against the Palestinian people." See "University of Sydney Palestine Solidarity Statement," accessed May 10, 2022, forms.gle/viy3XQBEUyNUFXvX8.

26. Lindsay Murdoch, "Academic Tells Conference Delegates Not to Upset Sri Lanka over Human Rights," *Sydney Morning Herald*, September 12, 2014, accessed May 10, 2022, www.smh.com.au/world/academic-tells-conference-delegates-not-to-upset-sri-lanka-over-human-rights-20140912-10fzdq.html.

27. Murdoch, "Academic Tells Conference Delegates."

28. See, for instance, "Shame on Sydney U: Stupidity & Ignorance," *Sri Lanka Guardian*, September 18, 2014, accessed May 10, 2022, www.srilankaguardian.org/2014/09/shame-on-sydney-u-stupidity-ignorance.html; "Expression of Concern at Exclusion of Sri Lankan Activists at International Conference," Forum-Asia: Asian Forum for Human Rights and Development (website), September 18, 2014, accessed May 10, 2022, www.forum-asia.org/?p=17697; Edward Mortimer, "An Open Letter to Participants of the 'Enhancing Human Rights and Security in the Asia Pacific' Conference," Sri Lanka Campaign for Peace and Justice (website), September 12, 2014, accessed May 10, 2022, www.srilankacampaign.org/an-open-letter-to-participants-of-the-enhancing-human-rights-and-security-in-the-asia-pacific-conference/. The present author was also a signatory to a letter to Professor Celermajer along similar lines coordinated by the Sri Lanka Human Rights Project and the Centre for Peace and Conflict Studies at the University of Sydney.

29. Celermajer, *Conference Report*, 33.

30. Evelyn Balais-Serrano, "Letter to Associate Professor Danielle Celermajer, Director Enhancing Human Rights and Security in the Asia Pacific, University of Sidney [*sic*] [dated September 16, 2014]," Forum-Asia: Asian Forum for Human Rights and Development (website), September 18, 2014, accessed May 10, 2022, www.forum-asia.org/?p=17697.

31. Mark Thomson, "[Open Letter to Associate Professor Danielle Celermajer – Geneva, September 14, 2022]," APT (website), accessed September 27, 2018, apt.ch/content/files_res/open-letter-apt-14-sept.pdf (original URL discontinued, available at web.archive.org/web/20190124115731/https://www.apt.ch/content/files_res/open-letter-apt-14-sept.pdf).

32. Richard Bennett, "[Letter to Associate Professor Danielle Celermajer, dated September 12, 2014]," *Sri Lanka Brief*, accessed May 10, 2022, srilankabrief.org/wp-content/uploads/2014/09/Amnesty-letter-to-Danielle-Celermajer.pdf.

33. Celermajer, *The Prevention of Torture*, 19.

34. Gilles Heuré, "'Les Décombres': fallait-il republier l'ouvrage de Lucien Rebatet?" *Télérama*, November 10, 2015, accessed June 30, 2022, www.telerama.fr/livre/les-decombres-fallait-il-republier-lucien-rebatet,133824.php; Florent Georgesco, "Un spectre nommé Maurras," *Le Monde*, April 19, 2018, accessed May 10, 2022, abonnes.lemonde.fr/livres/article/2018/04/19/un-spectre-nomme-maurras_5287426_3260.html.

35. Marie-Laure Delorme, "Antoine Gallimard au JDD: 'Je n'ai pas renoncé aux pamphlets de Céline,'" *Le Journal du dimanche*, March 3, 2018, accessed June 12, 2022, www.lejdd.fr/Culture/antoine-gallimard-au-jdd-je-nai-pas-renonce-aux-pamphlets-de-celine-3589427.

36. Sven Felix Kellerhoff, "29 Bände Propaganda, Verklärung und Haß," *Die Welt*, June 19, 2006, www.welt.de/print-welt/article223863/29-Baende-Propaganda-Verklaerung-und-Hass.html.

37. In an exception to this generalization, the French publisher Agone reissued a collection of Italian antifascist texts by Camillo Berneri in 2019: Camillo Berneri, *Contre le fascisme: Textes choisis (1923–1937)* (Marseille: Agone, 2019).

38. The founder of PEGIDA, Lutz Bachmann, was forced to resign in 2015 after a 2012 photograph was circulated in which he posed as Hitler. Björn Höcke, the AfD

leader in Thuringia, was just one AfD leader remarked for his unambiguous adoption of Nazi rhetoric. See Ellen Ivits, "So sehr verfällt die AfD in Nazi-Jargon," *Stern*, October 30, 2015, accessed May 10, 2022, www.stern.de/politik/deutschland/afd-verfa ellt-durch-bjoern-hoecke-frauke-petry-und-co-zunehmend-in-nazi-jargon-6524228. html; "Despite Holocaust Remarks, AfD Lawmaker Björn Höcke Allowed to Remain in Party," *Deutsche Welle*, May 9, 2018, accessed May 9, 2022, www.dw.com/en/ despite-holocaust-remarks-afd-lawmaker-bj%C3%B6rn-h%C3%B6cke-allowed-to-remain-in-party/a-43715394; Lizzie Dearden, "German AfD Politician 'Attacks Holocaust Memorial' and Says Germans Should Be More Positive about Nazi Past," *Independent*, January 19, 2017, accessed May 10, 2022, www.independent.co.uk/ news/world/europe/germany-afd-bjoern-hoecke-berlin-holocaust-memorial-shame-history-positive-nazi-180-turnaround-a7535306.html.

39. See Gideon Botsch and Christoph Kopke, "NS-Propaganda im bundesdeutschen Rechtsextremismus," *Aus Politik und Zeitgeschichte* 43–45 (October 2015), accessed May 10, 2022, www.bpb.de/apuz/213520/ns-propaganda-im-bundesdeuts chen-rechtsextremismus?p=all.

40. Martin Doerry and Klaus Wiegrefe, "Das Monstrum," *Spiegel*, January 8, 2016, accessed May 10, 2022, www.spiegel.de/spiegel/print/d-141171592.html.

41. Emma Henderson, "Anders Breivik Says Hitler's Mein Kampf Is Only Reason He Is Surviving Prison," *Independent*, March 16, 2016, accessed July 14, 2022, www. independent.co.uk/news/world/europe/anders-breivik-mein-kampf-only-reason-sur viving-prison-adolf-hitler-nazi-a6934336.html.

42. "Who Was Sweden's School Sword Killer?" *The Local SE*, October 23, 2015, accessed June 30, 2022, www.thelocal.se/20151023/who-was-swedens-far-right-school-killer-in-trollhattan/.

43. The book was discovered with other Nazi literature in the possession of the perpetrator of the machete and hammer attack at a supermarket in Wales in 2015. A copy was also found among the personal effects of Luca Traini, a white supremacist who shot six West African migrants in Italy in 2018, and in the backpack of the unsuccessful hostage-taker at the Deportee Memorial in Mayenne in the same year. See Elwyn Roberts and Steve Bagnall, "Zack Davies: Machete Man Who Screamed 'White Power' as He Attacked Asian Dentist in Tesco Guilty of Attempted Murder," *Daily Mirror*, June 25, 2015, accessed May 10, 2022, www.mirror.co.uk/news/uk-news/zack-davies-machete-man-who-5948162; Peter Sharp, "Italy Shooting: Hitler's Mein Kampf Found in Home of Suspect," *Al Jazeera*, February 5, 2018, accessed May 10, 2022, www.aljazeera.com/news/2018/02/italy-shooting-hitlers-mein-kampf-home-suspect-180205075642713.html; Martin Cotta, "Mémorial des déportés à Mayenne: Mein Kampf et des ouvrages d'Hervé Ryssen et Alain Soral retrouvés dans un sac à dos," *France Bleu*, April 25, 2018, accessed May 10, 2022, www.francebleu. fr/infos/faits-divers-justice/memorial-des-deportes-a-mayenne-mein-kampf-et-des-ouvrages-d-herve-ryssen-et-alain-soral-retrouves-1524665589.

44. Jon Henley, "Antisemitism on Rise across Europe 'in Worst Times since the Nazis,'" *Guardian*, August 8, 2014, accessed May 10, 2022, www.theguardian.com/ society/2014/aug/07/antisemitism-rise-europe-worst-since-nazis.

45. Melanie Staudinger, "'Selbst Erwachsene fallen auf Nazi-Hetze herein,'" *Süddeutsche Zeitung*, April 26, 2012, accessed May 10, 2022, www.sueddeutsche.de/

bayern/diskussion-um-hitler-buch-mein-kampf-selbst-erwachsene-fallen-auf-nazi-hetze-herein-1.1342227.

46. Doerry and Wiegrefe, "Das Monstrum."

47. "Russia Bans Hitler's 'Mein Kampf' over Fears It Fuels Rise of Far-Right," *Telegraph*, March 26, 2010, accessed May 10, 2022, www.telegraph.co.uk/news/worldnews/europe/russia/7528364/Russia-bans-Hitlers-Mein-Kampf-over-fears-it-fuels-rise-of-far-Right.html.

48. Martin Doerry, "Zünder raus," *Spiegel*, December 6, 2016, accessed May 10, 2022, www.spiegel.de/spiegel/dokument/d-148347090.html.

49. See the statement from Andreas Wirsching, Institut für Zeitgeschichte, "Die Zielsetzung des Editionsprojekts," accessed December 20 2020, www.ifz-muenchen.de/fileadmin/user_upload/Forschung/Mein%20Kampf/Text_Wirsching.pdf. In the first instance, the intention was to make the edition too expensive for widespread popularity: in 2007, the then IfZ director Horst Möller told the *Frankfurter Allgemeine Zeitung* that the higher price of the projected edition would exclude its use as right-wing propaganda: "Soll man 'Mein Kampf' edieren?" *Frankfurter Allgemeine Zeitung*, July 15, 2007, accessed June 11, 2022, www.faz.net/aktuell/feuilleton/buecher/interview-horst-moeller-soll-man-mein-kampf-edieren-1460152-p2.html.

50. Doerry, "Zünder raus."

51. This and all other quotations in this paragraph are from Wirsching's preface to *Mein Kampf: Eine kritische Edition*, vol. 1 of 2, by Adolf Hitler, eds. Christian Hartmann, Thomas Vordermayer, Othmar Plöckinger, Roman Töppel (Munich and Berlin: Institut für Zeitgeschichte, 2016), 4, my translation.

52. In October 2016, an online bookseller in Bavaria was fined four thousand euros for selling a Russian reprint of a 1943 edition of the work, and proceedings were also started against Leipzig publisher Der Schelm, which brought out its own unannotated reprint in 2016. See "Adolf Hitlers Pamphlet bleibt in Deutschland verboten," *Spiegel*, June 26, 2014, accessed May 10, 2022, www.spiegel.de/kultur/gesellschaft/adolf-hitlers-mein-kampf-verbot-bleibt-nach-justizminister-treffen-a-977582.html; Doerry, "Zünder raus"; Isabel Metzger, "Ein Schelm, wer Böses denkt," *Spiegel*, May 31, 2016, accessed May 10, 2022, www.spiegel.de/kultur/gesellschaft/adolf-hitlers-mein-kampf-unkommentiert-staatsanwaelte-ermitteln-a-1094377.html; Gaby Reucher, "Right-Wing Publisher Plans Unannotated Edition of Hitler's 'Mein Kampf,'" *Deutsche Welle*, June 6, 2016, accessed May 10, 2022, www.dw.com/en/right-wing-publisher-plans-unannotated-edition-of-hitlers-mein-kampf/a-19305191.

53. John Stuart Mill, *On Liberty* (New York: Barnes and Noble Book, 2004), 37.

54. Christian Hartmann, Thomas Vordermayer, Othmar Plöckinger, Roman Töppel, introduction to *Mein Kampf: Eine kritische Edition*, vol. 1 of 2, by Adolf Hitler, eds. Christian Hartmann et al. (Munich and Berlin: Institut für Zeitgeschichte, 2016), 11, my translation.

55. Christian Hartmann, "'Mein Kampf' Is the Shell, We're Removing the Fuse," interview by Felix Bohr and Steffen Winter, trans. Ella Ornstein, *Spiegel*, May 23, 2102, accessed May 10, 2022, www.spiegel.de/international/germany/german-historian-discusses-new-scholarly-edition-of-hitler-s-mein-kampf-a-834560.html.

56. Hartmann et al., introduction, 12, my translation.

57. Wolfgang Benz, "'Jews': See 'Poison Gas,'" trans. Angela Davies, *German Historical Institute London Bulletin* 39, no. 1 (May 2017): 38, www.ghil.ac.uk/publications/bulletin/bulletin-39-1/.

58. Hartmann, "'Mein Kampf' Is the Shell, We're Removing the Fuse."

59. Doerry, "Zünder raus."

60. "'Mein Kampf' verkauft sich 85.000 Mal," *Spiegel*, January 3, 2017, accessed May 10, 2022, www.spiegel.de/kultur/gesellschaft/mein-kampf-kritische-ausgabe-von-hitlers-hetzschrift-verkauft-sich-85-000-mal-a-1128343.html.

61. Martin Doerry, "Zünder raus." The Dutch translation of *Mein Kampf*, published in 2018, was reported to be at number two of the bestseller list in the Netherlands as of the end of September 2018: see Charline Vanhoenacker and Alex Vizorek, "Charline et Alex reçoivent Régis Laspalès," FranceInter (website), September 28, 2018, accessed May 10, 2022, www.franceinter.fr/emissions/par-jupiter/par-jupiter-28-septembre-2018.

62. Hartmann et al., introduction, 12, my translation.

63. The phenomenon was not simply German: in June 2016, the conservative Italian daily *Il Giornale*, owned by Silvio Berlusconi's brother and known for its hard line against refugees, put a translation of *Mein Kampf* on sale with its Saturday edition, justified with the familiar injunctions about the necessity of learning from the past. See "Il Mein Kampf in edicola: tutto quello che non sapete," *Il Giornale*, June 11, 2016, accessed May 10, 2022, www.ilgiornale.it/news/cultura/mein-kampf-edicola-tutto-che-non-sapete-1270279.html; "Hitlers 'Mein Kampf' als Samstagsbeilage," *Spiegel*, June 11, 2016, accessed May 10, 2022, www.spiegel.de/kultur/gesellschaft/mein-kampf-italienische-zeitung-liefert-hitler-buch-als-beilage-a-1097101.html.

64. Jeremy Adler, "Absolute Evil," trans. Angela Davies, *German Historical Institute London Bulletin* 39, no. 1 (May 2017): 19, www.ghil.ac.uk/publications/bulletin/bulletin-39-1/.

65. Maiken Umbach, "Mein Kampf: A New Edition," *History Today*, February 3, 2016, accessed February 27, 2017, www.historytoday.com/mein-kampf-new-edition.

66. Jürgen Kaube, "Das Wort hat Adolf Hitler," *Frankfurter Allgemeine Zeitung*, January 9, 2016, accessed June 30, 2022, www.faz.net/aktuell/feuilleton/debatten/die-kritische-mein-kampf-edition-14004595.html; "'Mein Kampf'-Ausgabe wird Bestseller," *DW*, February 27, 2016, accessed June 30, 2022, www.dw.com/de/mein-kampf-ausgabe-wird-bestseller/a-19078844; "'Mein Kampf' ist wieder Bestseller," *Zeit Online*, February 28, 2016, accessed June 30, 2022, www.zeit.de/wissen/geschichte/2016-02/adolf-hitler-mein-kampf-bestseller-nationalsozialismus-buch; "Hitler's Racist Manifesto Is a Bestseller in Germany Now. That's Actually Good News," *Washington Post*, March 10, 2016, accessed June 30, 2022, www.washingtonpost.com/posteverything/wp/2016/03/10/hitlers-mein-kampf-is-a-bestseller-in-germany-heres-why-thats-good-news/; Sven Felix Kellerhoff and Berthold Seewald, "Hitler ist wieder da – finden auch Historiker," *Die Welt*, September 24, 2016, accessed May 10, 2022, www.welt.de/geschichte/article158343706/Hitler-ist-wieder-da-finden-auch-Historiker.html; "Adolf Hitlers 'Mein Kampf': Der ungewollte Bestseller," *Stern*, January 3, 2017, accessed June 30, 2022, www.stern.de/politik/deutschland/-mein-kampf-von-adolf-hitler-eine-hetzschrift-als-bestseller-7264790.html; "Hitlers Hetze Is nur noch historisch,"

Tagesspiegel, January 7, 2017, accessed June 30, 2022, www.tagesspiegel.de/politik/ein-jahr-neu-edition-von-mein-kampf-hitlers-hetze-ist-nur-noch-historisch/19222686.html.

67. See the Facebook event "Mein Kampf ist zurück!" November 3, 2016, accessed May 10, 2022, www.facebook.com/events/214657008955232/.

68. Hans Riebsamen, "Hitlers Hass-Schrift bleibt im Giftschrank," *Frankfurter Allgemeine Zeitung*, January 7, 2016, accessed May 10, 2022, www.faz.net/aktuell/rhein-main/hitlers-schrift-mein-kampf-bleibt-im-giftschrank-13999333.html.

69. Quoted in Antoine Vitkine, *Mein Kampf: Histoire d'un livre* (Paris: Flammarion, 2009), 63, my translation.

70. Vitkine, *Mein Kampf*, 126–27.

71. The IfZ's conviction that the best way to combat Nazism was to facilitate, not impede, public access to *Mein Kampf* has periodically been shared on the left. The original French translation of the book was even secretly funded by the Anti-Racist League, a body established to fight against anti-Semitism, in the belief that publicizing Hitler's intentions could only boost understanding of the Nazi threat to France. Even Hitler himself had refused to allow his book to appear in France, fearing that the intense hostility expressed to France in its pages would reveal his hand too clearly. The political effect of *Mein Kampf*'s content cannot, then, be claimed to *necessarily* favor the far right: in the appropriate political context, it is reasonable to think that it might harm it.

72. Vitkine, *Mein Kampf*, 264–65, my translation.

73. Björn Hengst, "3700 Fußnoten gegen Hitlers Hass," *Spiegel*, December 21, 2015, accessed May 10, 2022, www.spiegel.de/kultur/gesellschaft/mein-kampf-in-kritischer-edition-3700-fussnoten-gegen-adolf-hitlers-hass-a-1068562.html.

74. Götz Aly, "*Mein Kampf*: A Scholarly Burial," trans. Angela Davies, *German Historical Institute London Bulletin* 39, no. 1 (May 2017): 28, www.ghil.ac.uk/publications/bulletin/bulletin-39-1/.

75. Florent Brayard and Andreas Wirsching, eds., *Historiciser le mal. Traduction, annotation critique et analyse de Mein Kampf d'Adolf Hitler* (Paris: Fayard, 2021).

76. Andreas Wirsching, "Hitler, Mein Kampf: A Critical Edition," *German Historical Institute London Bulletin* 39, no. 1 (May 2017): 16–17, www.ghil.ac.uk/publications/bulletin/bulletin-39-1/.

77. Nor could a decision not to republish the work be described as an attempt to forestall all "historical classification, contextualization, and explanation" of it, as Wirsching hyperbolically claimed: as we have seen, republication of the text in toto was never necessary to achieve these aims, especially when extracts from *Mein Kampf* had been included in German school history texts since the 1960s. Thomas Sandkühler, "'Mein Kampf' in der Schule – Den Aufstieg Hitlers verstehen," *Der Tagesspiegel*, January 14, 2016, accessed May 10, 2022, www.tagesspiegel.de/wissen/mein-kampf-in-der-schule-den-aufstieg-hitlers-verstehen/12827038.html.

78. Aurélien Mondon and Aaron Winter, *Reactionary Democracy: How Racism and the Populist Far Right Became Mainstream* (London: Verso, 2020).

79. "Joschka Fischer sieht 'viele Nazis' in der AfD," *Focus* (Berlin), March 3, 2018, accessed May 10, 2022, www.focus.de/politik/deutschland/ex-aussenminister-joschka-fischer-sieht-viele-nazis-in-der-afd_id_8556349.html.

80. In 2016, in one of a number of such incidents, an AfD campaign car was caught with the unambiguously Nazi numberplate "AH1818," Hitler's initials, corresponding to the first and eighth letters of the alphabet: "AfD Accused of Using neo-Nazi Symbols on Campaign Car," *The Local* (Germany), August 23, 2016, accessed May 10, 2022, www.thelocal.de/20160823/afd-in-leipzig-accused-of-using-nazi-symbols-on-campaign-car.

81. Dearden, "German AfD Politician 'Attacks Holocaust Memorial.'"

82. Jefferson Chase, "Local AfD Leader's Holocaust Remarks Prompt Outrage," *Deutsche Welle*, January 18, 2017, accessed May 10, 2022, www.dw.com/en/local-afd-leaders-holocaust-remarks-prompt-outrage/a-37173729; "Despite Holocaust Remarks."

83. *Manifesto for Germany: The Political Programme of the Alternative for Germany* (Berlin: Alternative für Deutschland (AfD), 2016), 47, accessed May 10, 2022, www.afd.de/wp-content/uploads/sites/111/2017/04/2017-04-12_afd-grundsatzprogramm-englisch_web.pdf. See also Melissa Eddy, "Alternative for Germany: Who Are They and What Do They Want?" *New York Times*, September 25, 2017, accessed May 10, 2022, www.nytimes.com/2017/09/25/world/europe/germany-election-afd.html.

84. "German Swastika Ticket Row as Hitler Play Opens in Konstanz," *BBC News*, April 20, 2018, accessed May 10, 2022, www.bbc.com/news/world-europe-43821564.

85. "AfD's Gauland Plays Down Nazi Era as a 'Bird Shit' in German History," *Deutsche Welle*, June 2, 2018, accessed May 10, 2022, www.dw.com/en/afds-gauland-plays-down-nazi-era-as-a-bird-shit-in-german-history/a-44055213.

86. Abi Wilkinson, "Kent Grammar School Plans 'Unsafe Space' Including Mein Kampf," *Guardian*, November 21, 2017, accessed May 10, 2022, amp.theguardian.com/uk-news/2017/nov/20/kent-grammar-school-announces-plans-for-unsafe-space-including-mein-kampf; Tom Batchelor, "Grammar School Accused of 'Legitimising Fascism' after It Creates 'Unsafe Space,'" *Independent*, November 21, 2017, accessed May 10, 2022, www.independent.co.uk/news/education/education-news/simon-langton-grammar-school-unsafe-space-fascism-hitler-mein-kampf-kent-political-correctness-a8067396.html.

87. See, for illustration, Sarah Al-Matary, *La haine des clercs: l'anti-intellectualisme en France* (Paris: Seuil, 2019); Luc Boltanski, "Pourquoi ne se révolte-t-on pas? Pourquoi se révolte-t-on?" *Contretemps: Revue de Critique Communiste*, September 17, 2013, accessed May 10, 2022, www.contretemps.eu/pourquoi-ne-se-revolte-t-on-pas-pourquoi-se-revolte-t-on/.

88. Rima Najjar Kapitan, "Climbing Down from the Ivory Tower: Double Standards and the Use of Academic Boycotts to Achieve Social and Economic Justice," in *Against Apartheid: The Case for Boycotting Israeli Universities*, eds. Ashley Dawson and Bill V. Mullen (Chicago: Haymarket, 2015), 148.

6. THE OPIUM OF THE EDUCATED

1. See, for instance, Artemy Magun, "Spontaneity and Revolution," *The South Atlantic Quarterly* 116, no. 4 (October 2017): 815–33.

2. Philip Mendes and Nick Dyrenfurth, *Boycotting Israel is Wrong: The Progressive Path to Peace between Palestinians and Israelis* (Sydney: NewSouth, 2015), 149.

3. Vladimir I. Lenin, "What Is to Be Done? Burning Questions of Our Movement," Marxists Internet Archive (website), accessed May 13, 2022, www.marxists.org/archive/lenin/works/1901/witbd/i.htm. For discussion, see Hal Draper, "The Myth of Lenin's 'Concept of the Party' or What They Did to What Is to Be Done?" Marxists Internet Archive (website), accessed May 13, 2022, www.marxists.org/archive/draper/1990/myth/index.htm.

4. Quoted in Shira Wolosky, "Teaching in Transnational Israel: An Ethics of Difference," in *The Case against Academic Boycotts of Israel*, eds. Cary Nelson and Gabriel Noah Brahm (Chicago: MLA Members for Scholars' Rights, 2015), 353.

5. Edward Said, *Representations of the Intellectual* (New York: Vintage, 1996), 10–11; Lenin, "What Is to Be Done?".

6. In a similar vein, Hagar Kotef speaks of the "academicwashing" that anti-occupation Israeli research might constitute: "In criticizing Israel, revealing its wrongdoing, showing its logic of control, we *demonstrate Israel's tolerance and democratic nature*." Hagar Kotef, "Fragments," *Critical Inquiry* 44, no. 2 (2018): 348, italics in original.

7. Noemi Casati, "Political Participation in a Palestinian University: Nablus Undergraduates' Political Subjectivities through Boredom, Fear and Consumption," *Ethnography* 17, no. 4 (2016): 525.

8. Jamal Khader, "A Moment of Truth: A Document of Christian Palestinians Calling for BDS," in *The Case for Sanctions against Israel*, ed. Audrea Lim (London: Verso, 2012), 142.

9. Kotef, "Fragments," 344.

10. Omar Barghouti, "Just Intellectuals?" in *BDS: Boycott, Divestment, Sanctions: The Global Struggle for Palestinian Rights*, ed. Omar Barghouti (Chicago: Haymarket, 2011), 101.

11. Sinéad Murphy, *Zombie University: Thinking under Control* (London: Repeater Books, 2017), 99–100.

12. See also Colin Barker and Laurence Cox, "'What Have the Romans Ever Done for Us?' Academic and Activist Forms of Movement Theorizing," in *Proceedings of the Eighth International Conference on Alternative Futures and Popular Protest*, eds. Colin Barker and Mike Tyldesley (Manchester: Manchester Metropolitan University, 2002), mural.maynoothuniversity.ie/428/.

13. For a defense of this position, Julien Benda's 1927 essays published as *The Treason of the Intellectuals* remain a key text. See Julien Benda, *The Treason of the Intellectuals*, trans. Richard Aldington (Abingdon: Routledge, 2017).

14. Umberto Eco, "Ur-Fascism," *New York Review of Books*, June 22, 1995, accessed May 13, 2022, www.nybooks.com/articles/1995/06/22/ur-fascism/. Anti-intellectualism is, however, far from restricted to the far right but is also found in anarchist and communist variants. See Sarah Al-Matary, *La haine des clercs: l'anti-intellectualisme en France* (Paris: Seuil, 2019).

15. Al-Matary, *La haine des clercs*, 219.

16. Lena Obermaier, "Far-Right Parties in Europe Have Become Zionism's Greatest Backers," *Jacobin*, September 8, 2021, accessed May 13, 2022, jacobinmag.com/2021/09/germany-afd-zionism-antisemitism-israel-nationalism; Adam Taylor, "Ex-Israeli Spymaster, Who Helped Capture Adolf Eichmann, Releases Video in

Support of German Far-Right Party," *Washington Post*, February 3, 2018, accessed May 13, 2022, www.washingtonpost.com/news/worldviews/wp/2018/02/03/ex-israeli-spymaster-who-helped-capture-adolf-eichmann-releases-video-in-support-of-german-far-right-party.

17. Alan Montefiore, "The Political Responsibility of Intellectuals," in *The Political Responsibility of Intellectuals*, eds. Ian Maclean, Alan Montefiore and Peter Winch (Cambridge: Cambridge University Press, 1990), 201.

18. Tiya Miles, "Fighting Racism Is Not Just a War of Words," *New York Times*, October 21, 2017, accessed May 13, 2022, www.nytimes.com/2017/10/21/opinion/sunday/fighting-racism-protesting.html.

19. For useful discussion of this point, see Matthew Abraham, *Out of Bounds: Academic Freedom and the Question of Palestine* (New York: Bloomsbury Academic, 2014), 2ff.

20. Jeff Halper, *Decolonizing Israel, Liberating Palestine: Zionism, Settler Colonialism, and the Case for One Democratic State* (London: Pluto Press, 2021), 111.

21. Edward Said, *Orientalism: Western Conceptions of the Orient* (Harmondsworth: Penguin,1995), 10.

22. See Jonathan Ofir, "New Israeli 'Ethics Code' for Academia Seeks to Combat BDS," *Mondoweiss*, June 21, 2017, accessed July 1, 2022, mondoweiss.net/2017/06/israeli-ethics-academia/. An English translation of the code can be viewed at dailynous.com/wp-content/uploads/2017/06/israel-academic-ethics-code-english-translation-alon-harel.pdf, accessed July 1, 2022. For Kasher's IDF ethics code, see appendices A and B of James Eastwood, *Ethics as a Weapon of War: Militarism and Morality in Israel* (Cambridge: Cambridge University Press, 2017).

23. Jean-François Sirinelli, *Intellectuels et passions françaises*: *Manifestes et pétitions au xxe siècle* (Paris: Gallimard, 1996), 375.

24. Hilla Dayan, "For Occupation Studies, to Cultivate Hope," *Critical Inquiry* 44, no. 2 (2018): 351.

25. John Dewey, *The Quest for Certainty*, in *The Later Works*, vol. 4 of 17: 1929, ed. Jo Ann Boydston (Carbondale and Edwardsville: Southern Illinois University Press, 1984), 17.

26. Nancy Koppelman, "'When You Want to *Do* Something, Join Us!' The Limits of the Social Justice Mandate in Higher Education," in *The Case against Academic Boycotts of Israel*, 202.

27. Antonio Gramsci, *Selections from the Prison Notebooks*, trans. Quintin Hoare and Geoffrey Nowell Smith (New York: International Publishers, 1971), 352. In this light, it is no surprise that Gramsci's main theoretical work was done when he was in prison, that is, when he was prevented from undertaking concrete organizing. The role of Israeli prisons as incubators of theoretical thought among Palestinians has been stressed by Ariel Handel and Ruthie Ginsburg, "Israelis Studying the Occupation: An Introduction," *Critical Inquiry* 44, no. 2 (2018): 336.

28. Carlos Fraenkel, for instance, has argued that "philosophy can save the Middle East," a view he attributes to Sari Nusseibeh and that he later qualified as a "rhetorical overstatement": Carlos Fraenkel, *Teaching Plato in Palestine: Philosophy in a Divided World* (Princeton: Princeton University Press, 2015), 3, 189.

29. Alberto Toscano, *Fanaticism: On the Uses of an Idea* (London: Verso, 2010), 48.

30. Max Weber, "Politics as a Vocation," in *From Max Weber: Essays in Sociology*, eds. H.H. Gerth and C. Wright Mills (Milton Park: Routledge, 1991), 78.

31. Charles Taylor, "Understanding and Ethnocentricity," in Charles Taylor, *Philosophy and the Human Sciences: Philosophical Papers 2* (Cambridge: Cambridge University Press, 1985), 133.

32. Gerhard Richter and Theodor W. Adorno, "Who's Afraid of the Ivory Tower? A Conversation with Theodor W. Adorno," trans. Gerhard Richter, *Monatshefte* 94, no. 1 (2022): 16. Official academic philosophy, for another Marxist philosopher, Paul Nizan, was even at root the expression of philosophers' *contentment* with the political status quo, and so entirely remote from any desire to reform it. As the accredited spokespeople of reason – "that dream-ridden machine whose sole function is to understand and explain, not to decide or choose" – philosophers, Nizan continued, would never be offended by any injustice; their attitude, that is, would always be "philosophical." Paul Nizan, *The Watchdogs: Philosophers of the Established Order*, trans. Paul Fittingoff (New York: Monthly Review Press, 1971), 67, 93.

33. Gramsci, *Selections from the Prison Notebooks*, 338–39.

34. Handel and Ginsberg, "Israelis Studying the Occupation," 341.

35. Jean Baudrillard, "For a Critique of the Political Economy of the Sign [1972]," trans. Charles Levin, in *Selected Writings*, ed. Mark Poster (Stanford: Stanford University Press, 1988), 76.

36. Toscano, *Fanaticism*, 48; Weber, "Politics as a Vocation," 78; Taylor, "Understanding and Ethnocentricity," 133.

37. Said, *Representations of the Intellectual*, 57.

38. Quoted in Haim Bresheeth-Žabner, *An Army Like No Other: How the Israel Defense Forces Made a Nation* (London: Verso, 2020), 232.

39. A critique of the limitations of social media as a forum for political campaigning is often de rigueur among grassroots activists: lonely figures behind the screen, it is thought, can feel nothing of the immediacy, energizing stimulus or solidarity that comes from participation with flesh-and-blood others in live political events. What is less often realized is that this critique applies more widely than just to the screen: it also applies to the quintessentially intellectual experience of reading itself.

40. Slavoj Žižek, *Violence* (London: Profile, 2008), 6.

41. Žižek, *Violence*, 6.

42. Shlomo Sand, *La fin de l'intellectuel français? De Zola à Houellebecq* (Paris: La Découverte, 2016), 153.

43. In his study of intellectuals and petitions in France, Jean-François Sirinelli names as a typical intellectual failing the "failure to recognize the national or international balance of forces." Jean-François Sirinelli, *Intellectuels et passions françaises*, 526.

44. From this point of view, James Eastwood makes an interesting criticism of the testimonial-based methodology of the Israeli non-governmental organization Breaking the Silence, which aims to raise awareness of the real nature of the IDF's operations in the occupied territories: James Eastwood, *Ethics as a Weapon of War: Militarism and Morality in Israel* (Cambridge: Cambridge University Press, 2017).

45. Noura Erakat, "The Case for BDS and the Path to Co-Resistance," in *Assuming Boycott: Resistance, Agency and Cultural Production*, eds. Kareen Estefan, Carin Kuoni and Laura Raicovich (New York: OR Books, 2017), 97.

46. It's worth noting that this is, in fact, exactly the same kind of simplifying that is characteristic of the physical sciences, which idealize and generalize – simplify – the empirical world in a way intended to reveal the most fundamental forces driving it.

47. Koppelman, "'When You Want to *Do* Something, Join Us!'" 215.

48. Miriam F. Elman and Asaf Romirowsky, "Postscript: BDS," *Israel Studies* 24, no. 2 (2019): 232; Cary Nelson, "The Problem with Judith Butler," in *The Case against Academic Boycotts of Israel*, 185; Donna Robinson Divine, "Word Crimes: Reclaiming the Language of the Israeli-Palestinian Conflict," *Israel Studies* 24, no. 2 (2019):10; John Strawson, "Colonialism," *Israel Studies* 24, no. 2 (2019): 41.

49. Susie Linfield, *The Lion's Den: Zionism and the Left from Hannah Arendt to Noam Chomsky* (New Haven: Yale University Press, 2019), 278–79.

50. Kieran Healy, "Fuck Nuance," *Sociological Theory* 35, no. 2 (2017): 119, 121, 123.

51. Erakat, "The Case for BDS and the Path to Co-Resistance," 93. See also Rashid Khalidi, *The Hundred Years' War on Palestine: A History of Settler Colonialism and Resistance, 1917–2017* (London: Profile Books, 2020).

52. David Shulman, *Freedom and Despair: Notes from the South Hebron Hills* (Chicago: University of Chicago Press, 2018), 8.

53. Mendes and Dyrenfurth, *Boycotting Israel Is Wrong*, 146.

54. Ramzig Keucheyan, *Hemisphère gauche: Une cartographie des nouvelles pensées critiques* (Paris: Zones, 2009), 87.

55. In Austin's theory of speech acts, an utterance's perlocutionary force refers to the actual consequences it has in the world. J.L. Austin, *How to Do Things with Words* (Oxford: Oxford University Press, 1962), 101.

56. Noam Chomsky and Ilan Pappé, *On Palestine* (Harmondsworth: Penguin, 2015), 96.

57. See, for example, Paul Feyerabend, *Against Method*, 3rd ed. (London: Verso, 2003).

58. Noam Chomsky, "Activism, Anarchism, and Power," interview by Harry Kreisler [*Conversations with History*, March 22, 2002], The Noam Chomsky Website, accessed May 13, 2022, chomsky.info/20020322/.

59. Shlomo Sand, *Les mots et la terre: Les intellectuels en Israël*, trans. Levana Frenk, Michel Bilis and Jean-Luc Gavard (Paris: Flammarion, 2010), 88; Abaher El Sakka, "Les universités palestiniennes: Entre hiérarchisations académiques et attente sociale," *Hérodote* 168 (2018): 145. See "About Community Service," Birzeit University (website), accessed May 13, 2022, www.birzeit.edu/en/about/life-at-bzu/volunteer/overview.

60. Pablo Iglesias, for instance, stresses the importance of jokes and insults to *La Tuerka*, the television program that contributed to the emergence of the Spanish political party Podemos. See Carolina Bescansa, Íñigo Errejón, Pablo Iglesias and Juan Carlos Monedero, *PODEMOS, Sûr que nous pouvons!* (Bouzigues: Indigène éditions, 2015), 38.

61. See Martin Plaut, "From Cecil Rhodes to Mahatma Gandhi: Why Is South Africa Tearing Its Statues Down?" *New Statesman*, April 16, 2015,

accessed May 13, 2022, www.newstatesman.com/world-affairs/2015/04/cecil-rhodes-mahatma-gandhi-why-south-africa-tearing-its-statues-down.

62. The term was originally adopted by German theology students in the sixteenth century to designate the enemies of students, just as the biblical Philistines were the enemies of the chosen Jewish people. See Alain Rey, ed., *Dictionnaire historique de la langue française* (Paris: Le Robert, 1998), under *philistin, ine*; and Friedrich Kluge and Elmar Seebold, eds., *Etymologisches Wörterbuch der deutschen Sprache*, 25th ed. (Berlin and Boston: De Gruyter, 2011), under *Philister*.

63. On the geography of reason, see Nelson Maldonaldo-Torres, Rafael Vizcaíno, Jasmine Wallace and Jeong Eun Annabel We, "Decolonising Philosophy," in *Decolonising the University*, eds. Gurminder K. Bhambra, Dalia Gebrial and Kerem Nişancıoğlu (London: Pluto Press, 2018), 71.

64. Gabi Baramki, *Peaceful Resistance: Building a Palestinian University under Occupation* (London: Pluto Press, 2010), 112.

65. Barghouti, "Just Intellectuals?" 104.

66. Steven Salaita, *Inter/Nationalism: Decolonizing Native America and Palestine* (Minneapolis: University of Minnesota Press, 2016), 62–63.

67. See Sand, *Les mots et la terre*, 88.

68. On infrahumanity, see Jamil Khader, "Rethinking Academic Palestine Advocacy and Activism: Academic Freedom, Human Rights, and the Universality of the Emancipatory Struggle," in *Enforcing Silence: Academic Freedom, Palestine and the Criticism of Israel*, eds. David Landy, Ronit Lentin and Conor McCarthy (London: Zed Books, 2020), 268.

Index

Abraham, Matthew, 61, 168n6
abstraction, use in politics, 73
Abu Dis, 16, 19, 20
Abusalama, Shahd, 83
academic boycott of Israel, 64, 81, 100, 110, 116, 129, 137; effect on students, 31–32; institutional character of, 28–33; Israeli countermeasures, 6, 48; and scientists, 181n49; selectivity, 36–41; as tactic, 38
academic boycotts, 35–52; of conferences, 46–47; harm to boycotters, 48; of institutions, 46–47; normality of, 44–49; of publications, 45–46; of rankings, 47; of Russia, 38, 45, 47, 50; of Serbia, 50, 54; of South Africa, 2, 5, 30, 38, 39, 44–45; of Strategic Defense Initiative research, 50; of UAE, 38; of US, 50; of weapons research, 50; within Israel, 47–48
academic community, 9, 36
academic freedom, 21, 35–40, 42–43, 49–55
academics: complicity with power, 112–13; disengagement from politics, 60–63; mutual collaboration, 53–55

Act.IL, 25
Addameer Prisoner Support and Human Rights Association, 18, 153n2
Adler, Jeremy, 123
Adorno, Theodor, 62, 136, 138
AfD. *See* Alternative for Germany
African Literature Association, 3
African National Congress, 44
Al-Arroub, 19, 20
Al-Ashqar, Essam, 19
Al-Azhar University, 15, 21
Al-Kiswani, Omar, 20
Allenby Crossing. *See* King Hussein Crossing
Al-Maskobiyya interrogation center, 20
Al-Quds Open University, 19, 21
Al-Quds University, 16, 19, 20
Al-Shaykh Muwannis, 22
Alternative for Germany, 120, 123, 125, 127, 128, 194n38, 199n80
Althusser, Louis, 93, 94, 192n82
Aly, Götz, 125
Ambassadors Online, 25
American Association of University Professors, 171n33
American Studies Association, 3, 181n48
Amnesty International, 116, 117, 153n2
Amos, Valerie (Baroness), 68
An-Najah University, 14

anti-boycott laws, US, 6
anticolonialism, 15
antifascism, 6, 119, 122, 125
anti-intellectualism, 12, 110, 111, 129, 135, 137, 147–49, 200n14
anti-Palestinianism, 4, 7, 21, 28–31, 38–39, 42, 84, 94, 96–97, 102, 105, 111, 148, 152n13, 189n57
antiracism, viii, 6, 7, 8, 21, 125, 132, 148
Anti-Racist League, 198n71
anti-Semitism, 6, 7–8, 35, 37, 47, 63, 76, 83, 119, 120
anti-Zionism, 7, 8, 84, 131
apartheid: Israeli, vii, 3–4, 13, 31–32, 58, 84, 123; South African, 2, 5, 13, 38, 46
Arab and Muslim Ethnicities and Diasporas Studies program, 84
Arab College of Applied Sciences, 21
Arabic, 19, 23
archaeology, 23, 46
Ariel University, 26, 28, 48
Asian Forum for Human Rights and Development, 116
Asian Human Rights Commission, 116
Association for the Prevention of Torture, 116
Association of University Teachers, 45
audience, 80–81, 87–91, 94, 99–102, 104, 145, 146; involuntary, 101; role in research, 110, 114; silence of, 79, 99
Austin, J.L., 103–4, 105, 190n72, 203n55
Australia: Aboriginal conversation conventions, 190n64
Australian National University, 45
Avnon, Dan, 167n151
Ayalon, Ami, 68
Azarova, Valentina, 66

Baramki, Gabi, 14, 19, 24, 32–33, 109, 149
Bard College, 99
Barghouthi, Imad, 19
Barghouti, Omar, 39, 53–54, 131, 149

Barghouti, Widad, 19
Bar-Ilan University, 26–27
Baroud, Ramzy, 64
Bauman, Richard, 87
Bavaria, 119, 120, 121, 196n52
Beersheba, 22
Begin-Sadat Center for Strategic Studies, 26
Ben-Gurion, David, 22
Ben-Gurion University, 3, 22, 24
Ben-Sasson, Menahem, 68
Berman, Russell, 53, 178n21
BESA Center. *See* Begin-Sadat Center for Strategic Studies
Bethlehem, 16
Bethlehem University, 18, 20, 154n10, 155n24, 155n27
Birzeit University, 1, 14, 15, 16–17, 18, 19, 20, 109
Bourdieu, Pierre, 113
boycotts: consumer, viii, 2, 176n90; cultural, viii, 2. *See also* academic boycotts
Breaking the Silence, 202n44
Brecht, Bertolt, 119
Breivik, Anders, 120
Briggs, Charles L., 87
British Society for Middle Eastern Studies, 3
Butler, Judith, 21, 43, 73, 93, 96, 103–6, 167n150, 170n30

campaigning, political. *See* organizing, political
Canada, 68, 82
Canary Mission, 66
Casati, Noemi, 131
categories, general, 71–73
Celermajer, Danielle, 114, 115, 118, 193n25, 194n28
Céline, Louis-Ferdinand, 119
censorship, 19, 43, 67, 84, 101, 112, 136
Center for Peace Research, 28
Centre for Palestine Studies, 184n11
Centre for the Study of Human Rights, 115

Chatterjee, Piya, 43
Chemerinsky, Erwin, 89–90
China, 37, 39
Chomsky, Noam, 111–13, 125, 142, 147
civility, 1, 43, 79, 149
collaboration, 53–55, 65, 115–16, 124, 146
Committee of University Heads in Israel, 24, 28
Commonwealth Human Rights Initiative, 116
communication, 79–81, 85–92, 97–98, 100, 103–4
community, 36, 54
convention, 79, 99–100, 105–6, 191n77
Cook, Jonathan, 83
Corbyn, Jeremy, 6, 7
Cornell University, 181
counterargument, 106–7
counter-boycotts, 49–51

Dabashi, Hamid, 70
Dahiya doctrine, 26
Darmon, Muriel, 74
Davis, Glyn, 68
Dayan, Hilla, 134–35
Dean, Jodi, 98
Defense Strategy for International Markets, 25
Der Schelm, 124, 196n52
Dershowitz, Alan, 50
Descoings, Richard, 68
despair, 143
Dewey, John, 135
dialogue, 31–32, 41–42, 53, 109–10, 115, 140
discretion, 41, 54, 69–76, 99
disruption, 77–86, 89–91, 96–102, 106, 140
Drezner, Daniel W., 60
Drummond, Susan, 83
Dyrenfurth, Nick, 143

Eastwood, James, 27, 111, 202n44
École normale supérieure, 82
Eher, 124

Elbit Systems, 24, 25
El-Haj, Nadia Abu, 23, 100
Elrom Center, 25
Elsevier, 45–46
Elyan, Derar, 18
Emek Shaveh, 23
enclosure, 58, 64, 65, 66–68, 112
Erakat, Noura, 39, 140, 141, 143
Estlund, David, 77, 86
ethics, 46, 111; codes, 28, 134
Europe, 3, 9, 10, 14, 23, 32, 45, 66, 83, 87, 119–20, 131, 152n13
European Union, 3
exchange schemes, university, 10, 30–31
exclusion: in academia, 42, 44, 52, 55, 63–64, 115, 178n25
expertise, 23, 79, 111–12, 125, 142

Facebook, 7, 82
Falk, Richard, 39, 184n11
far right, 4, 6, 99, 119–25, 127, 131, 198n71, 200n14
fascism, 119–20, 124–25, 128, 131
Fatah, 15–16
Finkelstein, Norman, 61, 66, 68
Finlayson, Lorna, 93
France, 3, 68, 82, 112, 119, 125, 202n43
free speech, 77–80, 82–86, 88–89, 98, 101–2, 104, 121
Free Speech Week, 47
Freire, Paulo, 74
French Communist Party, 112

Gallimard, 119
Gauland, Alexander, 127
Gaza, 1, 5, 14–16, 18, 21, 25–27, 32, 39, 42, 58, 82, 83, 90, 128
German Jews' Aid Society. See Hilfsverein der deutschen Juden
German Sociological Association, 47
Germany, 45, 82–83, 118–28
Gillman, Howard, 89, 90
Ginsberg, Ruthie, 136
Goebbels, Joseph, 119
Goethe University, 83
Gramsci, Antonio, 135, 136, 149, 201n27

grants, 32
Greer, Germaine, 75
groupthink, 11, 137, 143–45, 147–48, 150
Guérin, Daniel, 119
Gur-Ze'ev, Ilan, 23–24

Haifa, 22, 44
Haik, Hossam, 130
Halper, Jeff, 133
Hamas, 15, 25, 26, 40, 103–4, 156n40
Hamdallah, Rami, 68
Hammad, Mahmoud, 20
Handel, Ariel, 136, 201n27
Haraszti, Miklós, 112–13
Harawi, Yara, ix
Harris, Roy, 187n31
Hartmann, Christian, 121–22
hasbara, 6, 25, 30
hate speech, 84, 104–6, 121–22
headscarf, 16. *See also* hijab
Healy, Kieran, 142
Hebrew, 44
Hebrew University of Jerusalem, 22–25, 27, 54, 68
Hebron, 16–17, 19, 22, 143
heckler's veto, 101
Hessel, Stéphane, 82
hijab, 155n24
Hilfsverein der deutschen Juden, 44
Himmler, Heinrich, 119
history: ideological function of, 23
Hitler, Adolf Mein Kampf, 118–28
Höcke, Björn, 127, 194n38
Holocaust. *See* Shoah
HUJ. *See* Hebrew University of Jerusalem
humanities, 36, 59–61, 63, 69–76, 111
human rights, 37, 47, 53, 98, 114–18
Human Rights Watch, 116, 153n2
Human Terrain System, 111
Humboldt University, 78, 183n1

Ibreiwish, Ibtihal Khader, 20
ideology, 4, 23, 58, 64, 66, 74, 75–76, 80, 84, 86, 93, 98, 103–6, 111–12, 125–27, 136

IDF. *See* Israel Defense Forces
IfZ. *See* Institute for Contemporary History
Ignatieff, Michael, 68
IHRA. *See* International Holocaust Remembrance Alliance
Il Giornale, 197n63
Ilongot, 187n33
improvisation, 146–48
Im Tirzu, 25
Inbar, Efraim, 26
Indian Institutes of Technology, 47
Indigenous peoples, 6, 7, 37
Institut des Études Politiques. *See* Sciences Po Lyon
Institute for Contemporary History, 119–27
Institute for National Security Studies (INSS), 25–26
insults, 89, 189n57
intellectualism, 10–11, 109–28, 129–40, 148–49, 150
International Congress of Quantum Chemistry, 46
International Holocaust Remembrance Alliance, 6, 63, 83
international students, 17, 65, 68
interpellation, 93–100, 103, 105–7, 189n57, 190n70, 191n79
Iran, 7, 37, 57
Islamic University, 15, 21
Islamophobia, 7, 120, 148
Israel: Jewish state, 8; liberal image, 4, 57, 75; nation-state law, 20; normalization, 31–33, 128; universities, 21–33
Israel Defense Forces, 16, 19, 20, 24–27, 64, 90, 95, 111, 134, 138, 155n24
Israeli Air Force, 25
Israeli Anthropological Association, 48
Israel Institute of Technology. *See* Technion
Israeli Sociological Society, 48

Issawiya, 27
Italy, 66, 82, 195n43

Jakobson, Roman, 92–93, 94, 96
James, William, 88
Janasansadaya, 116
Jayyous, 19
Jenin, 20
Jerusalem, 16–17, 19, 20; Declaration, 152n13; East, 1, 16, 22, 27
Jewish Studies, 50, 175n83
Jongen, Marc, 99
Judaism, 131, 148
Justice for Peace Foundation, 116

KAIST. *See* Korea Advanced Institute of Science and Technology
Kant, Immanuel, 36, 124
Kapitan, Rima Najjar, 37, 128
Kasher, Asa, 134, 201n22
Kassis, Rifat Odeh, 32
Keucheyan, Razmig, 143
Khalidi, Muhammad Ali, 2
Khalidi, Rashid, 95, 96
Khan al-Ahmar: Bedouin community, 20
King Hussein Crossing, 17
Koppelman, Nancy, 135, 142
Korea Advanced Institute of Science and Technology, 46–47

Laborie, Armelle, 39
Lamont, Michèle, 70–72, 74–75
Langton, Rae, 104, 105–6, 188n40
language, 78, 84–99, 103–6, 133, 189n58; functions of, 91–92, 94. *See also* speech
La Sapienza University, 50
Latin American Council of Social Sciences, 3
Lebanon, 14, 19, 26
Lenin, Vladimir I., 130, 139
Levy, Amit, 23
LGBTQ people, 37, 46, 47
Linfield, Susie, 142
linguistics, 45, 71, 86, 88, 90

literal meaning, 87, 90–91
literary studies, 70–71
Lockheed Martin, 24–25, 47
London Metropolitan University, 47

MacKinnon, Catharine A., 104, 190n72
Macron, Emmanuel, 176n90
Madrid talks, 15
Maira, Sunaina, 43–44
Makdisi, Saree, 16, 21, 73, 78
Marshoud, Ola, 20
Marxism, 93, 130, 131
Matonti, Frédérique, 112
Maurras, Charles, 119
May 1968, 134
McDonald, David A., 95
Mendes, Philip, 143
Middle Eastern studies, 3, 23
Middle East Studies Association, 3
Miles, Tiya, 132
Military Medicine Program, 27
Mill, John Stuart, 85, 104, 121
Miller, David, 66
Minerva initiative, 111
Misgav, Chen, 24
Modern Language Association, 3–4, 62–63
Möller, Horst, 196n49
Morris, Benny, 23–24
Moshe Dayan Center, 26
Murphy, Sinéad, 131

Nablus, 14, 20
Nakba, 22
NASA, 46
Nasir, Hanna, 15
National Security Studies Center, 25
National Security Studies Program, 25
National Women's Studies Association, 3
Nazism, 118, 119, 120, 122, 125, 127–28, 198n71
Nelson, Cary, 39–40, 51, 59–60, 61, 69–70, 73, 154n18, 167n150, 182n61

neoliberalism, 57, 58, 62, 64, 68–69, 141
Netherlands, 82, 197n61
New Historians, 23–24
Newman, David, 41, 47, 167n151
New Public Management, 67, 74
New York University, 51
New Zealand, 7
Nielsen, Kirstjen, 47
Nizan, Paul, 202n32
no platforming, 81
NPD party, 120
Nussbaum, Martha, 50, 52, 53

Oklahoma, 47
Open Society Justice Initiative, 116
Open University of Israel, 18
Operation Guardian of the Walls, 25
Operation Protective Edge, 24
organizing, political, 3, 91, 135, 143–47, 150
Oslo talks, 110
Otto, Götz, 123

PACBI. *See* Palestinian Campaign for the Academic and Cultural Boycott of Israel
Palestine: Jewish inhabitants, 8
Palestine Legal, 83, 186n16
Palestine Technical College, 21
Palestine Technical University, 18–20
Palestinian Authority, 40, 110, 143, 156n40
Palestinian Campaign for the Academic and Cultural Boycott of Israel, 3, 4, 31–32, 42
Palestinian Council for Higher Education, 3
Palestinian population: youth, 18
Palestinians, prejudices against, 23, 73, 93–94. *See also* anti-Palestinianism
Pappé, Ilan, 23–24, 112, 146
Patriotic Europeans against the Islamization of the West, 119–20, 194n38

peer review, 44–46, 70–72
PEGIDA. *See* Patriotic Europeans against the Islamization of the West
performativity, 54, 76, 103–5, 190n70, 191n77
pessimism, 143
Pessoa, Luiz, 88
Pettersson, Anton Lundin, 120
philistinism, 110
philology, 23
Plessner, Martin, 23
Podemos, 203n60
politics, 5, 7, 40, 81, 88, 99, 101, 113, 127–40, 147–50; of higher education, 1, 46, 51, 55, 58–63, 76, 125; and students, 31
pornography, 104–5, 191n77, 192n83
Powell, Enoch, 119
praxis, 131–33, 135–38
Prevent scheme, 66–67
Primoratz, Igor, 54
Prinz, Jesse, 88
prison, 201n27
publishers, corporate, 178n24

Qalandia checkpoint, 16
quietism, political, 63, 110, 132, 149

Rafael Advanced Defense Systems, 24
Ramallah, 16, 17, 19, 155n27
rankings, academic, 47
Rebatet, Lucien, 119
reclamation, 106–7
refugees, 5, 8, 25, 37, 41, 68, 197n63
Reichmann University, 25
Reinhart, Tanya, 49
Renn, Ludwig, 119
resignification, 106, 191n79
Rhodes Must Fall, 148
right of return, 8, 25
Rights Now, 115
Right to Life, 115
Rodin, David, 30, 35, 44
Romania, 46
Rubinstein, Ariel, 48

Russell, Conrad, 43
Russia, 38, 45, 47, 50, 120

Said, Edward, 60, 102, 111, 112, 113, 125, 134, 138, 142
Salaita, Steven, 7, 9, 36, 37, 41–42, 66, 68, 79, 110, 140, 149–50, 170n30, 181n48
Salim, Ahmad Abd al-Jaber Muhammad, 19
Sand, Shlomo, 94, 112, 139–40
San Francisco State University, 84
Sapir, Edward, 88
scholarship(s), 14, 26, 43, 61, 63, 71, 76, 110, 113, 133, 135, 137
scholasticide, 13, 21
school education, Palestinian, 16, 44, 95
science, 203n46
Sciences Po Lyon, 82, 83
Sciences Po Nancy, 82
settlements, Israeli, 6, 23, 25, 28, 48, 96, 103–4, 142
settler-colonialism, 6–7, 37
Sheffield Hallam University, 83
Shihade, Magid, 50–51
Shin Bet, 27, 68
Shoah, 127
Shulman, David, 143
Siboni, Gabi, 26
silencing, ix, 21, 51, 104, 116
simplification, 141
Sivan, Eyal, 39
Six-Day War, 14
smartwashing, 64, 130, 139, 141–42, 150
Snow, C. P., 36
social media, 202n39
social sciences, 111
sociology, 23, 142
South Africa, 2, 5, 13, 30, 35, 38, 39, 44–45, 46, 50, 148, 153n2
Soviet Union, 57, 112–13
speech, 31, 43, 61, 78, 77–106. *See also* free speech; hate speech; language
Sri Lanka, 37, 114–18

Sri Lanka Campaign for Peace and Justice, 116
Stanford University, 46
strikes, 18, 47, 51, 78, 130, 139
Students against Right-Wing Hate, 83
Summers, Larry, 68, 69

Tabori, George, 127
Takriti, Abdel Razzaq, 2
Talpiot program, 27
Tamils, 37
Tantura, massacre in, 29
Technion, 22, 24, 25, 44, 130
Tel Aviv, 17, 31, 57
Tel Aviv University, 22, 25–28
Thailand, 46
theorizing, 11, 70, 110, 112–13, 129–48
Thouqan, Ghassan, 20
Tibet, 37, 39
Toolan, Michael, 90
Töppel, Roman, 123
torture, 18, 114–18
Traini, Luca, 195n43
Treves, Angelo, 124
Trotsky, Leon, 119
Trump, Donald, 38, 46–47, 60, 82–83

UK, 3, 45, 47, 65, 66–68, 82, 119, 127
UK Lawyers for Israel, 66
Ukraine, 38, 45, 47, 50
Uniform to Studies scheme, 26–27
universals, 72
universities, 35–48, 52–53, 57–76, 79, 82–84, 99, 109–12, 132–34; European, 83; French, 82; Israeli, 21–32; Palestinian, 14–21, 40
Universities UK, 67
University and College Union, 47, 62
University College of Applied Science (Gaza), 21
University Jean Jaurès, 82
University of Aix-en-Provence, 82
University of California, 180n46
University of California, Berkeley, 47, 177n11

University of California, Irvine, 78
University of California, Los Angeles, 46, 47
University of Central Lancashire, 184n11
University of Colombo, 115
University of Glasgow, 45, 83
University of Haifa, 24, 27, 29, 68
University of Illinois at Urbana-Champaign, 181n48
University of Johannesburg, 3
University of Leicester, 47
University of Melbourne, 47
University of Palestine, 21
University of Paris 1, 82
University of Paris 8, 82
University of Reading, 179n38
University of Santiago de Compostela, 83
University of Sydney, 37, 75, 167n151, 193n25, 194n28
University of Tel Aviv, 22, 25, 26, 27, 28
University of Toulouse 2 Le Mitrail, 82
University Paul Valéry, 82
USACBI. *See* US Campaign for the Academic and Cultural Boycott of Israel
US Campaign for the Academic and Cultural Boycott of Israel, 184n8
Uyghurs, 37

Vitkine, Antoine, 125
Voloshinov, Valentin, 90

Weißensee Kunsthochschule Berlin, 83
Weizman, Eyal, 63, 138
Weizmann, Chaim, 22
West, Cornel, 66
West Bank, 5, 14–18, 22–26, 28, 32, 39, 48, 65, 82, 95, 110, 133
White, Ben, 39
Wirsching, Andreas, 120, 121, 126, 198n77
Wise, Phyllis, 181n48
World Archaeological Congress, 46
World Health Organization, 47

Xinjiang, 37

Yehya, Rabie', 20
Yiannopoulos, Milo, 47
Yissum, 24–25
YouTube, 82
Yudkin, Michael, 30, 35, 44

Zionism, 2, 4, 7, 8, 23–24, 30, 58, 69–72, 75, 83, 92, 93, 110, 112, 131, 142, 147
Žižek, Slavoj, 86, 139
Zoom, 82

About the Author

Nick Riemer is senior lecturer in the English and linguistics departments at the University of Sydney and a Palestine solidarity and trade-union activist. In addition to his academic work in semantics and the history and philosophy of linguistics, he has written for *The Guardian, Jacobin, Al Jazeera English, The Australian, The Sydney Morning Herald* and other publications.

www.ingramcontent.com/pod-product-compliance
Lightning Source LLC
Chambersburg PA
CBHW021841220426
43663CB00005B/343